Fatal Risk

Fatal Risk

A Cautionary Tale of AIG's Corporate Suicide

Roddy Boyd

WILEY

John Wiley & Sons, Inc.

Published by John Wiley & Sons, Inc., Hoboken, New Jersey.
Published simultaneously in Canada.

For general information on our other products and services or for technical support, please contact our Customer Care Department within the United States at (800) 762-2974, outside the United States at (317) 572-3993 or fax (317) 572-4002.

Wiley also publishes its books in a variety of electronic formats. Some content that appears in print may not be available in electronic books. For more information about Wiley products, visit our web site at www.wiley.com.

Library of Congress Cataloging-in-Publication Data:

Boyd, Roddy, 1968-
    Fatal risk : a cautionary tale of AIG's corporate suicide / Roddy Boyd.
      p.   cm.
    Includes index.
    ISBN 978-0-470-88980-0 (hardback); ISBN 978-1-118-08429-8 (ebk);
    ISBN 978-1-118-08427-4 (ebk); ISBN 978-1-118-08428-1 (ebk)
      1. Insurance companies–United States–History.   2. American International Group, Inc.– History.   3. Federal aid–United States.   4. Financial crises–United States.   5. Global Financial Crisis, 2008-2009.   I. Title.
    HG8540.A43B69 2011
    368.006'573—dc22

                                                                          2011001512

Printed in the United States of America

10 9 8 7 6 5 4 3 2 1

To Laura: More than 20 years ago we said that even if we didn't have money or a plan, we had each other and that better days would come. We still have each other, and the better days are here. To enjoy them with you is a treasure and a privilege.

Contents

Cast of Characters

AIG

Martin Sullivan   Chief executive officer of AIG until 2008
Steven Bensinger   Chief financial officer of AIG until 2008
William Dooley   Head of AIG's Financial Services Division
Ernie Patrikis   General counsel of AIG until 2006
Anastasia Kelly   General counsel of AIG until 2009
Chuck Lucas   Risk management chief of AIG until 2001 (consultant until 2007)
Robert Lewis   Risk management chief of AIG until 2010
Kevin McGinn   Credit risk management head of AIG
Win Neuger   Global investment chief of AIG until 2009
Michael Rieger   Mortgage-backed securities fund manager at AIG until 2007
Richard Scott   Head of global fixed income at AIG until 2008
Elias Habayeb   CFO of financial services
Chris Winans   Vice president of media relations until 2008
Nicholas Ashooh   Head of corporate communications until 2010
Edward Liddy   CEO of AIG 2008–2009

International Lease Finance Corporation

Steven Udvar-Hazy   CEO of ILFC until 2009

AIG Financial Products

Howard Sosin   Cofounder, CEO of AIGFP until 1992
Randy Rackson   Cofounder AIGFP until 1992
Barry Goldman   Cofounder AIGFP until 1992
Tom Savage   CEO of AIGFP from 1994 to 2001
Joseph Cassano   CEO of AIGFP from 2001 to 2008
David Ackert   Former head of Transaction Development Group and Energy Group at FP until 2007
Jacob DeSantis   Head of Equities and Commodities at FP until 2008
Jon Liebergall   Former head of Municipal Group and co-head of North American Marketing at FP
Andrew Forster   Head of Asset Finance Group
Alan Frost   Former head of U.S. investment bank and structured securitizations effort
Gary Gorton   (consultant) Yale finance professor and author of FP CDO risk software
Eugene Park   Corporate marketer and former head of structured securitizations
Kelly Kirkland   Consultant and former head of European business at FP

AIG Trading

Gary Davis   Former cofounder AIG Trading
Robert Rubin   Former cofounder AIG Trading
Barry Klein   Former cofounder AIG Trading

AIG Board of Directors

Robert Willumstad   Former AIG CEO and chairman of the board
Frank Zarb   Former AIG chairman of the board
Carla Hills   Former U.S. trade representative
Richard Holbrooke   Former senior U.S. diplomat

Frederick Langhammer   Former CEO at Estee Lauder Cos.
Stephen Bollenbach   Former CEO of Hilton Hotels

C. V. Starr & Co. (ex-AIG)

Maurice "Hank" Greenberg   Former AIG chief executive officer (until 2005)
Edward Matthews   Former AIG vice chairman, finance
Howard Smith   Former AIG CFO
Bertil Lundqvist   General counsel at C. V. Starr

Goldman Sachs

Gary Cohn   Goldman president and chief operating officer
Lloyd Blankfein   COO
Craig Broderick   Risk management chief
David Viniar   CFO
Andrew Davilman   Managing director, sales
Ram Sundaram   Managing director, prop trading
Daniel Sparks   Partner, mortgage trading

Boies, Schiller & Flexner LLP

David Boies   Lawyer for Greenberg
Lee Wolosky   Lawyer for Greenberg
Nick Gravante   Lawyer for Greenberg

Simpson Thacher & Bartlett

Richard "Dick" Beattie   Outside adviser to AIG board

Sard Verbinen & Co.

George Sard   Public relations adviser to AIG

The Federal Reserve Bank of New York

Timothy Geithner   President FRBNY
Sarah Dahlgren   Head of supervision FRBNY
Thomas Baxter   General counsel

Kynikos Advisers

Jim Chanos   Kynikos general partner
Chuck Hobbs   Kynikos research chief

Gradient Analytics

Donn Vickrey   Cofounder and research chief

Fatal Risk

Introduction

Robert Willumstad viewed himself as one of the good guys. Most men do, of course, but he had tried to be one: forthright, a by-the-book kind of guy. He took pride in his handshake being valued in New York and even more pride in his hard work at being the engineer to Sandy Weill's dreamer in the construction of Citigroup. At that banking and financial giant, his unit was most assuredly *not* the one where the Securities and Exchange Commission and attorney general had had a field day; he generated *profits*, not subpoenas.

In a town full of executives, Willumstad was a businessman, or at least he tried to comport himself like one. Executives were appointed, carried out orders, and were paid what they were paid. A businessman built an enterprise, something that would outlast cycles and trends and perhaps even the man who built it. An executive focused on his mandate and cared for little else; a businessman had to be concerned with the totality of the company. Willumstad had always sought to keep perspective, to think a few moves ahead and solve the problem. That he

1

had tried to do it as a human being and not a glory hound was a point of pride.

He thought of this as he sat in a lovely waiting room outside the president of the New York Federal Reserve's office in the middle of September 2008 for a chance to speak to Timothy Geithner. Willumstad, the chief executive of AIG, was there to inform the Fed president that all attempts to secure a solution in the private market were failing. Cash was running out, and when their debt was down-graded on Monday they were going to have to come up with at least $50 billion, maybe more. No one was willing to buy key units of the company and there were no loans possible. Recently stung by the public outrage over its role in setting up a $30 billion portfolio to take Bear Stearns's more troubled mortgage bonds off J. P. Morgan's books, Geithner had been very blunt in telling Willumstad that no Fed help was forthcoming.

Willumstad hadn't really wanted any. He had tried every route they could think of, including trying to become one of the 18 banks and securities firms that buy and sell bonds directly with the Fed. He had hoped this would allow AIG to access some of the funding programs the Fed had set up for these "primary dealers" to keep the markets vibrant. He never heard back. Hell, he couldn't even get Geithner to focus on the $2.5 trillion in derivative exposure AIG had when he had brought it up to him earlier in the week.

So now he was there to frame out for Geithner and his staff what had been unimaginable for all of his more than 40 years in the banking business: AIG was going to die. Hank Greenberg's company, the cor-nerstone of both the New York and American business communities, was going to die. Competitors and customers alike had once admired its verve and audacity, but now they just feared whatever crater it made when it died.

As he stared at the floor, he was struck at the spectacle of it all. The CEO of one of the most important companies on earth was stuck in a chair trying to grab a few minutes with a central banker to explain just what might happen to the American economy and the global capital markets when that company died.

A final thought crossed Willumstad's mind: he was hoping that he ran his own meetings more punctually than this. He did not want to think that he often kept people waiting; now that the shoe was on the other foot, he found he didn't really like waiting all that much.

■ ■ ■

While much was surprising about what we now call the Credit Crisis of 2008, much fundamentally was not. A secret straw poll in 2005 of the globe's public- and private-sector financial leadership about which global firms would be in dire straits should there be a sustained real estate–driven liquidity crisis would have likely put Bear Stearns and Lehman Brothers at the top of the list. From there, the picks get more fractious, but eventually all would have had some combination of the other American investment banks—Morgan Stanley, Goldman Sachs, and Merrill Lynch—followed by the Bank of America, Royal Bank of Scotland, and UBS. Having access to cash and the short-term loan markets, balance sheet strength, and flexibility, the financial requirements for corporate survival in a market crisis were—then as now—widely seen things the major money center banks had in abundance. The investment banks, chief among them Goldman Sachs, would always be better places to work in the short and medium runs because of their incredible profit-generation capabilities, but a commercial bank could weather the proverbial "thousand-year storm."

Next to this in the firmament of the world's financial luminaries was AIG.

AIG simply stood apart. Everything that brought the globe closer together, or moved it away from the blood-drenched ideologies and feudalisms of the previous century, AIG seemed to have a piece of. The emergence of Russia and the Eastern bloc from its Communist brutality into a global trading partner was made much easier with AIG standing ready to insure what they had to trade. The same is true of China and other Southeast Asian states.

Where other underwriters of insurance and risk would not go, AIG gladly went on the view that someone willing to engage in commerce was a reduced threat to global safety. In a sense, no other company so readily represented American postwar power—the ready allure of national wealth via trading and the promise of safety from multinational engagement and cooperation. All of the globe's business leaders reckoned with AIG at some point in their workweek. Incredibly, one man had built it from its Chinese roots into a global company that every day insured more skyscrapers in Dubai or fuel exploration off the coast of Louisiana or Scotland even as its sprawling capital markets operations traded instruments unimaginable just months prior.

Maurice "Hank" Greenberg built this company according to a vision he alone seemed to possess, and yet he managed to keep its operations and business lines, ever more sprawling and diversified, under his thumb from his suite of offices on the 18th floor of AIG's 70 Pine Street headquarters. Eventually, though, mistakes in a litigious age got him removed from the company that he still views as his very flesh. The reins were turned over to men whose experience was narrow and who possessed none of the animal fear and innate aggression that he did.

The troubles of succession from business founder to the next generation are among the oldest dilemmas in human endeavor. But in AIG's case, there was an added wrinkle: In a bid to increase earnings and diversify from the risks that AIG had faced in being one of the largest insurance companies in the world, Greenberg led AIG into capital markets.

The returns were extraordinary, and cemented the reputation of Greenberg as a visionary without peer in industry. Yet as AIG grew in this area and allowed more of its balance sheet to be used in the guarantee business, as opposed to trading or insurance, the world's most important financial company became the terminus of its financial risk. In the late 2000s, that risk was defined by real estate, an asset that was often bought and traded based on leverage and borrowing costs.

More dangerous than that was that the men running AIG saw little of this risk for what it was, nor did they believe it when it was pointed out to them. The new stewards of AIG had had little of Greenberg's ruthlessness when faced with risk and none of his knowledge of business or markets.

And there was nothing Greenberg could do about it, since he had been banished from the kingdom he had built.

■ ■ ■

All of this was what brought Bob Willumstad to the New York Fed in mid-September 2008. Warnings had been ignored while Greenberg and

AIG's management fought an all-consuming civil war. As management basked in bull markets that drove earnings to record sums and compensation packages hit the stratosphere, layer upon layer of risk was added to the balance sheet, and trading schemes devised by the Devil himself were implemented.

AIG was created to handle risk that others could not or would not. It prospered because its managers, Greenberg chief among them, correctly judged that while some Nigerian oil wells might explode or some Brazilian executives might be kidnapped, they would be the exception, not the rule. Yet they priced the coverage as if it were more than likely the case that oil wells and executives would be in trouble. The only way to guarantee that a company could be around to handle future risk was to earn a strong profit on the risk they insured today.

The collapse of AIG, Willumstad had learned, was an inside job. The men who had run AIG had forgotten a basic premise of risk: all risk was dangerous, but there were some risks that were more fatal than others.

Chapter 1

The (Noncorrelated) Dream Team

In May 1997, a young man armed with a keen mind and a desire to succeed got out of a taxi at a leafy office park on Nyala Farm Road in Westport, Connecticut. Despite its location across from the busy Connecticut Turnpike, it was a surprisingly serene locale. Visitors from the concrete canyons of Manhattan's financial district always remarked that they couldn't believe they were only an hour from Grand Central Terminal. In every sense of the word, it was the very embodiment of the phrase, "the nearest far-away place."

Andrew Barber, a 25-year-old options trader who had recently joined Prudential Securities, was more thankful than most to be enjoying the scenery. The breeze whistling through the trees, the absence of packed streets, and the quiet all were a thankful break from a big New York trading floor's steam-kettle life. Born and raised in a small western New York town not far from the Pennsylvania border, he loved getting out of the city and hoped eventually to move back there. For now, though, there was no small amount of work to be done. Heading up an embryonic trading desk in a securities trading outpost of a vast insurance colossus, he was grateful for the opportunity to get in front of some people he believed might know where he was coming from.

There was potential here, Barber thought, though he had no idea what sort of business he might plausibly drum up. The men he was going to see did not much care about Prudential's ability to sell securities in dozens of different countries, its huge balance sheet, or its boilerplate about putting the needs of the client first. They had heard variations on that pitch for around a decade now, and from men who had been at this game far longer than he had.

No, thought Barber, as he walked in the doors of a company called AIG Financial Products, none of those things appeared to matter very much to this place at all. Still, he was there, and just maybe that was enough.

Things happen here, Barber thought. It struck him that just getting in the door at places like this was a victory.

■ ■ ■

There was no way for Barber to know it at the time but he had walked into a business that was arguably one of the most distinctive in the global financial landscape. Possessing no real corporate mandate—other than to make money without risking its gilt-edged, triple-A credit rating, the place, to Barber's way of thinking, was the financial equivalent of the National Security Agency. You were aware of it, but you had no idea what they did or how they did it. AIG Financial Products simply did as it pleased, whenever people there felt it was opportune, dealing with whomever they chose to, in the pursuit of making a buck however they saw fit.

AIGFP, or simply FP, as employees called it, had to do precious little. They had no need to pick up the phones to the big trading desks in New York and demand bids and offers for blocks of stocks and bonds, they had no outside investors fretting over last month's earnings numbers, and no corporate managements were seeking their advice on strategy. It is no understatement to say that you could have a pretty successful career on a Wall Street trading desk in the 1980s and 1990s and would never have once encountered AIGFP on the other side of a trade. As a number of its founders acknowledge, this was all part of their plan.

But with each passing month, it became more apparent to the observant that AIGFP was a very large player in parts of the financial landscape. Investment bankers would come down to the trading floor with puzzled looks, describing conversations they had just had with equally baffled public finance officials who were using AIGFP to manage their interest rate exposure. It seemed to the bankers—and their municipal clients—that AIGFP was somehow making a killing in offering towns and cities the ability to swap their fixed-rate debt costs out for an interest rate that floated as borrowing costs rose or sank. This swap idea was hardly new, but was rarely used since someone—and it was almost always the municipal borrower—invariably got killed when rates ran up and debt that had once been cheap became suddenly quite expensive. For an investment bank, it was a public relations headache, another example of the Street's sharks preying on the unsuspecting.[1] As the story went, though, AIGFP managed to hedge out its risk and was happily taking the other side of these trades. For a fee, it even helped the cities and towns hedge their exposure to this sort of volatility, minimizing costs from swings in interest rates.

In the early 1990s, bankers to technology companies began to tell their colleagues that their clients in the Silicon Valley and along Massachusetts's Route 128 were using AIGFP to turn their large blocks of company stock and options into ready cash. Instead of taking out a cash loan from a UBS or J. P. Morgan against their equity stake (a strategy fraught with risk since the bank could demand cash collateral or even seize the executive's stock when the value declined enough), AIGFP used options to help corporate executives raise cash from their holdings overnight without making investors worry over the message sent by the CEO's stock sales, or incurring the wrath of the taxman, who fretted over whether the stock had truly been sold and risk transferred.[2]

That interesting and lucrative things were happening at AIGFP was evident to a certain type of curious Wall Streeter—the sort who asked questions about why things were really happening, or conversely, why they were not. It was just that no one outside of Westport had answers to these sorts of questions.

This is where Andrew Barber came in because, like any dream factory, AIGFP needed a constant flow of dreamers. In this case, they needed puzzled bankers from Wall Street's transaction factories to make the pilgrimage to Westport and unpack their dilemmas. Usually, it was a client with a certain sort of problem not amenable to the typical Wall Street banker cure-alls: the issuance of stock or bonds, a merger or sale of a unit. Rather, bankers and corporate officials came to them with the thorniest of problems: an international corporation with huge tax liabilities in one currency and large tax benefits in another that needed to have its tax payments risklessly normalized and then converted into a third currency, a privately held company that needed to rapidly (and without the hassles of Securities and Exchange Commission [SEC] registration) turn its huge and profitable holdings in some publicly held companies into some ready cash without surrendering its equity stake. Wall Street, and thus the men and women who worked there, were the canvas for AIGFP to conjure up new ways to use AIG's rivers of cash and its titanium balance sheet to reap profits where others could not or would not.

A bright and creative thinker, Barber was just the sort AIGFP liked to deal with in the 1990s: smart enough to be doing the type of highly quantitative trading and analysis that was the sine qua non of their daily life, yet honest enough to know its limitations. Despite his relative youth, Barber was trying to build a business and was willing to talk to most anyone to see if he could get something going. This entrepreneurial spirit was a virtual necessity, since Prudential Securities—though part of a massive insurance company—was in reality a second-tier player (at best) in a financial system where first-tier firms like Goldman Sachs, Morgan Stanley, and Merrill Lynch garnered the lion's share of customer trades and investment-banking work. On a given day, Barber would trade, research his own trading ideas, peddle a few trades to his growing book of customers and then grab a quick sit-down with the corporate finance department to explain how options and other derivatives could factor into getting some corporate client business done. It was, he had come to realize, a job that was equal parts exhilarating and utterly thankless.

Word gets around quickly on Wall Street when someone's thinking is fresh or different. Astute investors remember when a sell-side trader challenges their assumptions or gets them to frame an investment dilemma in a different fashion. Traders are too often depicted as aggressive rogues, using bravado and ample amounts of capital to reroute a whirlwind market and carve out profits. The precise opposite is more often true: they are content to (nearly risklessly) execute trades between clients with differing investment views and goals and to hopefully earn a few cents' profit between the bid and offer prices. Many sell-side traders and sales staff are quite good at providing clients market intelligence but much less efficient at helping clients use current conditions to frame a sober view of the future. As such, rather than the proverbial "Masters of the Universe" stereotype, they are more akin to hot-dog vendors on a Manhattan street, competing in a ruthlessly efficient and crowded market, earning a precarious living on heavy volume and narrow margins.

Not Barber.

So when a marketer at AIGFP got wind of a guy who was looking at equity options and derivatives differently, a quick phone call was made and Barber happily hopped a train to Westport.

Passing through the doors, what struck Barber was what he didn't see at the place that a generation of Americans has now come to view with varying degrees of infamy. There were no packed trading floors, nor was there any false bravado or bonhomie among the people he met there. People were courteous, not because they particularly wanted anything from him—and he was in no position to be granting much in the way of the expensive, wheel-greasing perks institutional investors favor, like sports tickets or travel junkets—but because they seemed decent.

In fact, the more Barber thought about his time there, the feeling he got was that this was the most intentionally designed place he had ever been to in his life. Very little expense had been spared to create the perfect anti–Wall Street feeling: the main trading room, if indeed that's what it actually was, he thought, had been set up as a series of interconnected, but free-standing desks to intentionally avoid the institutional trading desk vibe. (To get a sense of what the place really was, he had to force his eyes to track the roughly congruent layout of stacked computers and Bloomberg terminals.)

The walls of the room contained row after row of books, from arcane academic works covering the mathematical shape of interest rate curves to works on admiralty law and even copies of the corporate tax code from the 1940s. They weren't for show; they were bookmarked, haphazardly stacked, and dog-eared, Barber noticed, and freshly so. People here wanted to know everything about subjects he hadn't much presumed existed, let alone seen as ripe for some money making.

There was a platoon's worth of dutiful analyst types studying those books, taking notes, comparing and contrasting things between volumes and between the book and their computers. Barber assumed they were the paralegals, junior assistants, and first-year researchers that all financial firms seem to run on. He would, in short order, learn how wrong he was.

The flatness of the organization was apparent almost immediately. While speaking with Jake DeSantis, one of the young derivatives traders he had come to know, one of the few senior managers there ambled by and, unprompted, opened up about a series of ideas he had. People walked by and talked about land purchases and shale, leases, and tax credit. Others floated into the conversation, and senior people ducked in and then out.

Were these potential trades or deals he was talking about, or simply random musings? Was Jake being asked to look into something, or was this just FP's version of water cooler talk? At FP, he would learn, these sorts of distinctions could be immaterial. The next trade or the next deal could come from anywhere, in any asset or market sector, so everyone was open to exploring anything.

Again, the contrasts between large Wall Street firms like Prudential (and PaineWebber, where he had started trading) were striking. At those places, you could occasionally have a rewarding conversation with a supervisor, but there were so many managers and so many different corporate and political distractions that it was easier and safer to limit your contact with them. Making solid money was the safest way to avoid becoming a casualty in some investment bank's corporate restructuring or a boss's ego power move, but even then, there were no guarantees. Wall Street, he was coming to learn, offered many ways to die.

There was an aquarium there—one of the largest freestanding saltwater tanks in the world—that contained a decent-sized shark.

A remnant from a previous tenant, the tank and its shark soon disappeared; when Barber asked why, he was told simply, "It's just not who we are." FP was wholly detached from the cultural norms of Wall Street and its boxing leagues, after-work drinking and strip clubs at conferences. Everything that was important to Wall Street simply got in the way at FP.

Barber would come to learn that AIGFP worked because it had the precise opposite ethos of the Wall Street salesmen who courted its business. The hustlers could keep their quick one-eighth- and one-fourth-point profits on a deal, or the extra nickels and dimes they captured on the spread between interest paid and interest received; AIGFP told people like Barber they wanted the risk because it was so often mispriced. This was a nicer way of FP's saying that they felt they had the brain and computer power to look five years down the road and make a profitable assumption about the likely range of a stock's price. A company with balance sheet, talented people, and a creative bent could make handsome returns over time when an executive, wanting to turn his options grants into some cash, allowed FP to strip out the volatility component of his options grant in return for cash.[3]

The surpassing strangeness of all this would only occur to Barber years later. In über-competitive Wall Street, where everything to do with business was held to be a secret or some proprietary formula, a customer had happily told him he could keep short-term profits and then told him that they make money—real money, into the tens of millions per trade—because they value something entirely differently than he does. Then, to complete the through-the-looking-glass aspect of it all, they told him how they do it.

On the way back to Prudential after a visit in 1998, Barber reflected on it. Am I a customer of theirs, or are they a customer of mine? He would learn the answer during his first transaction with them, a convoluted deal involving a method to extract the value from a rich dot-com executive's stock holdings without selling the stock or risking a decline in value or tax liability.

The answer was in their worldview: AIGFP had no customers, only counterparties. As cordial and engaging as everyone there was, as willing as they were to give away the things that everyone else on Wall Street valued, Barber quickly saw that they did not negotiate on the structure of a transaction. Ever. When Barber inquired about perhaps changing a minor point here or a detail there, the answer was a firm "no."

Everything AIGFP did was a "principal" transaction because AIG's balance sheet and credit were always theoretically at risk. In this environment, every deal is constructed to very exacting risk tolerances, and everything and anything was a possible threat.

He would see this utter aversion to risk in action. A dozen years later Barber says he is still astounded to recall it. There were conference calls with FP that spawned more conference calls, which in turn led to meetings and calls with tax lawyers who would ask the initial risk-review-type questions but from a tax-law precedent angle. After they were done, the corporate finance lawyers weighed in. Then accountants ran the numbers to scenarios that Barber viewed as more satire than fact—wholesale shifts in the tax code back to 1970s levels, huge swings in the stock market, total corporate disruption. After that, there were people who seemingly had no connection to the transaction but who had clearly studied the deal closely and had strongly held opinions. It never really ended. Line by line, word by word, the deal's papers were gone through, with the FP people always asking, "Do you understand?" and "Will there be a problem here?"

They were modeling the deal, he surmised, to protect themselves in the event Prudential or its customer weren't able to live up to their obligations for any reason known to man. This struck him as odd, since Prudential in 1998 had $200 billion in assets and their customer was, at least on paper, worth hundreds of millions of dollars. "How," he would ask colleagues many months later, "do you even develop a worldview that could model a trade to make money if a $750 billion institution failed?"

With a vetting process like this, Barber concluded, AIGFP's concern was the opposite of his—and thus the opposite of Wall Street—in that they did not fret over where revenue was going to come from; they fretted over whether they had properly analyzed and modeled the risk that everyone else supposedly did not understand. In the vernacular, Wall Street, and all of American business, looked at transactions and worried about "upside," wondering where additional profits could come from. At FP, people cared only about "downside," or what could go wrong, better known as "the fat tail."[4]

As he got tired, the legions of FP people who flocked around one of the smaller deals they would do in that time frame gathered strength and revisited things that had been signed off as settled simply because they wanted to. An investment bank, given that much time, could presumably have merged the United States and Canada.

Someone with whom he had struck up a dialogue at FP told him they did things this way because they were part of an insurance company and all the risk they took was in writing coverage, not in helping dot-com millionaires placate their boards while getting cash to buy vineyards and more houses. Barber took the point.

After another meeting, Barber rode the train back to New York and thought of his experiences with AIGFP. He knew that the only other company that had a unit doing financial deals wholly apart from their main business was Enron. The comparison made Barber laugh; these guys were so unlike Enron it was ridiculous. The Enron guys would slit your throat for a dollar bill they found on the floor. The AIGFP guys would politely bend down and give it to you.

Years later, when AIGFP became a name more well known in Washington, D.C., than it was in Westport (and later Wilton), Barber recalled a conversation he had with a group of AIGFP traders later that autumn about Ramy Goldstein and the blowup of UBS's high-profile equity derivatives desk, a story that was the center of every trading desk's chatter.

In brief: Goldstein, a brilliant, Yale-educated PhD and former Israeli paratrooper, had led a team of equally talented traders who made markets in seemingly every option, at prices and in sizes no one else could match. Over four years, Goldstein's London-based desk seemed to capture every trade on the Street, booking hundreds of millions of pounds of profit before giving it all back (and more) in 1997 when a series of the group's longer-dated options trades went wrong and about $430 million was lost. Tales were emerging from former colleagues at UBS about a mind-bending concentration of risk that was neither understood by management—nor really disclosed to it—and about reliance on trading models and risk management programs that were programmed with the most ludicrous assumptions. Because of the debacle, UBS, for centuries one of the world's most storied banking franchises, had been forced into a hasty and unequal marriage with Swiss Bank Corporation, allowed to keep only its name.[5]

The reaction of the AIGFP traders was one of total, utter shock, Barber remembers. To a man, they would all question how even one of those problems could have occurred in a properly run firm—where was corporate management and their risk-controllers? How could anyone assume that volatility would always be in their favor? What about the hedges? Didn't anyone else at UBS understand these trades?

More elementally: How could one trading desk do a series of trades in such volume that the firm itself was at risk?

At AIGFP, you were forced to spend hours vetting the minutiae of ideas and trading strategy with, well, anyone who asked. From unit chief Tom Savage, to his deputy Joe Cassano, to risk management in New York, and (more often than you might suppose) the boss of bosses, CEO Maurice "Hank" Greenberg himself. It was a process that a 15-year veteran of FP described as "a sociopathic hunt for risk. It forced you to drop ideas you really liked for the ones that really worked. Along the way, you became an expert in every facet of the deal."

What happened at UBS seemed, to the outsider at least, that no one questioned Goldstein because he made so much money, and only when that ended did questions about his strategy surface. A consensus emerged: a firm like that didn't even truly deserve consideration as a professional operation.

No one ever mentioned to Barber what he thought might be the obvious reaction: that it couldn't happen at AIGFP. Even in bantering about UBS's foibles, it seemed, there were things that were just beneath discussion. They might have answered the phones or called themselves "FP," but no one ever seemed to forget that the letters "AIG" preceded them. To the age-old question, "What's in a name?," Barber had come to realize that when it came to AIGFP, the answer was, "a lot."

■ ■ ■

It is the mid-1980s and Hank Greenberg and Ed Matthews (the man who was, effectively, his second in command) are obsessed with diversification. Broadly, of course, all large businesses are. McDonald's pushes salads, bottled water, and yogurt to capture customers when periodic nutritional concerns erupt over their fries, burgers, and shakes. Merrill Lynch, whose army of retail brokers and massive stock- and bond-trading desks traditionally had anchored the firm's profit line to the direction of the market, broadened out into managing retirement funds for unions, advising corporations on mergers, and processing trades for hedge funds.

They hunt for diversification because it often works: a whole new set of people came into McDonald's, stayed a while, and took their wallets out; Merrill got steady earnings and cash flows from businesses that required little real risk to its capital. In the language of finance, it was called noncorrelated earnings, and investors would readily pay a higher price-to-earnings (P/E) ratio for them.[6] The diversified earnings didn't have to be massive, and in their own way could be cyclical, but they had to be on a different economic footing than the primary businesses of the corporation.

There was a catch. The quest for these elusive earnings flows put the corporate chief on the horns of a dilemma. If he went too far out on the limb for diversification, then he risked owning a business that he had no native expertise in for the sake of having its earnings. This was called *conglomeration* and brought a whole new set of headaches. Investors, at least since the 1960s, were dubious of conglomerates and would not pay a higher PE multiple for them, reasoning that the sum of the parts was almost always less than fair value. (In other words, they were buying a business that was not managing its assets effectively since it was too big.)[7]

Greenberg distrusted this theory of diversification as a way of managing the risk of particular business cycles. His business was risk and nothing else. Seen coldly, AIG was the endpoint of the financial equation every time an earthquake, car accident, or fire happened in more than 100 countries. AIG, as he conceived it, was a continent whose shores were buffeted by huge oceans of risk. So far, they had been fortunate. AIG was relentless in its geographic expansion and obsessed with writing the insurance others would not. He was baffled that his competitors still saw the consumer business in England or Canada as diversification; to him, Nigerian oil fields and Vietnamese small business was closer to the mark. Anybody could write life insurance for a lawyer in Scarsdale; he was writing it along the northern Manchurian border since the 1980s. This, combined with decent underwriting practices, had acted as natural brakes on local and regional recessions. A keen student of the earnings of AIG's competitors, he knew he was better off than most, but that wasn't good enough. On good days, he knew AIG could do better, that there was always some other option to generate excess capital that they hadn't considered; on bad days, he pondered grimly what he always suspected would someday come—a fearful symmetry of concentric catastrophes and economic woes that could cut even AIG off at the knees.

What that nameless, shapeless evil was, he could not say. But Greenberg was a man who had detailed contingency plans for AIG's survival in the event of nuclear attack on New York City and for the collapse of the American political system. If diversification was gnawing at him, then it was for a good reason, even if he couldn't fully enunciate it yet.

So, throughout the mid-1980s, he and Ed Matthews pressed for options. There was no particular reason why that juncture in time saw Greenberg so concerned about diversification, other than to say that it was raw animal instinct. Sharks sensed the slight electrical pulses generated from a struggling fish a mile away, and Greenberg felt looming risk. It mattered nothing to the shark what was thrashing, only that he moved toward it; Greenberg did not reflect on why he badly needed to diversify in the winter of 1986, only that it be done.

Still, it was a problem not easily solved. They had grown large, very large, and he was not shy about telling Matthews that the days of swimming against the tide were long past. As Robert O'Harrow and Brady Dennis reported in a three-part *Washington Post* investigative series on the rise and fall of AIG Financial Products called "The Beautiful Machine" (December 2008–January 2009), Greenberg told Matthews, "We are the tide now."

While Greenberg was worried, he was also optimistic. Every time he faced a seemingly insolvable problem in business, Greenberg had seen his hard work, his eternal restlessness and curiosity pay off and a solution emerge. Suggestions to help AIG diversify, however, were met with a scowl. The idiots on Wall Street—the analysts and their constituents, portfolio managers—always thought consolidation and size were the answer. This left him agog. What good was massive size when a recession was in full swing and 20 percent of your customers were behind in their premiums, and another 20 percent were scaling back coverage or not paying at all? If you wanted to move away from commercial insurance risk, he wasn't quite seeing the utility of being pitched a merger with a commercial insurer.

He formulated his responses with some decorum (having long ago learned to curb his desires to address the more clueless questioner—who, as he saw it, was simply passively phrasing a statement or a demand as a question—as "Moron" or "Jackass") and replied that while scale certainly did have its place in business, simply becoming big in a sector was not always best for the enterprise longer term. He argued that even the largest life insurer in the United States or the largest financial services firm in western Europe, was going to have problems when those markets turned south and stayed there for three years.

Still, bankers proposed mergers, with each one—to the minds of Matthews and Greenberg—appearing stupider than the next. With his hands folded across his chest, he frowned as the bankers unfurled their spiel.

"Thirty percent growth!"

"New markets!"

"Cost savings!"

The bankers spewed their buzzwords, but Greenberg only saw trouble. How did a transaction help you pay a workforce you had grown 30 percent and who expected salary and benefits regardless of the economic cycle? Was this company doing something in some market that AIG wasn't? If you have just gotten bigger—and are having to consider a period of wrenching and expensive layoffs to boot—how are you saving on expenses?[8]

That's why so many of his competitors were in the end just crappy companies never too far from death or a merger—they couldn't even think a proposition this far through. They made deals because deals, they thought, were what they were supposed to make. The shape of the business in five years if the markets didn't grow as planned? An unlikely consideration.

Still, there was the not-so-small matter of diversification. Greenberg needed something that could be a sustainable business, where capital could be responsibly deployed to generate solid returns and yet was totally unconnected to insurance cycles. The capital markets were the natural answer, but here—more so than even in the realm of potential competitor acquisitions—his natural instincts and the arched eyebrows of Ed Matthews warned him off. A naturally amiable and engaging man, the Princeton-educated Matthews had an excellent business mind and easily spotted the risks in the details of an issue that Greenberg hadn't.

A senior partner as an investment banker at Morgan Stanley in the late 1960s and early 1970s, Matthews was broadly considered to be among the handful of men who were in the running to helm the firm in the mid-1970s and beyond. An unapologetic partisan for the old, clubbier Wall Street, he had no love for its evolution into trading floors and cutthroat banking. He found honor in being a traditional investment banker and he was astounded at how many young bankers looked at the client's needs as an opportunity for a quick fee or, increasingly, an opportunity for their firm to take advantage of. Matthews shook his head at the explosion of capital deployed on the trading desks at Goldman Sachs, Salomon Brothers, and Morgan Stanley. Did any of the leaders at the big firms really get it? Did they understand that trading your equity-capital base several times over each day on three or four different continents was a recipe for disaster?

Matthews knew in his bones that it was almost certain to bring down one, if not more, of these shops. He had seen dozens of the old-line, preppy banking partnerships folded into the bigger firms— especially Merrill Lynch, which seemed to acquire an old-line firm weekly in the 1970s—when trading commissions were deregulated in 1975, with their partners happy to sell out for a fraction of their equity value. But this was different. If Goldman or Salomon collapsed, they would turn the marketplace upside down, all because they were chasing an extra buck.

This was premonition, though, and AIG was a place you didn't run on premonition. Moreover, Matthews shared Greenberg's view that they were missing something in the markets. The world was changing; having major units in London or Asia was no longer exotic. Capital flowed across borders in the dozens of billions of dollars every minute, offering limitless opportunity to the company with the strength and expertise to take advantage of discrepancies in asset prices. Greenberg had put him in charge of this project, if they could call it that, but Matthews was unsure how to go about it.

They had legions of traders, portfolio managers, and analysts at AIG investment management, and he couldn't see any of them coming up with any ideas on how to generate large amounts of revenue doing things unconnected to the capital markets cycle. Nor could he see them doing it without big-time risk.

This was not to knock them—as chief investment officer he was their boss, after all—but simply to say that looking to make more money doing more of what everyone else was doing could not work: trades became very crowded, and the larger you were, the harder it was to get out. They had grown mightily since he joined in 1973, and now they were the big fish, the whales, and they needed very deep water to maneuver. There were not many places left to find that sort of deep water in the 1980s without breaking new ground. Again, a dilemma emerged since AIG was an insurance company, and insurance companies, whatever one may say about them, were not known or valued for their commitment to financial innovation.

Matthews told Greenberg and his colleagues that having lots of cash was nice and having a triple-A rating gave them a head start in doing anything, but in the end, you simply made a few extra cents doing what everybody else was doing because you could do more of it or you could do it for a lower cost. They were looking to do something special, something no one else was doing, and finding those people was a rare thing.

Finding the concept would come, Matthews had thought to himself, but he fretted over the people issue. He couldn't recall how many great business plans he had seen wilt because people wanted more power, more credit, and, always, more money. There was no doubt about it.

As a former Wall Streeter himself, he would ensure that when they found what they were looking for in the markets, there would be no investment bankers and traders around to really screw it up.

■ ■ ■

In the winter of 1986, Abraham Ribicoff—the long-serving former Republican senator from Connecticut working as a senior adviser at the law firm Kaye Scholer, and who practiced the sort of law that was popular in certain Washington, D.C., and corporate circles, in which his substantial Rolodex was deployed matching people with needs and problems to the people who could address them—called Hank Greenberg. Insofar as Greenberg had personal friends, Ribicoff was one—a sensible and level-headed senator who, as befitting a legislator from Hartford, had always worked hard to protect insurance company interests in Washington. Of course, Ribicoff had been a good ally for Greenberg, but he found the senator legitimately intelligent, able to see solutions to complex foreign policy problems. This was no minor compliment. AIG, with operations in over 100 countries in 1986, was tremendously levered to American foreign policy, and Greenberg spent much of his waking time navigating AIG through one political-diplomatic-financial brushfire after another. A person like Ribicoff, whom Greenberg saw as clearheaded and not given to cheap posturing, was valuable to AIG's interests.[9]

Greenberg took the call immediately. The senator, rather than calling in a small chit (another specialty of retired politicians) or passing on a tip about some pending nonsense in D.C., got right to the point.

"Hank, I wouldn't bother you with business issues," Greenberg remembers Ribicoff saying, "but there are a few fellows that I think you'll want to meet." He went on to tell Greenberg that a man named Howard Sosin had come to see him and that he seemed to be a mighty impressive fellow, even allowing for the fact that he had no real idea what the hell it was he did for Drexel Burnham Lambert, that high-flying Wall Street firm that was in the news all the time.

Ribicoff said Sosin was looking for an introduction to Greenberg and he was inclined to extend it, but that in listening to the man, it was really clear that he was, in a word, different. His resume included a stint at Bell Labs, then the most prestigious technological corporate research facility in the world and a PhD in the mathematically heavy field of derivative pricing theory. Though demonstrably brilliant, he presented himself well and seemed to have a very strong vision of what he wanted to do. To an outsider to the financial world, Ribicoff had said, he seemed more like an inventor who had come up with something no one else had dreamt of.[10]

Greenberg took the meeting and ordered Shake Nahepetian, his longtime assistant, to set it up straightaway. The premise of the meeting was an idea he had for a form of derivative, something that at first pass left Greenberg cold. Still, they were in the market to do something different, and Ribicoff was a good sort, so he followed through.

After meeting Sosin, Greenberg recalled, "I told Ed to handle that since I had no deep-seated grasp of what they were going to do."

"I guess what impressed me," said Matthews, "was that he really was on to something that no one else was." He continued, "They had a specific program no one else had . . . they had really thought it through. They didn't care about other lines of business or what other people were doing."

Both men's affections would later shift, but pressed on the matter they acknowledged Sosin's command of the subject matter and above all, his risk aversion. Greenberg and Matthews, veterans of hundreds of money-scheme pitches, were impressed with his emphasis on risk control and bear-market scenarios.

What Sosin was "on to" was to engage in long-dated interest rate option swaps. "Rate swaps," or more colloquially, "swaps," were not new to Wall Street; there was always someone wanting to swap out their floating rate (an interest rate that moved up or down according to some predetermined benchmark, such as 90-day Treasury bills) exposure for the predictability of a fixed rate. There just wasn't really anyone interested in doing it for more than two years, and most market players wouldn't conceive of it beyond one year. The reasoning, circa 1986, was fairly simple.

As an example, assume Corporation A pays a floating rate of about 4 percent for three-year debt and wants to swap into fixed-rate debt of 4.25 percent to better manage its interest expenses. Corporation B agrees to assume the floating-rate debt expense in return for receiving 4.25 percent in interest from Corporation A. If rates stay about the same, everyone is happy: Corporation A gets to better plan for its financing costs, and Corporation B is making 0.25 percent (or 25 basis points) on the swap. But rates rarely stay the same. If rates go to 5 percent, 6 percent, or more, Corporation B is losing cash every second of every day. Depending on the size of the loan, this could amount to some serious risk. Worse, there was no real secondary market for these loans, nor were there many ways of hedging this risk. To do the trade in a world like this, Corporation B would have to have a nearly religious conviction that rates weren't going to go above 4.25 percent.

In 1986, there were very, very few financial managers willing to bet that rates couldn't increase sharply. After living through the massive interest rate increases of 1979–1980, when the Federal Reserve boosted interest rates to 17 percent in the fight against inflation, willingly assuming floating-rate risk for a long period of time with no real hedging ability was akin to a professional death wish.

But Sosin, as a veteran academic and trader, knew full well that fear did not necessarily translate into unwillingness. Since 1982, he had been on the other side of the phone from Drexel's corporate and trading-desk clients and a very interesting subset of them did indeed want the ability to convert some of their fixed 5- and 10-year debt into floating rate. They wanted it badly, in fact, and, he reasoned, likely would not be too hung up on the short-term cost of trading with whoever could facilitate this for them.

As hard as Sosin had worked to come up with a plan that made good business sense, Randy Rackson had labored to develop the sort of software that could easily and accurately calculate the costs and risks of doing those interest rate swaps. Barry Goldman, the quietest and most reflective of the three, had been busy as well. Drexel's interest rate option research chief, he had constructed any number of transactions they could offer potential clients and had, in conjunction with Rackson, looked at ways of developing software programs that took into account ways these deals could be hedged.

If Drexel seemed an unlikely place to have begun the mathematical and financial odyssey that would eventually put Sosin and his colleagues into Hank Greenberg's office—and the firm's fortunes were indeed tethered to the then-booming junk bond market—the practical structure of a place like Drexel made the threesome's ascension incrementally less baffling.[11]

Shot through with ambition to overtake the likes of Goldman and Morgan Stanley as the banker to America's elite, Drexel (under the oversight of chief executive Fred Joseph and junk bond guru Michael Milken) was willing to invest its massive junk bond profits in the trading and underwriting of numerous securities that were then at best sidelines for Wall Street. Included in this was the then embryonic trading of interest rate swaps.

Joining the firm in 1982 after the bitter collapse of the options-trading partnership he had put together while at Columbia Business School (he would leave the school's faculty the same year) as a government bond arbitrage trader, Sosin had impressed his bosses and colleagues with his ability to theorize new uses of options and futures in hedging techniques. In this, Sosin and Wall Street were growing up at the same time. The path to success on Wall Street's trading floors had long been the willingness to take risk to execute large trades, which in turn brought in customers and their lower-margin but higher-volume business. As derivatives took hold in fits and starts in the early 1980s, customers became more eager to trade with the firms that had the most effective strategy for deploying them for risk management. And it was just fine with Sosin if everyone else at Drexel was focused on things like leveraged buyouts (LBOs) and the issuance and trading of junk and convertible bonds for their cash-desperate client base's designs on the American corporate landscape.

Though no one's idea of a traditional salesman, Sosin was direct and absurdly intelligent and looked at things—the interest rates, volatilities, and funding needs and liabilities that corporate treasurers and chief financial officers (CFOs) had to wrestle with—differently than the bankers most corporations dealt with. He actually, in the words of a former colleague, proposed solutions for the interest rate management problems of corporations that they hadn't necessarily heard a thousand times before, a small miracle in the herdlike confines of Wall Street. (That any solution Sosin proposed involved trading or banking with Drexel was both obvious and beside the point to the corporate executives.) The plain fact is that Sosin and a desk full of his colleagues built a derivatives business that was profitable from the get-go, grew in stature (and profits), and, increasingly, was doing business not with the fast-growing, junk debt–addicted companies that Drexel did most of its business with, but members of the establishment like IBM, Chase, and Phillip Morris. The operation Sosin built began to separate itself from the great mass of Wall Street trading desks, all of which were proficient at executing customer orders, by becoming problem solvers. He had come to understand that the real money on Wall Street wasn't in just doing what others were not, but in having some form of advantage that dissuaded customers from doing business with all the competition that was sure to spring up.

By this time he and Rackson were close friends, and they would stroll lower Manhattan's harbor front during lunch breaks or after client meetings and wonder aloud about working for themselves. They pondered, and then rejected, an investment partnership—what we now call a hedge fund—since raising capital wasn't the biggest need they would have. They needed balance sheet. From there, they just had to calculate who had both the appetite and resources to handle what they were pondering on those walks.

None of that made him a man who, in the course of events, would ordinarily wind up being able to do business with Hank Greenberg, who controlled a company whose market capitalization in 1986 made it one of the largest in the Standard & Poor's 500. It did, however, ensure that Sosin had been battle tested. The academic theories from Bell Labs and Wharton that had intrigued him so had either been adapted to fit the reality of the market's violent crucible or they had been thrown out. Sosin had come to see something that was very important to Matthews and Greenberg: things went wrong, terribly and horribly wrong, in the markets and you had to have a good idea of how to get the hell out of whatever trade you started before you did some serious damage.

It did not hurt Sosin's cause that when asked about his views on trading strategy, he replied that he didn't have one. Before they could get a frown off, he told the pair that he thought trading as a way to make money was dangerous and ultimately counterproductive and that he planned on making money from hedging out risk and capturing price and cost-of-funding inefficiencies. This actually understates Sosin's antipathy to trading. Having sat on a Treasury-bond trading desk, he was appalled at how otherwise bright men wagered capital on bonds based on their guesses as to how the market reacted to any one of two dozen economic statistics. This wasn't a rational business; it was playing lottery tickets for a living.

Matthews, who was one of the handful of corporate executives in the United States in the 1980s who had taken part in some longer-dated swaps (though not with Sosin), saw true potential. AIG could make money acting as a matchmaker, pairing up companies who could swap with each other directly; they could make money taking the other side of a transaction and hedging out the risk; they could make money trading different parts of the hedges; they could, in the safety of a business pitch on the 18th floor of AIG's headquarters, make money doing anything.

Something else was apparent to all involved: there was no law that said the software and business plans that were developed for interest rate swaps couldn't be applied to dozens of other thorny money problems. Businessmen first and foremost, Greenberg and even Matthews were certainly lost after about 15 minutes speaking to Sosin, Rackson and Goldman, but that mattered little. They would happily trade a disadvantage with the minutiae of mathematical jargon for a direct shot at having a captive customer base that included the world's largest and most prolific borrowers: the big banks, multinational manufacturing conglomerates, airlines, governments, Fannie Mae, and Freddie Mac.

They would all have to come to AIG. Better yet, they would all want to.

In private, Greenberg and Matthews began to sense that the three men from Drexel not only had a plan that took into account market corrections, but they were bringing in customers who really wanted the product. And while managing risk was a wonderful thing, making money was altogether more wonderful.

Hank Greenberg is often quoted as having said, "All I want from life is an unfair advantage."[12] He was about to get it—for a while at least.

■ ■ ■

The papers were drawn up as a joint venture. At the end of a round of negotiations, Sosin, his two colleagues Rackson and Goldman, plus another seven Drexel options and futures trading pros would become something called AIG Financial Products, and they would receive 38 percent of their net income. Ownership of the company would be 80 percent AIG and 20 percent Sosin. No one had ever driven a bargain anything like that with Greenberg—before or since—but at the outset he didn't complain. Five-eighths of a monopoly is still a pretty handsome competitive position.

Ribicoff, the battle-hardened veteran of decades of broken commitments and promises, told Sosin, "You let us draw up your marriage. Let us handle your divorce," according to the *Washington Post*.[13]

There was a quirk to the structure of FP. From a regulatory perspective, it fell between most every crack. Though any U.S. domiciled institution is subject to any federal law, practically speaking, on a daily basis, it was as if FP didn't exist. It wasn't a money manager or a bank, so its operations would leave no real paper trail, and since it sought no commerce with the public or even most corporations, there was no sales or marketing literature to be filed. Its business activity would, according to plan, be something that most corporations would rarely disclose nor investors or media seek answers to. Even a hedge fund has a prime broker who clears its trades and secures its financing; FP wasn't going to do much trading, and if anybody had any question about their credit quality, well, the phrase "triple-A" directly cleared up matters. There is no record of Sosin's having designed this as such, but there is ample evidence that on many levels he was pleased with this sort of structure.

In late January 1987, Mike Milken made an impassioned phone appeal to keep Sosin, proffering a larger share of his profits, more power, guarantees, appealing to loyalty ("Hadn't Drexel been fair to him?" and "What more could they do to keep him happy?"). Traders on his desk were impressed, as Milken rarely made a direct pitch like that. In the days before the explosion of private equity and hedge funds, leaving a plum position like Sosin's was a risky move. Sosin was a partner in the firm and owned several million dollars of stock, in addition to his million dollars plus in annual compensation. In late 1986 there were rumors that Drexel would go public and, like Salomon Brothers in 1980, its partners would reap multiples of book value for their equity.[14]

But Sosin politely and quickly rejected the appeals, sharing little about his future plans, shaking hands, packing his boxes, and leaving.

When it became clear that Sosin was going, Drexel's management offered Rackson a $2 million guarantee (he had earned over $1 million the previous two years) to run the department. He turned it down straightaway. Close with Sosin since the early 1980s, when he was at an economics consulting shop called Data Resources International, trusting Sosin had worked out brilliantly for him. Having turned down an impressive guarantee from his then employer, the First Boston Corporation, of $350,000 to stay there and co-run their financial futures department, he declined and took a salary of $125,000 with no guarantees of a bonus in order to continue to ponder risk, derivatives, and the software they both felt was the future of Wall Street.

A year later, he was a millionaire.

They had crafted an oral agreement since Rackson's first day on the job in 1985. In return for being Sosin's junior partner, Randy would be paid 50 percent of whatever Sosin made. A certain type of trader would reject that deal out of hand, but that trader wasn't privy to what Rackson saw: everywhere Howard Sosin had been allowed to let his thoughts and visions play out, a lot of money had been made.

What Sosin didn't know, of course, was how close Drexel had come to suing him and AIG for "raiding" the firm. He took 10 men with him, all key producers or senior operations and analytics staff. Drexel went from a respected competitor in a high-margin business to virtually out of the business in the short term.

It would later (much, much later) be learned that Howard Sosin was a different sort of employee. He could make many millions of dollars for you in ways that you hadn't imagined, but when he left, there was a big crater and bad blood to spare.

Chapter 2

Who Dares, Wins

L ike the starving given a meal, or the parched a sip of water, the men who founded AIGFP had gotten what they had dreamed of and were determined to not let it slip away.

Decades later, several of the initial AIGFP founders still talk about their first impressions of life at AIGFP in one phrase: the balance sheet. It changed the way they thought about business, value, and risk. In turn, they would seek to use this asset to do a sort of business that had never been done.

It is one thing to propose a joint venture with the likes of an AIG for the purposes of doing what had never been done before, but when a triple-A-rated balance sheet is laid before you on Wall Street, the theoretical becomes instantly possible. In the finance business, the advantages of having a triple-A-rated balance sheet are so profound that most people in the industry can only understand them conceptually. To begin with, in every transaction, the triple-A-rated company has a pronounced advantage in borrowing and carrying costs; they can get into a trade at a lower price than the competition and stay there longer.

It goes without saying that a triple-A can also put on bigger positions than its competitors.

The ability absorb the market's blows is the difference between failure and glory on Wall Street. In a milieu where an asset might increase or decrease in value 25 percent or 50 percent in three months, funding a trade more cheaply lowers your cost basis, which in turn increases your ability to exit it profitably at your discretion.

Those are just bottom-line considerations, however. Practically speaking, you don't go to people—people come to you. Concessions in price or risk are made to get you into the deal and then to keep you there. Investment banks compete bitterly to win your business and, as often as not, front their own capital or bring you their best deals to curry your favor. In a sense, you are the port in the storm: you are offered transactions from the desperate and the discreet that others never even see or hear of.[1]

Seemingly trapped in a cycle of virtue, it's also incrementally harder to get in deep trouble with a triple-A rating since commercial banks, like their investment-bank cousins, compete greedily to provide credit facilities into the multibillions of dollars. When others starve for credit, you have it at your fingertips.

As with most things, it turns out that size does matter.

■ ■ ■

These were wonderful, new things to Sosin and his colleagues but they didn't make the venture work. From day one until the crisis of 2008, the reason for FP's success—the only aspect that separated them from the herd of Wall Street proprietary trading desks and hedge funds—was AIG's unconditional triple-A guarantee of every contract they entered into. Without it, they would have to trade because they couldn't hold securities or enter into deals for any length of time.

Oddly enough, capitalization for the unit was almost a nonissue since trading was an afterthought. Actually, the only corporate mandate the unit had from AIG was to handle its tax "issues." Though this sounds more nefarious than it was in practice, the fact of the matter was that AIG—like any corporation with operations in about 130 countries—had massive amounts of tax liabilities in one currency and ample tax breaks in another because of underwriting losses. One of FP's jobs was to try and employ various investment strategies to help even their corporate tax bill.

This was now Howard Sosin's realm in late 1987. He had become accustomed to watching others profit from his innovations and strategies because they had the wherewithal to stick around in a deal to the point where the serious money got made. Now other people could fight investment banks for a few pennies of profit in some trade; he and his team became focused on how risk was mispriced.

The three leading lights of AIGFP, Sosin, Goldman, and Rackson, arranged their computers in early February 1987 in some spare office space at 667 Madison Avenue and quite literally launched on day one. Sosin, as a former colleague recalls it, was on the phone with the treasurers and financial officers of his former clients immediately.

Both Rackson and Goldman would initially get compensated at 20 percent of Sosin's compensation level. Though it seems lopsided, the entire joint venture was between AIG and Sosin, allowing him to control and allocate bonuses based on the 38 percent of profits due FP. Both men recognized that they were going to be dealing with transactions and profits the size of which they had never dreamed, and that there was *zero* chance that Howard Sosin was going to underpay himself.

It took a little convincing to get corporations to do some swaps beyond two years' length (known as *tenor* in Wall Street parlance), but as predicted corporate treasurers were only too happy to avoid having to face an investment bank as a counterparty in anything for more than a year.[2] With the continuing growth of an interest rate swaps market pegged to something called LIBOR (short for London Interbank Offered Rate), the interest rate that banks borrow from each other in London, they could (per Rackson's models) hedge these trades.[3]

Under their joint-venture agreement with AIG, they had the right to claim the profits from a swap transaction at the origination of the transaction. Nothing astounding about that, since many transactions allow for revenue recognition at this point. What Ed Matthews, chief financial officer Howard "Howie" Smith, and Hank Greenberg apparently had not recognized, though, was how, in Smith's words, "[FP] was taking all the profit out on day one and then leaving AIG with a 30-year exposure to a swap. We might not have known as much about swaps as Howard, but we sure understood open-ended liability. We didn't allow it in the insurance units so why should we have tolerated it there?"

But it wasn't, in 1987, a hill to die on. They made about $50 million that year (in which, rather memorably, the equity market crashed and wiped out much of Wall Street's trading profits). Perhaps more than anything else, this ability to generate profit entirely unrelated to the rest of the capital markets stayed the hand of Greenberg and Matthews in the face of "downstream" risk they would never ordinarily have tolerated. In any event, Sosin was doing exactly what he had laid out in his presentations. In 1987, AIG booked over $1.13 billion in pretax profit in its general and life insurance businesses so Sosin's developing business didn't occupy much thought at 70 Pine Street.

If there were grumblings out of Howie Smith's finance department about the construction of the swaps market trades, they were outweighed by the realization that as arcane as the FP swaps book was, Sosin had instilled in everyone there the commitment to thoroughly hedging out every form of market risk conceivable. No one at FP was going to use its balance sheet to express a strongly held view of interest rates or currencies. From time to time, they were offered large blocks of stocks or bonds at attractive prices but turned them down, despite the allure of a built-in profit, because it wasn't the business they were in. When a deal presented itself, if a hedge could not be found, structured or invented, FP would not do the transaction.

Nor did many understand that every swap had a ratings clause embedded in it. If FP's counterparty was downgraded, no matter where the swap was in its 30-year life cycle, FP had the right to back out.

Tom Savage, a former colleague of Sosin's from Drexel who had been asked to join with the original 10 (and had declined, only to join several months later in the winter of 1988 as Drexel's prospects continued to deteriorate), says that the money made at FP was a function of originality and "who we were," that is, their inventiveness and their low cost of capital.

"I don't think enough people appreciated that about Howard's time. Leaving the "directional" bets to others became an FP hallmark."

One of the unique features of Sosin's tenure was the institute of a risk-management function called Trade Review (TR). In practice, it was simplicity itself: a group of FP employees reviewed every aspect of every deal the day it was booked. To ensure objectivity, you could not review your own trades.

Given that AIG was engaged in long-dated swaps where it was directly exposed to the credit quality of a company that was (to varying degrees) less solid than AIG, upon the development of a new swap opportunity, a group of AIGFP employees would review the trade and the swap contract. All FP professionals had to take turns a week at a time in serving on TR, which met every evening after the lawyers provided had prepared the necessary documentation. Needless to say, it often took several hours of work. An offshoot of the peer-review process during Sosin's career as an academic, it was an attempt to apply common sense, or "distributed wisdom" in the words of sociology, in the vetting of a risky, arcane proposition.

Sosin was looking for commonsense mistakes or bad assumptions, reckoning that if a risk modeler felt uncomfortable with the interest rate assumptions embedded in a swap, maybe the person who put the deal together should reconsider it or, at the least, defend it publicly. If a marketer hemmed and hawed or became defensive, that was a red flag. Trade Review was even more elemental: Sosin was looking for examples of "hive mind" or "group think." In other words, he was looking for someone who *hadn't* spent dozens of hours on the trans-action to point out where it appeared FP had done something for the sake of earning a quick few bucks. A transaction done because the numbers fit or because it was in vogue was a transaction that *didn't* get done at FP. No one had to do anything at FP for the sake of showing a short-term profit; all that had been left behind at Drexel.

It's difficult to overstate the singularity of this approach. Not only would this not occur at a Goldman Sachs or Merrill Lynch, but the proposal of the idea would be heresy and, quite possibly, professionally dangerous to any who suggested it.

■ ■ ■

Once moved out of the city to Nyala Farms road in Westport—about three miles from Sosin's home in Southport—the growing staff of Financial Products sought to expand beyond swaps by concentrating on whatever struck their fancy. It really was this simple: for $150,000 base salary plus health care and an oral agreement that Sosin would be fair at bonus time, they sat around and dreamed up new ways of marrying their balance sheet to profit opportunities. In this pursuit of doing what others were not, FP had a big advantage in the person of Barry Goldman.

One of the prize pupils of Nobel laureate and options-pricing model developer Robert C. Merton (often called "the Father of Modern Finance Theory"), Goldman had authored numerous articles—including at least one with Howard Sosin—on options pricing and finance theory. Though having had a prestigious academic career was hardly unusual at FP, Goldman was seen as a breed apart not just because he had worked so closely with Merton (though that was a tremendous credential in the then-emerging shuttle between academia and Wall Street,) but because he was able to translate the theory of finance into something that would bring in profits.[4]

"That Barry was the smartest of the bunch is for certain," said Savage. "You could sit around and talk to him about the philosophical implications of a problem in finance that bugged you for 10 years and he would look up at the ceiling and solve it. In 10 minutes. He did that a lot."

So-called quants (short for quantitative-modeler) and rocket scientists, with their multiple science and math degrees from prestigious universities, were thick on the ground in and around Wall Street by the late 1980s, but they proved to be a mixed blessing. Adept at dreaming up or handling volumes of complex math and computer problems, many proved sharply less valuable in dreaming up lasting ways for the investment banks to make money.

This was not Goldman's problem.

According to Savage and another key FP executive from the early days, Bob Litzenberger, Goldman could readily dream up deals and navigate through three or four valid obstacles that a prospective swap counterparty would face.[5] Litzenberger said that Goldman, despite his pedigree, looked at problems like an ordinary businessman, with a keen sense of how good intentions and hard work can go awry in an instant. A hallmark of Goldman's, according to former colleagues, was the embedding of a zero-coupon interest rate option in longer-dated swaps, which proved to be quite lucrative for FP over the life of a swap.

It is no secret that Goldman was perceived as something of an eccentric to his colleagues, many of whom recall with amusement his regimen of ice cream for breakfast, slavish devotion to the Boston Red Sox, and an absence of worldly interests outside of reading and listening to music. Rather unlike Sosin and Rackson, however, he seemed quite content with his by-all-traditional-standards handsome compensation of nearly $50 million between 1987 and 1992 and happily retired from Wall Street in the mid-1990s to do, in the words of several former colleagues, "apparently nothing."[6]

One of the issues that Goldman (and his colleagues) found fertile soil in was the previously mundane realm of municipal securities. No former FP executive seems to recall precisely who made the initial pitch to the treasurers of America's cities to do business with AIGFP, but it proved to be a remarkably effective profit stream and source of cheap capital.[7] As noted earlier, only doctors and dentists eclipsed municipalities as the easiest marks for Wall Street's sales machine. Generations of city, county, and state treasurers got reamed when they exchanged fixed-rate debt costs for an investment banker's promises of floating-rate bliss, only to see rates shoot up and losses mount shortly after the ink dried.

AIGFP had a way around that.

They would swap rates with a city or town, but with a twist: FP had found a way to hedge out most of a municipalities risks using specifically designed swaps. Moreover, because of the unique tax-exempt nature of dealing with a municipality, AIGFP was able to find corporations that were all too happy to reduce the risk of an increasing tax rate and take the other side of an interest rate swap with a municipal debt issuer.

In interviewing a host of former FP executives, it is clear that the municipal securities business was a source of great profit for the unit because (to make an achingly complex series of interlocking hedges and swaps simple) they were able to capture a handsome spread between their exposures on muni swaps and their hedges in the taxable world by understanding the excruciating details of both markets. Better still, for the municipality to lock in fixed long-term interest rates as anticipated. More than 23 years on, with hundreds of separate muni swaps done, it does not appear than any municipal issuer has sued AIGFP—a truly remarkable feat.

The reasons for this are obvious, according to documents detailing AIGFP's internal calculations, since their muni swap customers often saved as much as 50 basis points (or one half of a percentage point) in interest rate expense over the life of the swap. This could add up to material savings when, for example, you consider that a half-point less interest expense on a $200 million swap saved the taxpayer $1 million per year on what were often 30-year borrowings. It wasn't a fortune, but when compared to how most cities fared after contact with Wall Street, it must have seemed like manna from heaven.

Where FP hit its stride was with a foray into something that, along with the long-dated interest rate swaps, came to define their presence in the capital markets (at least until the credit-default swaps imbroglio). Beginning in 1988, AIGFP began to get heavily involved in something called municipal guaranteed investment contracts, or MGICs as they were known within the unit.

A variation on the guaranteed investment contract, a long-standing insurance company offering, where a customer's deposit earned a prevailing risk-free interest rate in return for nearly Treasury bond level of security, these instruments were a favored way for insurance companies to raise pools of cash to invest at higher rates of return. Except AIGFP wasn't guaranteeing Mom and Pop the 90-day T-bill rate plus 20 basis points, they were dealing with state highway departments and boards of education.

Here's what AIGFP figured out: A city that was building new schools and had raised the funds via debt wasn't going to spend the capital all at once, but would release it in stages as the projects approached completion. Rather than keep it sitting in a bank earning a short-term savings rate, the finance officials were receptive to AIGFP—a triple-A U.S. insurance company subsidiary—pitching them AIGFP's version of a GIC. They got a near bank level of security, liquidity to draw at par at any time for their required purposes, and a much higher interest rate than the trustee bank's negligible overnight sweep account rate; AIGFP tapped into a galaxy of ready cash that it could deploy in whatever strategy it wanted to. The risk-adjusted borrowing rate for FP was often higher than its alternative borrowing choices; however, the advantage of muni borrowings for FP was that it tapped into a sizeable niche market for cash that it could deploy in its corporate transactions without restraints of competing in the public markets with its parent company.

All of these deals—and others simply too arcane for our purposes—made AIGFP approximately $1 billion between 1988 and 1992. They had, as one former executive put it, a printing press in the basement. Of that figure, more than $380 million was Sosin's to allocate. Rackson and Goldman were paid nearly $50 million each; Sosin took home more than $125 million.

Then, depending on whose history you believe, one of two things happened. Either madness ensued and AIG—in an eerie foretelling of a future inability to manage AIGFP—shot itself in the foot and forced out the people who were on the cusp of creating the most profitable financial enterprise in the history of the capital markets. Or management, alone in finally realizing the long-term risk that was under way in Westport, got wise and put some serious restraints on FP's ability to structure long-term swaps. Either way, by Christmas 1993, Sosin and most of his brain trust were gone, despite (incredibly) having earned more than $650 million that year.

Technically, the reason that the place one of Sosin's closest confidantes called "Heaven on Earth" was unwound was due to a series of snafus related to an epically complex deal—more a series of transactions—with Edper, the Bronfman family's then highly rated Canadian conglomerate.[8]

In the fall of 1992, AIGFP wound up effectively loaning Edper about $200 million via long-term floating-rate debt. Not only was there no market then for long-term floating-rate debt, thus ensuring that whatever value FP set for the transaction was driven by their models, but fundamentally, they were a direct counterparty to an ambitious, dynastic conglomerate with a boundless appetite for financial opacity. To complicate matters, they also wrote a series of credit-sensitive swaps on another class of Edper debt.

Everything was fully hedged, and, like always, a nice chunk of profit was realized at the initiation of the transaction. And then the hammer fell: Edper was downgraded. Immediately, all of the native intelligence and market savvy at FP came to naught. The unit was stuck with a direct exposure to a real estate company whose prospects looked shaky. What was worse, the direct exposure was in a floating-rate security for which no market existed, and they were locked into a swap that looked like its liabilities were endless.

Sosin, Rackson, and Goldman were mature men, and they had all, as the expression goes, "seen combat." They understood losses came with the territory and proposed a series of measures and countermeasures to limit exposure. Greenberg, Matthews, and Smith had also "seen combat," though—plenty of it, literally, in Greenberg's case—and countermeasures were the least of their worries. To the FP leadership, this was a classic example of a good deal turned sour. To the AIG leadership, the deal being good or bad was immaterial: Sosin's group was doing increasingly risky, if not erratic, transactions that they were going to have to stand behind. Howard Sosin was a very rich man, as Howie Smith would tell Ed Matthews and Hank Greenberg repeatedly, and getting richer every day because *they* guaranteed everything FP did, sight unseen.

There was no way he could have known it, but the screw-up with the Bronfmans was the precise entry AIG's leadership had been looking for to force a sea change in how FP conducted business. Truth be told, Greenberg and FP had been on a collision course since about January 28, 1987, the day after its doors were opened.

Greenberg had long fretted over the deal he signed: ceding 38 percent was ceding a lot of money, but that was barely the tip of the problem. The fact of the matter was that they had written a very simple contract with Sosin—they would guarantee *anything* he did. They couldn't even really ask questions. In his darker moments, he would analogize it to letting someone you don't know very well keep a copy of your checkbook in their drawer.

Of course, they had every right to walk away from it with the appropriate notice, but therein lay the dilemma that agonized Hank and Ed. If they got Sosin out, a major risk factor walked out of the door, but so did an earnings stream that was approaching a half-billion dollars and had been growing at a steady 20 percent annual clip.

Greenberg had war-gamed it incessantly in his mind. No more possibilities of an endless and eternal risk from some deal he and Ed couldn't truly figure out if they spent a week on it. But no more of that "capital lite" nine-figure earnings stream either.

He had tried to fire Sosin once before, in mid-March 1990, when he objected strenuously to a plan he and Matthews had to set up a currency and commodities trading operation with a group of former traders from Drexel. Sosin objected furiously, arguing that the trading of anything that had a derivative component to it, especially commodities and currencies, was his bailiwick. Greenberg had tried the formal approach man to man, had tried reasoning with him as a colleague, and had even been his charming best, all to no avail. This was so appallingly infuriating to Greenberg that it virtually fascinated him.

"How on earth," he would reflect, "am I tolerating this from a guy I am in a fucking joint venture with?"

Smith and Matthews had asked each other a version of the same question more or less every day for the past several years. Smith couldn't understand how AIG had ever gotten comfortable with allocating the profit from a deal on day one; Sosin would be out of the business, if not dead, when some of these deals closed and AIG would still have guarantees in effect.

"Tell me how one of these deals doesn't come back to kill us. Just one. Tell me how they [FP] got every credit [analysis] right on every counterparty and nothing changes or deteriorates over the next 20 or 30 years," Smith reflected. "There simply has to be a better way of [handling this] than taking all the money out on day one."

For Ed Matthews it was more personal. In complete seriousness, Matthews would recount for hours how Sosin was the hardest person he had ever dealt with in his career. He didn't understand how anyone could be so terrible to deal with on every issue on every occasion; the principles of statistics, he argued, would dictate that at least a few times their interactions would have been agreeable.

One story Matthews recounts is that in the middle of a discussion over the AIGFP bonus pool that was rapidly turning south, Sosin said that he had to wrap up the conversation since he had promised to take his family to a Mets game. Late afternoon slipped into the early evening, and pretty soon game time was fast approaching, with Sosin continuing to press his points. Matthews put his foot down and tersely informed him that the conversation was over. When Sosin refused to end it, Matthews told him that he couldn't negotiate with a man who would leave his little son sitting with his mom at a ballgame in Queens.

Sosin hung up.

Another time, their conversation deteriorated into rank insults. Within minutes of phoning Matthews, he was calling the number two man at AIG, and his notional boss, "a devious son of a bitch." Astounded, Matthews got down to his level and called him "a goddamn liar." So it went, with the 61-year-old Matthews reduced to schoolyard epithets, straining to best one of the most brilliant men in the capital markets in the use of profanity and vulgarity, until he realized that this was all going to wind up in court one day and hung up.

The answer was money. Whatever else could be said of Sosin, the man knew how to make money, and that was something that Greenberg and Matthews were wise enough to understand did not come along every day.

The key to understanding Sosin, Greenberg had learned, was that he viewed his contract with AIG as the inviolable writ of God. If it said that all derivatives would be traded by FP, then absolutely no one else within AIG could so much as look at anything more complex than a standard convertible bond. That his contract essentially said these very things drove Greenberg mad. Of course, discounting the fact that no one had any idea that the market for derivatives would explode—along with Drexel, throwing hundreds of good traders into the job market—Greenberg had no one to blame but himself and his lawyers for drawing up the contract this way.

To Greenberg, who viewed AIG as an old-line partnership—albeit one where he was the general partner with unusually broad powers—this was heresy. He had built a company where of a moment, should you be asked to sacrifice something for the good of the firm, "Yes!" was just about the only answer that mattered. He had risked his balance sheet and credit rating so that Sosin could get his operation going; why was Sosin preventing AIG from hiring a bunch of traders who were in markets he had nothing to do with?

Sosin's reply to these concerns was "a deal was a deal." From his perspective, allowing AIG to force modifications on him at their will would—in the fashion of the camel's nose and the tent—hurt their business and could culminate in the inevitable stripping of all of FP's rights. He had taken a lot of risk leaving Drexel and made AIG a small fortune doing things his way; there hadn't been any valid reason given to him for change. There was also the fact that he was not an AIG employee, so the lectures of Matthews and Greenberg about "the good of the company" were utterly immaterial to him.

But the Edper losses changed everything.

■ ■ ■

There was one risk that needed no legal explication in Sosin's contract-obsessed worldview: a threat to AIG's credit rating. So, in December of 1992, Greenberg drew up a new contract that was little more than an ultimatum: a series of limits on long-dated swaps and a change in the way revenue was recognized. For Sosin, the decision was easy.[9]

Within a few weeks, toward the end of January 1993, Sosin formally notified Greenberg that effective at the end of the year, he would be dissolving the partnership. He would take a core group with him, including Rackson and Goldman and a handful of other loyalists. They had a remarkable track record: since February 1987, AIGFP had earned about $1.1 billion pretax, making them responsible on a regular basis for between 10 percent and 15 percent of the corporation's earnings.[10] The importance of this to a certain kind of very influential money manager—the sort who prizes growth above all else—cannot be overstated. That none of them had the foggiest idea of what the hell AIGFP was up to is beside the point.

Sosin, it was clear, had every right to be very confident that another very deep-pocketed AIG rival was out there ready and willing to get into business with him. All that remained was for Sosin to get his $250 million incentive fee, portion it out among his colleagues, take his cut, and proceed on to the next chapter.

AIG had different ideas. They had been running what the *Washington Post* called "a covert operation"[11] and had begun to reverse engineer all of the deals of which Sosin was so protective. They struck first and marked the Edper bonds and swaps to zero, took the charge against earnings, and announced to Sosin that, because of these events, the bonus pool was zero.

In short order, Sosin sued AIG; AIG countersued Sosin, and what was an acrimonious business relationship became a spectacular divorce. In reality, AIG's gambit was just that: the classic corporate tactic of the rich and the strong in many legal battles. When well-heeled corporations seek to avoid an expensive liability and their counterparty is weak, litigation and a settlement is often an economically sound (if ethically dubious) approach. And settle is precisely what AIG did in early November 1993, paying Sosin just under $200 million, saving over $50 million from his contract-mandated payout.

One of the casualties of this affair was the relationship between Randy Rackson and Howard Sosin. Once best friends—no mean feat since Sosin, in the words of Tom Savage and many others, was "not the most amiable of men"—Rackson was godparent to two of Sosin's children and his closest business confidante.

Sosin's court battles were not over. According to legal documents Rackson filed in 1995, despite turning down repeated overtures from Ed Matthews to run the unit after Sosin's departure—for more than $20 million per year—Sosin stiffed him on his 1993 pay. In a running five-year legal battle that received none of the press that the initial split from AIG received, a jury eventually ordered Sosin to pay Rackson over $16 million.

Despite walking away from his AIGFP years with around $150 million in total compensation, Sosin never managed to catch that lightning in a bottle again. His next arrangement, with Spain's Banco Santander, lasted about three years and ended in acrimony as well. Personally, the reclusive Sosin, who never sought to promote himself within the media nor sought influence within AIG, suffered the embarrassment of a bitter divorce becoming public, replete with details over his finances and his wife's affair with another man.

The bitterness with which Smith, Matthews, and Greenberg view the Sosin period at AIGFP is perhaps understandable from a personal standpoint but makes little sense from a business standpoint. There can't be much said against the man and his operation from a risk-management perspective, and his group's innovation and execution on behalf of its clients was excellent.

■ ■ ■

Sosin had no way of knowing this, but he became vitally important to what AIG was not only becoming, but what it became. In developing a unit that would become 10 percent to 15 percent of pretax profit, the ruminations of Greenberg and Matthews were validated—there was indeed "something else" out there to be done that could provide the desperately sought-after noncorrelated earnings. His legal pleadings against AIG could have plausibly emphasized his contribution to the market cap expansion.

AIG's stock continued to appreciate handsomely, going from $68 in early 1987 to $88 and change in late 1993. Though the insurance subsidiaries continued to grow nicely, especially the foreign units, an extra horse added to the draught-team—one that was capable of growing north of 20 percent annually—was what caught investors' eyes. If 95 percent of investors had never heard of AIGFP or Howard Sosin, so much the better for Greenberg since they loved AIG.

At a price of $88 in late December 1993, 16 times its expected 1994 earnings, AIG was trading well above its competitors in the insurance realm, which was standing tradition on its head, since it was increasingly being viewed as less of a pure play in insurance and more of a hybrid insurance-finance combination. Better still, AIGFP allowed it to generate revenues in finance without the ugly work of retaining armies of brokers, bankers, and traders. Greenberg was getting investors to pay a higher price for AIG stock because they were enthralled with the colossal insurance machine he had helped build, but a growing slug of this profit was coming from the markets, an area where investors refused to pay up, because of the risk involved. For AIG and because he was Hank Greenberg, people were willing to forget about these concerns.

AIG, after the so-called Decade of Greed in the 1980s merged away dozens of former blue-chip stocks, had thus become a "widows and orphans" stock, a core holding for those interested in long-term safety of their investments.

However, AIG management's handling of their launch into Wall Street deserved mixed grades. Sosin's claim that much of what animated the growing hostility of Greenberg and others to him was simply the strong deal he drove for himself in 1987 may well be valid. AIG's insurance units had been built on Greenberg's precise oversight and control, something like FP, that relied so heavily on AIG's strength yet was still separate from his direct control was surely a bitter state of affairs. When it became clear that they could have long-term "tail risk" from

FP's deals (in theory, if not in reality), they moved quickly, bordering on ruthlessly, to change the terms of the joint venture. Their arguments may not hold much water 17 years later, but it is difficult to fault them for being farsighted and ruthless in protecting corporate credit quality.

Yet, like Sherlock Holmes's "dog that didn't bark," AIG's managers were willing to loudly declaim the risks of FP, yet remained unwilling to exit the business. Quite the opposite. As Sosin and his team of luminaries decamped, Greenberg, Matthews, and Smith had already furiously expanded AIG's efforts in the capital markets and asset finance sectors.

With virtually every passing day, AIG's massive ship sailed farther from the plain, if profitably familiar, shores of the world of insurance and into the kingdom of money.

Chapter 3

The Man with the Plan

It is simplistic to say that FP's losses on a single trade mattered so much to Hank Greenberg, because nothing mattered so much to him as not losing—a contract, money, market share, or credit rating. But not by much. He was and remains supremely competitive, even among an executive class where to sustain loss and defeat are considered character flaws. But that's not the full picture, either. And, to be fair, by the early 1990s, he really disliked and mistrusted Howard Sosin, so to have booked millions in losses (even if Sosin had made him hundreds of millions of dollars) from a man he wanted to be rid of two years earlier was a bitter pill to swallow.

A more accurate sense of the matter might be that the losses hurt Hank Greenberg because anything that hurt AIG wounded him: there was no appreciable difference between AIG as an enterprise and Hank Greenberg as a person.

Any number of chief executives are considered virtually interchangeable with the companies they founded and ran: Ted Turner and Turner Broadcasting, Warren Buffett and Berkshire Hathaway, and Bill

Gates and Microsoft are just a few examples. But Greenberg's case is different. Buffett is first and foremost a (brilliant) investor and Bill Gates is a (brilliant) engineer and software developer; it is a coincidence that they are good managers, or more truthfully, had the sense and humility to hire good managers. Ted Turner is a more apt comparison. In building CNN, Turner revolutionized media and made the world, in a sense, smaller, but his passion was only for building; by 1996 he had happily sold out to Time-Warner and was content to become a rich liberal philanthropist and, when it suited him, controversialist. He remains liberal, charitably inclined, and controversial, but after becoming an enthusiastic supporter of the Time-Warner–AOL merger in 2000, assuredly the most epic boondoggle in corporate history, he is much less wealthy.[1]

Greenberg is more along the lines of Federal Express's Fred Smith, another combat veteran who revolutionized and internationalized a centuries-old industry, and which, in its own way, facilitated greater global trade and a more peaceful world order. Except Fred Smith founded Federal Express thinking he might be able to run a business profitably if it was incrementally more efficient than the military logistics and postal services he had observed during two tours of duty in Vietnam.

Maurice Greenberg, on the other hand, knew that if AIG was built according to his vision, it would change the world.

■ ■ ■

Born in May 1925 to lower-middle-class parents in New York City, his cab-driver father was killed in an accident in 1930 and, after she remarried, his mother promptly relocated the five-year-old from Queens to Swan Lake, New York, a part of the marginally larger Liberty, about 100 miles north of the city. It was a Depression childhood in a rural setting as opposed to a Depression-era childhood in an urban setting. Presumably, like many a bright teenager in a Depression-era rural setting, planning on getting the hell out of there probably occupied a fair amount of his time.

As the Second World War exploded, he got his chance. The fast-thinking 17-year-old got his then girlfriend to help him fake a birth certificate; when that came to naught and the enrollment officer didn't believe him, he admitted to faking his mother's signature attesting to his being aged 18. "It turns out that I was younger than the age on my enrollment form," he has said wryly.[2]

Tricking a harried enlistment official was perhaps the last fast one Greenberg was to pull on the Department of the Army. Assigned to a communications support unit for a Ranger battalion, he was to land a few hours after the infamous first wave on Omaha Beach in the Normandy invasion of June 6, 1944. As the initial assault units were dispersed or cut to ribbons, his landing craft operator decided not to land on the appointed sector—the "Dog Green" sector that was graphically portrayed in the movie *Saving Private Ryan*—but took them instead to "Dog White," an incrementally quieter landing site 1,000 yards down the beach.

Greenberg has over the years acknowledged to a (very) few colleagues that whatever he was slated to do in supporting communication lines soon gave way to the reality of war. Given the attrition American troops experienced in the peculiar Normandy countryside, Hank Greenberg became a rifleman. Two of his long-standing colleagues have said that Greenberg has admitted that one of the lessons that combat impressed upon him was that plans are handy but matter little once the fight starts, where skill and determination and a willingness to suffer count for more.

Colleagues who have heard him discuss these experiences say that he remains angry at his unit's supply situation, still stuck more than 60 years later on the cold, hunger, and exhaustion that is the lot of the foot soldier. Regardless, he fought on, wet, cold, and hungry, like millions of soldiers before and after him. There was, he tells people, nothing else to do. What Greenberg won't discuss, of course, is more than made clear in the casualty lists of the forward combat units in the slog across northern France.

Eventually, his unit fought through Europe and landed in a non-descript village just outside of Munich called Dachau.[3] Arriving within a day of its liberation, Greenberg experienced the full panoply of its horror: the pits of decaying corpses, the walking skeletons, the open sewage. If Greenberg is dismissive of attempts to discuss the war, he is contemptuous of questions about Dachau. Still, a few of his more senior colleagues say that it is one of the few things he is emotional about, astounded that such things happened in broad daylight in Germany.[4]

After managing to get a GED, BA, and JD in a little less than five years, war again came to Greenberg's world when the Korean war broke out. Again, his efforts to serve in a less dramatic fashion came to naught when an appointment to a judge advocate general unit evolved into commanding an infantry platoon in the mountains between Seoul and the North Korean border, where he was ultimately awarded a Bronze star. He talks about his Korean war experience about as much as he does Dachau. According to the handful of colleagues he has ever discussed it with, Greenberg was involved in some of the most savage fighting of that war, defending positions in the months-long bitter winters against human wave attacks.

The most interesting aspect of Greenberg's early tale is that within three days of his discharge from the service, he was hunting for a job in New York. There was no extended rest or relaxation, no processing of what he had just experienced. He got down to work. In 1952, he walked unannounced into the Continental Casualty Insurance Company and, in trying to talk his way into a job with the personnel director, felt he had been rudely treated. He stormed out of the office and into the offices of a now-forgotten vice president and informed him, in front of a host of colleagues, that his personnel director was "rude and a jerk."[5] The initiative, aggression, and propriety impressed the executive, and Greenberg was offered a job as a trainee at $75 weekly.

In 1959 he became the youngest VP at Continental and would have presumably worked his way up the ladder there save for a conversation Continental's boss, Milton Smith, had with a fellow insurance chief named Cornelius Vander Starr, who had been inquiring about where he could get his hands on a fellow who understood the U.S. accident and health business well. He'd need a self-starter, an entrepreneurial type who could build something on time and under budget. Starr was wondering if Smith knew of anyone fitting the bill. As it happened, Smith let slip that he had the perfect man in one Hank Greenberg—why he mentioned this to a rival remains unknown—and in short order Starr hired Greenberg to run these product lines for his own company.

■ ■ ■

The complete history of AIG is worthy of Hollywood treatment, but falls outside of this book's scope. Still, even the barest outline of its launch reads like a Horatio Alger story for free marketeers.

AIG was founded by a patrician-looking, modestly resourced, 27-year-old wanderer from California named Cornelius Vander Starr. His background included a brief stint selling handmade ice cream, wrapping cigars, a tour in the First World War army, and passing the California bar exam. He wound up peddling insurance at a unit of a local realty firm.

After taking a clerkship with the Pacific Mail Steamship Company, which didn't work out too well, Starr wound up sailing to Shanghai, with only, as the story has it, a few hundred yen in his pocket.[6] Notwithstanding that he almost certainly had more than that (having founded and profitably sold a few businesses) one point rings clear from his earliest days: Starr was an inveterate entrepreneur, adventurer, and risk taker who gave little credence to what the establishment said was prudent or popular. (So is every other founder of a long-lived business, but Starr was simply more so. To analyze his actions from an 80-year remove is to conclude that he must have spent a great deal of time studying the operations of more established insurance companies and then done the precise opposite.)

With nothing more than what people described as a quiet self-confidence, Starr commenced operations as an underwriting manager for the overseas operations of English and American insurance companies. Called American Asiatic Underwriters (it later changed to its current title, American International Underwriters), Starr did something that no other American or European company was doing at the time, or for many years after: he hired middle-class Chinese to conduct and manage his business.[7] Starr embraced the untraditional in hiring practices, which became a theme of AIG's even after questions of race became a largely settled matter.

AIG is a treasure trove of stories about hiring people and situations that would ordinarily exist more in the realm of fiction than an insurance company. Here is one, recounted in Ron Shelp's *Fallen Giant*[8]: Starr had an admiration for the Russian expatriate community in Shanghai and liked to hire from within it because of their high levels of education and their multilingual capabilities. While seeking a prospective hire in a Russian refugee camp in Shanghai, a Polish cavalry officer who spoke very little English but who was desperate for work heard of the opportunity and beat the Russian to the interview. Banking on the fact that Starr couldn't tell the difference between a Pole and a Russian, and with his head wrapped in a bandage, he used what little English he knew to tell Starr that he was suffering from a terrible toothache and couldn't much talk. Starr, as the legend goes, caught on to the ruse quickly enough but hired the man on the spot, reasoning that, if nothing else, he had no shortage of courage and initiative.[9]

Oddly enough, despite the fact that Starr was operating in what was a Victorian-era colonial carve-up in Shanghai (under an 1840 treaty, foreign-owned businesses were given a chunk of Shanghai in which to own land and trade nearly tax free), his business practices and principles appear to have had more in common with, say, a local organic food cooperative or Ben and Jerry's Ice Cream than even the most purportedly enlightened public company of today.

Circa 1940, at a time when Jews and other minorities had to set up a parallel social structure in the United States because they were omitted from most institutions, and racial segregation was more or less the norm in wide swaths of the country, Starr's burgeoning empire was a virtual tower of Babel. Men from perhaps a dozen countries, every walk of life, and nearly every religion did business all over the world.[10] As Shelp notes in *Fallen Giant*, Starr assuredly did not shy away from hiring bright and talented Ivy Leaguers and other establishment sorts—many of whom were given substantial responsibility—but his record of meritocratic hiring and promotion (often having more to do with intuition than anything else) still had no analogue in business or government from that period and would remain ingrained in what became AIG's culture.[11]

One of the more striking aspects of dealing with AIG executives, both current and former, is the preponderance of people from modest backgrounds. For every Ed Matthews, who sits on the board of Princeton University, there are dozens of men and women who were likely fortunate to attend local branches of a public university. Greenberg, though inescapably now a man of the upper social and cultural strata, stood out as a manager for his willingness to recruit, promote, and ultimately share equity with men and women that many high-profile corporations broadly ignore.

Starr was more than a fellow with an open mind; he gave his local managers and sales staff, as well as his secretary and accountants (and even his wait and kitchen staff) ample equity in the various companies he controlled. The effects were immediate: in an age of seven- and eight-hour workdays and three-martini lunches, his employees worked 12-hour days six days a week to drum up new business; moreover, with "skin in the game," they were immensely loyal to Starr and often enough proved nearly impossible for rivals to poach.

Finally, 50 years before Peter Drucker and other management gurus by the boatload would preach decentralization as the premier management tool for the modern office environment, Starr made it the centerpiece of his managerial style. Managers—many of whom had precious little insurance background—were given responsibilities that far outstripped their titles. It was not uncommon for Starr to allocate $50,000 or perhaps $75,000 to a key associate and have him handle the opening of an office to underwrite risks in a nation like Italy. With that, the employee would be responsible for literally every aspect of the operation, including dealing with regulators and obtaining licenses, staffing, building up clients, and executing policies. There would be the occasional exchange of telegrams and cables, perhaps annual visits, but in every meaning of the term, Starr's man on the ground in Cuba or Argentina was on his own.

The only real thing that mattered to Starr centered on the pricing of risk. He would happily consider underwriting just about any kind of risk, but was not willing to do it for just any price. He insisted that the combined ratio—essentially the amount of expenses and incurred losses divided into the earned premium—be low, the clearest sign of profitable underwriting. Naturally, every insurance executive solemnly proclaims this—indeed, so does every businessman—but Starr and his companies had a key advantage that allowed them to translate this from lip service into practice.

In taking on Chinese shipping companies or Philippine manufacturers as clients, especially in the 1920s and 1930s, C.V. Starr and his companies obtained something akin to a soft monopoly. Being the only company writing policies covering loss from pirates along the Indonesian coast, currency revocations, or risk of loss from coups in nations that were then Imperial pawns gave them the ability to adjust premiums to levels that virtually assured profits. It also gave them a lot of repeat customers.[12]

Not that Starr's companies weren't taking risk—they were. It's just that he saw things differently than his competitors ensconced in comfortable offices in New York or Boston. Thousands of ships and boats, after all, would insure against theft and piracy to ply the tens of thousands of miles of Indonesian coastline, but only a few would actually be hijacked. Moreover, the losses from these claims could be offset with new business written as *some* of these companies grew their operations given the expansion of Asian markets.

Given his favorable competitive position, Starr's companies were able to develop what would emerge as the second defining feature of AIG: a legendarily thorough claims unit (almost certainly the first of its kind in Asia) using the latest scientific and forensic methods to determine the validity of a claim and defend against fraud.[13]

That's where his open-minded attitude toward foreign nationals came in quite handy. Unlike American and European insurers, who tripped over each other prospecting in the expatriate business and diplomatic communities, Starr used connected and ambitious locals to weed out weaker customers or frauds, and to bring in a steady flow of growing businesses that were happy to insure with a profitable American firm.

Greenberg proved a prescient hire. His masterstroke was turning around American Home Assurance, a then perpetually listless unit, to record profitability in several years. The task, it should be noted, was assigned to him because he had spoken up at an executive committee meeting dealing with the money loser in 1963, upbraiding his colleagues—including Bill Youngman, Starr's then CEO—as "goddamn fools . . . who didn't understand the basics of insurance."[14]

As the 1960s progressed, Greenberg's bluntness was tempered by a certain creative touch. According to a *Fortune* magazine article from September 2008, he pushed mightily to break into the Soviet Union, and after convincing the powers that be he wasn't a CIA plant (though later years would see him become very close to it), AIG was awarded the license. AIG's profile was raised in Japan when he got a company that sold hats to children to also sell accident policies, and to market this coverage by putting the insurance broker's name across them.[15]

The combination of a willingness to alternately to pound tables and make internal enemies to turn around a losing business unit, while happily trading with enemies past and present, made him an understandable choice to take over as president in 1968 as Starr's health deteriorated.

The good news was that Starr bequeathed Greenberg and his partners an insurance empire; the bad news was that it was both far-flung and not terribly profitable. There was Delaware-based C. V. Starr, which handled domestic insurance needs for U.S. companies, and Panama-chartered Starr International Co. (SICO), specializing in underwriting foreign risks for U.S. companies.

It was all the very picture of unwieldiness, so Greenberg sought to consolidate and streamline the diverse network of operating units. As a remedy, a multistep transaction was structured, whereby C. V. Starr and SICO exchanged their operating assets into what would become AIG in 1970, receiving blocks of newly issued stock in return. The same thing was then done for C. V. Starr.

Greenberg successfully argued that SICO and C. V. Starr & Co. shouldn't be eliminated. As part of its stock swap, SICO, the more profitable of the two companies, got a block of what became AIG stock. The owners of SICO, including Greenberg and other senior executives, had the right to liquidate SICO and distribute it equally among themselves, giving them each a multimillion-dollar payday. Presumably, with large payouts in the bank, they could have run C. V. Starr & Co. and made a very pleasant life for all involved. But Greenberg led the effort to combine the units and move forward as AIG. At the time, this was seen as sound business judgment and in the best interests of enterprise building; in an age of initial public offering (IPO) millionaires, it seems odd to have deferred a massive one-time payday for the privilege of working an additional 35 years.

With dividends reinvested, the value of this block eventually grew to some $22 billion in 2005. C. V. Starr & Co., which retained a few specialty insurance lines that the fledgling AIG didn't need, also took what became AIG stock, eventually worth about $5 billion.

Greenberg was able to make C. V. Starr and SICO the proverbial brass ring for a generation of AIG employees. That's because AIG's top management used shares of the units as incentive pay, doling them out to the company's top performers. The hook was a doozy: the units could be converted into AIG stock and sold only when a recipient reached age 65 or retired. That kept 35 years of AIG employees loyal.

The logic and choice were stark: a key manager, recruited to another company, could opt to leave and earn an extra $50,000 or so a year, or he could cash out his shares at the end of a career for many millions of dollars. It kept a thousand AIG employees from 1970 onward working 60-hour weeks, traveling the globe, and working for many thousands of dollars less in salary than their competitors because when they retired, a multimillion-dollar nest egg would be waiting for them.

To legions of AIG employees, it lent a sense of connection to their employer and a meaning to work that is frankly rare. However, with the CEO of AIG granted chairmanship over both of these companies, per their charters, Greenberg had almost godlike powers over the fates of his employees, and effective control over more than 17 percent of the shares outstanding. Thus, there were no palace coups or political intrigues directed at him. He appears to have used this power benevolently in that hundreds of SICO and C. V. Starr shareholders were allowed to retire earlier than 65 and keep their shares.

As the 2008 *Fortune* magazine article would note, Greenberg also conceived of SICO as "a corporate reserve for a 'very major rainy day.'" Memos to Greenberg spelled out as far back as 1980 that SICO could be a possible "survival vehicle," an offshore entity that would allow AIG's survival in the event of a "nuclear explosion detonated within the U.S.A." or "open rebellion of a sector of the US population."[16]

Greenberg made his mark on the newly consolidated company in other ways. Starting immediately in 1969, AIG began to reinsure much of its risk and, according to David Schiff, the long-time publisher of *Schiff's Insurance Observer* and a student of AIG's history, "They pretty much hit it perfectly. Whatever they laid off risk-wise seemed to result in claims and it was during a period where reinsurance was fairly cheap. They got the best part of the deal, by far." Because of AIG's foreign roots, it developed a U.S. underwriting presence somewhat later than many of its peers. This was fortunate because making a major domestic push for commercial business in the late 1960s and early 1970s allowed them to avoid much of the asbestos and environmental liability that devastated the industry. Also, with niche insurance lines like director and officer coverage, they were able to benefit from near-monopoly pricing power and, in many cases, use it as a wedge in the door to pry key sections of commercial coverage away from competitors.

After a few generations, most corporations have little more than a passing connection to the men and families who founded them. The legacy of Starr and his bootstrapping construction of what became AIG is more than an interesting footnote to a corporation's arc, however, in that it is pretty much exactly what AIG continued to do.

Greenberg was the perfect heir to Starr because he fully embraced Starr's restless quest for diversification. Throughout the 1970s, AIG continued to add opportunistically to its offerings, either by developing a product line itself or acquiring rival underwriters, each one offering another sort of coverage line or with a license in a specific geographical area. AIG's insurance operations became, in effect, self-hedging: as Europe's growth slowed down and premiums contracted, the United States and especially Asia would compensate. The world in 1987, and especially in 1993, offered little such opportunity for an insurance company to grow. There was eastern Europe, but the economic growth of its linchpin, Russia—at least prior to the boom in commodities— was no certain thing in the early part of the 1990s. Away from that, there wasn't much that could take an insurance company into the realm of double-digit growth, which was the sort of growth analysts wanted.

This left Hank Greenberg, at the end of 1993, with his bruises and headaches from his first go-round with FP still fresh, with little choice but to trust that his ability to move AIG into the business of money was going to work. He had worked harder than any man in business to generate the consecutive earnings increases that earn investor con- fidence. He would, he reasoned, be able to surmount this challenge. There would just be more and more businesses he and Ed would have to keep an eye on. Still, it gnawed at him. The money business was not like insurance, at least the way he played it. Dealing from strength, his capital position, and his triple-A credit rating would allow him to dominate where others could not.

Still, the risks in the money business were wholly unlike insurance. The risk in a business where you used your credit rating to win was always aimed directly back at the credit rating. You could underreserve or undercharge for insurance risk and still, given the pooled nature of the business, when all was finished and paid out, you could almost always limp away. When you bet that the guy you were swapping interest rates with would have the same credit rating in 26 years, well, that was something else.

All the guarantees in the world couldn't convince him that they weren't going to pick some bad apples for swaps. The worst thing was that he wouldn't know it until it was too late.

■ ■ ■

As 1994 dawned, there was some obvious math behind Hank Greenberg's worries over entering the money business. In 1989 he had about $6.8 billion worth of different financial assets on his balance sheet; at the end of 1993 he had over $25.5 billion and was adding more every day. He knew those assets were earning returns—Financial Services revenues had neatly tracked the mercurial growth of the balance sheet, passing $1.5 billion in 1993 with $390 million in operating profits (earnings before interest and taxes), but that was the problem: those assets were twinned up next to liabilities, and those were growing at north of 20 percent as well.

The relationship between balance sheet growth and financially driven profits was so clear that he was now hearing more calls, both internally and from investors, to get bigger. In fact, it was obvious to Greenberg that outside of Ed Matthews, Howie Smith, and a half-dozen or so AIG long-timers, absolutely no one gave a crap about the liability side of the equation. This is called the "bad-things-happen-to-other-companies" school of thought. They used every tool at their disposal to monitor credit, market, and liquidity issues like hawks, playing with debt denominations, maturities, and interest rates to ensure that no one area of their debt profile would prove dangerous. He even upbraided his unit managers who thought the liabilities were AIG's, making sure that everyone who ran a unit that had debt knew it was *their* problem and its repayment was coming out of *their* cash flows.

Assets grew, liabilities grew, earnings grew, and it was all wonderful, Greenberg reflected, until either earnings slowed or assets proved less useful and he was stuck with liabilities. At that point, as the early 1990s gave way to the middle part of the decade, Greenberg and his team couldn't sit around and occupy themselves with the shapes of possible clouds on the horizon. Investors liked the increase in returns and let

Hank know about it. Here again came more headaches. An iron rule of business was that when businesses·heeded the call to get bigger, they generally weren't terribly picky about how they got there. This was done by buying competitors, throwing balance sheets around, and the obligatory high-profile public relations campaign, all of which inevitably resulted in a series of executive dismissals and a nice plump charge to earnings a few years down the road.

It was, as the economist Joseph Schumpeter might have put it, the darker side of the process of creative destruction. Huge commitments in time, energy, and capital were made and inevitably thrown away as a new leadership team chose not to saddle themselves with the problems of the predecessors. Good money and the careers of talented men were wasted without concern until the next big corporation swept up the wreckage of its rivals to staff its own ill-considered efforts to dominate business in some venture.

To Greenberg, pursuing growth this way was an idiocy of the highest order. It had a thousand roots, but it all came from the chief executive and his key staff being appointees to their jobs rather than businessmen. They listened to the media; they listened to analysts; they listened to whatever money manager came in the door with demands to provide them whatever returns their own managers demanded. They did everything but plan and execute strategy that would suitably reward their capital-at-risk.

Greenberg reserved a *special* measure of contempt for this sort of chief executive and the companies and boards that allowed it. To his way of thinking, they barely rated the term *businessmen*. Capital was precious. You clawed and scratched to make it grow, and when you put it at risk you did anything to protect it. Having been raised without too much, he probably would have this worldview, but under C.V. Starr, Greenberg learned that true business success can be had if you are smarter with your capital and the risks you take with it (over a longer period of time) than your competition. Starting without much capital, in other words, isn't half the impediment in business that poor decision making was. And poor decision making was always a function of a misappreciation of the risk in something. In his mind, that would not be his problem, but still, it was not lost on Greenberg that investors fired CEOs and not the other way around.[17]

The herdlike investor pressure for ever greater returns, Greenberg's own relentless drive to expand and conquer all that was new and interesting to him, and a view on capital formation and preservation that was every bit as philosophically deeply rooted as that of Warren Buffett and Charlie Munger, formed a nexus as AIG became a global financial power.[18] Of course, AIG was going to press forward and grow, in finance as in all else, because that, in the end, was what businesses did.

And the markets blessed Hank Greenberg for his every decision in this area. Seven years after entering the money game, the returns in the Financial Services unit make it clear enough why investors happily went along for the ride. Rare is the CEO who shutters a unit compounding its growth into the double digits, and rarer still is the CEO who does that when that compounding is leading to pretax income of over $400 million.

But the market in 1994 should have put everyone on notice. Few "slipped up" with the instruments the large multinational trading firms now were playing with and lived to trade another day. During 1993–1994, the old-line securities firm Kidder Peabody virtually collapsed when its head government-bond trader was found to have mismarked a huge government-bond portfolio and lost $490 million. A pair of Japanese currency traders working at separate oil producers lost more than $2 billion each trading currency futures. England's oldest bank, Barings, disintegrated under a $1.78 billion futures trading loss in Singapore. One of Germany's largest conglomerates, Metallgesellschaft, lost $2.25 billion and was merged away when its oil price hedges proved disastrous. Orange County, California, long one of the richest in the United States, declared bankruptcy when its treasurer, Robert Citron, lost $2.38 billion speculating in a massive mortgage derivatives bet.[19]

Every last one of these institutions was considered well capitalized and/or professionally managed, with access to the latest analytic tools and specially trained consultants. Moreover, the losses themselves came from the portfolios of their star traders and from their best units. In this world, there were no Cassandras offering informed skepticism and doubt. These institutions were healthy and respected one day and (financially) listing or sunk the next.

The post–Cold War globalization of markets ensured that 10 and 20 times the capital of even the late 1980s were piling into trades, ensuring that prices could be propelled up to astronomical levels, and then, when some indeterminate inflection point was reached, collapsing through the floor as investors and short-term traders sprinted for the exits. Large numbers of foreign banks were entering the markets, building up trading desks from sleepy, customer-facilitating backwaters to profit centers. Staked with piles of cash, they lacked the trading—and trading management—experience and institutional relationships of their investment-bank and hedge-fund competitors. So, too, were U.S. and Western multinational corporations, who were finding to their (pleasant) surprise that the newly open eastern Europe and China markets had a healthy appetite for their products, and who sought to hedge their expanding sales in dozens of different currencies. In both instances, derivatives were seen as the fastest way to achieve their goals.

Technology, the interstate highways of capital flows, was inefficiently applied to the dilemma that the expansion of derivative flows posed. Newer and faster programs were built to execute and process trades, using chips that processed sequentially larger amounts of information in shorter amounts of time, but, at least anecdotally, traders on many desks simply hadn't developed or mastered the necessary software, reverting to variations on standard options analysis programs. Nor were trading managers and operations staff at many brokers and funds privy to software that gave real-time, accurate information about derivative values. Because traders often traded on software programs several years old, they proved unable to properly analyze an effective hedging strategy for derivatives that were multiplying in complexity and number.

Also, there was innocence. In case after case, traders failed to not only comprehend the extraordinary leverage of derivatives to sudden price movements in their underlying assets.

In the example of Orange County, Treasurer Bob Citron made a massive bet on inverse floaters, a security carved out of mortgage-backed securities that carry floating interest rates, which decrease in value as interest rates rise. As such, Citron was making a bet, using leverage in massive amounts from the brokers who were selling him this paper, that rates would stay the same or decrease. They didn't. So when the Federal Reserve began raising rates in February 1994, Citron's positions in inverse floaters were wiped out and the brokerages, desperate to make up for losses on their credit lines, seized the under-lying collateral in the rest of the portfolio. This set off a daisy chain of (then) substantial losses across Wall Street's bond departments as firms tried to offload their own bad trades. General Electric, the corporate parent of mortgage-bond powerhouse Kidder Peabody, was so dis-gusted with the combination of the hundreds of millions of dollars in mortgage-bond losses and the high-profile scandal on its government-bond trading desk (see above) that it sold the nearly century-old firm at a fraction of its book value to PaineWebber.

Rule makers, regulators, and politicians around the globe (especially overseas) were helpless, still stuck on trying to comprehend the basic structure of derivatives and unable to agree on anything more than the basics of trade settlement. The regulators' power of subpoena, the most potent weapon in their arsenal, was useless because they appear to have been baffled at what the discovery process provided.

The use of derivatives has also benefited massively from a form of regulatory arbitrage. Consider this now-standard chain of events: a London-headquartered broker-dealer's New York–based trading desk engaged in a rate swap with a European hedge fund that is domiciled for tax purposes in the British Virgin Islands. Which national regulatory body has *de facto* oversight of this transaction? Don't feel badly if it's baffling to you; the regulators couldn't figure it out either.

Investors, who all too often stumbled on the basics of income statement and balance sheet analysis, were forced to analyze a three-month-old (at best) snapshot of a company's derivative exposure in a quarterly report. As most derivatives were kept "off balance sheet" and referenced in the footnotes toward the rear of purposefully obscure and ambiguously worded corporate filings, it probably mattered little.

Against this backdrop of the cornerstones of finance crumbling in days, if not mere hours, Hank Greenberg soldiered on, confident in AIG's exceptionalism, its ability to remain apart from this fray as it had so many times before in so many crises, would continue. He spoke of a powerful "enterprise risk management" system, and in Chuck Lucas he had a risk manager who had not only overseen a trading desk—the Federal Reserve's, as it turned out—but had literally been there at the beginning of the derivatives market, writing sage white papers on systemic risk for the Fed that were roundly ignored in both the public and private spheres as regulators struggled to understand why balance sheets across Wall Street grew exponentially with the things he had been warning about in one way or another since the early 1980s. Lucas was given wide-ranging powers in the mid- to late 1990s and he reported directly to Greenberg, who afforded him an open door.

But any analysis of AIG's risk management begins and ends with Greenberg. Like a brilliant professor with a cluttered office, he knew where everything was and what it all meant. He was the risk management terminus, the ultimate arbiter of what was and was not acceptable. The problem was not that it didn't work, but that it worked so well. A generation of AIG employees learned to measure the risk they took so that it would be congruent with what Hank would tolerate. Investors and analysts happily assumed that a system like that would be in place forever more.

It wouldn't be.

■ ■ ■

The earnings were sweet and the stock price increase sweeter, but there was little real magic to building a first-rate finance business, for AIG or anyone else. Finance subsidiaries would purchase assets using corporate-guaranteed commercial paper or medium-term notes and try and make a difference on the spread.[20] This has been the DNA of finance since the European monarchies staked explorers in order to bring back the gold, spices, and silk that propelled their mercantilist economies upward.

It was a little different for Greenberg, though.

His "explorers" were buying aircraft, shorting commodities, and entering into 30-year swaps in the name of earnings diversification. By 1994, unlike the Renaissance explorers' treasures, there was little scarcity value to what AIG did. The debt half of the equation would always have to be paid in full and on time. Greenberg was confident, but not certain, that if push came to shove, most of these assets could be sold quickly enough to forestall some serious losses. As an insurance man, he had certainly developed a clear-eyed view of what was broadly known as *liquidity*. AIG's life insurers had long held substantial amounts of government and the highest-rated corporate debt as a way of earning extra returns on policy premiums. If they could beat the returns on

Treasuries (the so-called risk-free rate of return) by a percentage point or two over time, he was happy enough. The crucial thing was to be able to sell whatever you needed to *when* you needed to sell it. He knew, in other words, that if anything ever happened to the recently purchased International Lease Finance Company (ILFC) unit, as one of the (then) three major aircraft lessors around the globe, being able to sell a dozen planes quickly at a price that was beneficial to AIG was simply not going to happen. (In fact, in a narrow and highly competitive landscape like commercial airliner leasing, if ILFC ever got into trouble, it was *guaranteed* that his competitors and customers would bid sharply below market for their inventory of planes, knowing full well they had nowhere else to go.)

A fair worry, to be sure, until quarterly numbers came out and the reason they bought ILFC in the first place was reinforced to them because, as was abundantly clear, ILFC was something akin to a juggernaut. In the prior two years, ILFC had been running at about a 21 percent increase in annual revenues—in 1992 it had generated $690.9 million and in 1993 boosted it to $879.1 million—while sustaining operating margins of between 25 percent and 27 percent. Business theory would teach that the opposite is traditionally the case: as an enterprise matures, its revenue growth slows and its profits contract as competitors flood into the space and offer goods and services more cheaply.

But, at ILFC, business theory was stood on its ear.

Started in 1973 with a $50,000 stake among three Hungarian immigrants—father-and-son team Leslie and Lou Gonda and Steven Udvar-Hazy—they built it into one of the largest aircraft leasing operations in the world by the mid-1980s. At its helm was Udvar-Hazy, a then 44-year-old graduate of UCLA whose knowledge of the minutiae of his business made him in every sense the aircraft finance equivalent of Greenberg. His incredibly close working relationships with the manufacturers, who would, in short order, contract to just Boeing and Airbus, extended to their giving him input into their design processes.

Together, they turned an underfunded competitor to GE Capital Aviation Services and Guinness-Peat Aviation (GPA) into an industry leader that was the most profitable of the three. So when Ed Matthews got a call in the spring of 1990 from James Wolfensohn, the former Salomon Brothers partner and former World Bank president with his own eponymous investment-banking boutique, asking him if he'd be willing to meet with ILFC, Matthews was happy for the chance.

Again, like Greenberg, the restless quest to diversify as both a business model and a risk-management mechanism was at the center of their thinking.

"I figured we could possibly diversify Financial Services beyond purely capital markets," says Matthews. More importantly, they understood the leasing business and had wide experience insuring aviation of all stripes. So Greenberg, Matthews, and the then head of Financial Services, Alan Fishman, flew to Los Angeles to meet the Gondas and Udvar-Hazy secretly at a Beverly Hills estate owned by an Australian friend of Udvar-Hazy's.

There was a comic element to the meeting, according to Matthews. Since the estate was just a few blocks from the Beverly Hills Hotel, where the three were staying, they decided to walk there. Apparently, they were off by a house or two in their calculation and had knocked on a few wrong doors where friendly but harried Beverly Hills housewives assumed they were Mormon missionaries and offered them water. Leaving the second wrong house, Greenberg had to apparently restrain himself from blurting out that they weren't Mormons, but rather, "Two Jews and a WASP from New York, looking to spend a billion on a jet-leasing company."

Eventually, they found the proper estate and settled in for the give-and-take of buying another business that was new to them.

"I felt like I was in a movie," said Matthews. "There the three of us were lined up on one couch, and there the three of them were on another couch opposite—staring at us, perfectly dressed and very formal. Whenever anything was said that interested or worried them, they would confer among themselves in Hungarian, we'd be looking at them, blankly, trying to read them. I knew we were getting somewhere when Udvar-Hazy asked us who he'd have to clear money decisions with and I said, 'You're looking at them. These are the only three people who can say no to you at AIG.' As it happened, they had had a meeting with GE the week before, saw the GE organization chart, and had been sickened."

Several weeks after that, AIG's $1.26 billion tax-free acquisition of ILFC propelled Udvar-Hazy and the Gondas into the ranks of Beverly Hills' wealthiest, if least well-known, residents.[21]

If everyone involved smelled opportunity in the marrying of AIG's balance sheet to ILFC's business model, the human element was going to require some massaging. At a celebration dinner Udvar-Hazy staged at his palatial Beverly Hills home, and which Matthews and Greenberg attended, the guests were summoned by trumpeters wearing white tail tuxedos to the dinner table from his terrace where cocktails were served.

Surveying the spectacle of a traditionally staged Hungarian royal feast, Matthews turned to Greenberg and said, "Well Hank, we are paying for this now."

"Don't remind me," said Greenberg, looking away angrily.

The deal itself was an old-fashioned purchase. AIG bought their profits and management expertise and hoped they would continue their remarkable streak; the owners became rich and hoped that AIG's stock, of which they now owned tens of thousands of shares, continued its ascent.

ILFC, at its core, ran a fairly simple business: They issued debt and used the cash to buy a slew of planes from manufacturers at deep discounts to list price (often 25 percent or more) and then leased them out. Unlike their rival GPA (which effectively collapsed in 1993), they were very crafty about timing the placement of their purchases and diversifying their customer base, selling into either growing aviation markets or those markets with a high percentage of business travelers.

The very opposite of their initial experience with Financial Products in many ways—for starters, Udvar-Hazy was both courteous and open—there was one area in which ILFC's business model overlapped. Without an AIG guarantee, business would be much tougher. Granted, ILFC's leadership had made a handsome go of it without AIG, but funding the business on their own, after the debt-market tremors in 1989 and 1990, as first Drexel, then the savings-and-loan crisis, and finally wide swaths of the commercial real estate market collapsed, proved pretty alarming. Buying $5 billion of aircraft at a clip is not without its risks and Udvar-Hazy had watched his rivals at GE Aircraft, backed by GE's triple-A rating, get leases done on terms that ILFC just couldn't match.

ILFC's management takeaway was correct: even a well-run, profitable business like theirs had no guarantee that they could sell debt at the prices where profits could be locked in, or even that they could sell debt at all if markets became troubled. No debt at an aircraft lessor meant little business getting done. The debt markets were not a cruel mistress; they were a bitch. To have to fund a business on debt meant planning for stretches when that funding went away. Selling out was a no-brainer.

AIG couldn't control the debt markets or what happened to interest rates, but when it wanted money, it got it. Under AIG's umbrella, Udvar-Hazy could ensure that business would always get done.[22]

In one big area, however, Udvar-Hazy's plans put him on an annual collision course with AIG's financial management. In his perfect world, he would borrow a large percentage of his capital expenditures in the commercial paper market or other short-term credit markets and pay a sharply lower interest rate, thus ensuring that his spread (what ILFC paid out versus what it charged the airlines they leased to) was maximized. AIG had two beefs with this: The first was that it kept ILFC permanently in the market issuing debt, captive to the appetite of other banks for its obligations. The second was that while funding short worked wonderfully for ILFC as long as rates stayed low, if they went higher they would be forced to scramble to issue debt at higher and higher rates, with no assurance that they could sell the amount they need.

AIG counseled (and, occasionally, when the objections got louder, demanded) issuing a larger percentage of ILFC's funding needs in longer-maturity obligations to standardize their interest rate expense, in other words, a trade-off between fatter profits and a more stable funding stream. Udvar-Hazy lost every funding duration battle for the 15 years he dealt with Greenberg, Matthews, and Smith, but as Matthews noted, he was "a smart operator and a very good businessman. By yielding to us, he was putting more in his pocket over the long run."

The only other issue IFLC ran into with AIG was the classic asset-financing conundrum: with (implied) access to one of the world's great balance sheets, Udvar-Hazy felt it was time to get a lot bigger and make up for the contracts they had lost out on. Ed and Hank saw it a little differently. As Ed Matthews recalls it, he would have a conversation every so often with Udvar-Hazy to the effect of, "If you want to buy more planes, Steve, you'll have to sell some first." And he would.

This "separate peace" strategy worked perfectly for AIG and, given that the stock price flirted with $100 late in the year, presumably for the Gondas and Udvar-Hazy. In 1994, the first-year investors could see detailed segment information in the 10-K annual report, revenues at ILFC increased a perfect 20 percent to just under $1.1 billion in 1994 and operating income grew almost 12 percent.

Again, the predicates of AIG's risk management held: sharp unit operators with plenty of skin in the game, combined with relentless corporate oversight, allowed ILFC to stay ahead of risk. When those variables were removed, life changed for ILFC.

■ ■ ■

Investors, being inherent optimists, and research analysts, being inherently gullible and disinclined to seek out the troubling, probably didn't go much farther south in the 10-K than the AIG Financial Services segment information, which told them the units grew revenues about 15 percent and operating income 4 percent in 1994. If they had, however, gone about three pages lower, they would have seen *how* these numbers grew. ILFC increased its commercial paper borrowings 26 percent to $1.21 billion, its medium-term notes program issuance 12 percent, notes and bonds payable rose 13 percent, and loans and mortgages payable grew a whopping 88 percent. (The 10-K was careful to note that none of these were obligations of AIG; bond salesmen, peddling ILFC debt to money managers, were just as careful to note to their clients that there was no way Hank Greenberg was going to allow ILFC to get into trouble. Both assertions were correct.)

Other AIG units were not immune to borrowing now and paying later. A new trading business called AIG Trading grew loans and mortgages payable by $750 million, and FP increased its notes and bonds payable borrowing by more than $500 million.

That these were debt levels AIG had never taken on before, to support assets that were simultaneously volatile and outside their management experience, cannot be argued. Ratings agencies, investors, corporate rivals, and analysts just stood aside as Greenberg's growth machine spun out $3 billion in operating income in 1994, 13 percent of which was from a unit that didn't even exist a decade prior. They also stood aside as total liabilities grew 13 percent on its balance sheet.

Surely, some investment bank junior analyst, alone in an office late at night, noted it as he crunched his spreadsheet for the senior researcher on the insurance team. Perhaps he even scribbled some notes in a margin or on a legal pad for his boss, something to tell the giant institutional money manager clients, the Fidelity Managements and Putnam Investments, in the morning. Likely, the notes said something that concluded AIG was in "a growth phase" of unspecified duration and was using debt to build scale, a plausible scenario (and one that AIG's investor relations team happily spoon-fed the harried analyst).

Perhaps.

The laws of finance are never kind to companies fond of "growth phases," however. The only way possible to handle the double-digit percentage growth in debt levels is to increase operating income at an even greater percentage rate. In a globally interconnected market, where employees and customers come and go, nearly perpetual double-digit operating profit growth is impossible as market volatility and competition conspire to level returns out. The only feasible way to do that was for AIG's growing number of capital markets operators to go out and take risk. After that bridge is crossed, you can just hope they were more right than wrong at year's end. With its debt and operating income growth roughly tracking each other for a multiyear period, AIG was en route to a vicious cycle (albeit one that would, given its size and profitability, take years to play out).

We can surmise that this was a big problem if Hank Greenberg was being true to the thousands of conversations he had had over the better part of the previous 30 years, in which he told anyone who would listen that he didn't want outsized risk in the capital markets since all he did with every day in insurance was take risk.

■ ■ ■

A few months before they struck a deal with ILFC, Matthews and Greenberg got struck again with worries over diversification. This time, given that they were operating in over 130 countries, there was, as

Matthews recalls it, "something they were surely missing in commodities. There was no way we weren't leaving money on the table in currencies or were managing all those risks well enough."

"Something missing" to most businessmen usually called for something to be studied or considered, perhaps even an action plan being drawn up. Not to those two. It was time, in other words, to set up a broker-dealer to trade commodities, currencies, and energy. Drexel Burnham Lambert would again provide the raw material.

A triumvirate of former Drexel partners, Gary Davis, Robert Rubin, and Barry Klein, were knee-deep in the interview process with Greenberg and had at a point let him know that they were considering an opportunity with German energy trader Metallgeschellschaft. Sizing up his competition with brevity, Greenberg bellowed:

"Why would you go with the Germans? They get drunk at dinners and sing old Nazi songs!"

Laughs aside, it was food for thought for the three observant Jews.

Tipping the scales in AIG's favor for the trio was the fact that Greenberg, as all would later remember, directly understood what they were trying to do and had an immense understanding of international capital flows and of currencies in particular. Coming from Drexel, whose balance sheet was toxic from 1987 onward, with a boss like Hank and a triple-A balance sheet, Rubin and Davis couldn't engineer a scenario where they could lose.

Thus, AIG and its shareholders entered the energy, metals, and foreign-exchange businesses in a big way with the creation of AIG Trading Group.

■ ■ ■

Unlike their former Drexel brethren, this would be no "capital lite" model. AIG Trading would put nothing on their new parent's balance sheet that it took an astrophysicist to explain—let alone value—but Trading Group from day one needed to maintain a trading inventory for its roster of clients. It was no ordinary roster. In addition to utilities; gold producers; and oil, coal, and gas companies, Davis, Klein, and Rubin had a series of relationships that had been waiting for a pairing with a real balance sheet to be fully exploited.

Foremost were the apex predators and the most-sought-after customers of the capital markets in the early 1990s, the macro hedge funds: George Soros's Soros Fund Management, Michael Steinhardt's Steinhardt Partners, and Julian Robertson's Tiger Management chief among them.[24] These three controlled a measurable chunk of the capital allocated to the then-nascent hedge fund industry and had longstanding relationships with the ex-Drexel traders (most especially Davis), but they were much happier to trade with a triple-A-rated counterparty.

Having a good relationship with the trading desks at a place like Soros meant that order flow, the lifeblood of a brokerage operation, would flow freely. On any given day, the fund's traders were involved in every sort of commodity and currency play and AIG Trading was happily matching their buy and sell orders with other clients and making commission plus, on occasion, some spread between the trades.

There was a cost of doing business with the biggest volume traders in the market. They could get order execution from anyone—they wanted instant liquidity and in size. As derivatives gained in prominence, these funds wanted to "face" AIG Trading as a counterparty on their various swaps and hedges. *Liquidity* is a Wall Street code word for using a firm's balance sheet to buy and sell large blocks of securities, and it was the coin of the realm in this case. Immediately upon its founding, AIG started putting tens of millions of dollars' worth of commodity and currency options, futures, hedges, and short-dated swaps on their corporate books. They made decent cash—its first four years saw Trading earn more than $250 million in operating income—and every night of those years, Matthews, Smith, and Greenberg could go to bed understanding exactly what they were doing and why.

But the debt was piled on. It was not a steady thing, like ILFC, nor was there the vague sense of permanent attachment that came from having one of AIGFP's 30-year swaps on, but AIG Trading had to go out and borrow hundreds of millions of dollars to fund its nearly billion of dollars' worth of inventory. And, as noted earlier, the real risk in AIG Trading, like most financial companies, was the risk that what they were putting on the balance sheet as assets to offset their liabilities was going to be a lot less valuable at a moment's notice.

But Davis, Rubin, and Klein were not Sosin, Rackson, and Goldman. They had no inclination at all to do a transaction that would last a generation. To their way of thinking, if they put something on a balance sheet, they were damn sure going to sell it at a higher price than where they bought it. To traders, the end of a day, week, month, or quarter was a perfect scorecard to how you were doing. There were, AIG Trading officials would say (very) quietly to themselves, no accounting rules that allowed them to take all the profit on a deal up front; they earned their money by coming up with good ideas and providing more and better liquidity to the smartest and most important players in their markets. Years later, after AIG collapsed, Davis would acknowledge that the trader's sense of impending doom, of death around every corner, helped them from confusing the roles of trader and financial guarantor.

No one from AIG corporate was going to mistake the tone of AIG Trading for that of AIG Financial Products. Howard Sosin might have had an ego to match his earnings, and no small amount of paranoia to boot, but his management style and work habits made FP seem like a particularly driven department of finance at a leading university. There was no way that using raw fear would get a better decision from the team pricing out risk scenarios for a proposed 95-year swap with Amgen.

At AIG Trading, Gary Davis, then traveling in London, a veteran of the Darwinian world of Wall Street trading floors in the 1970s and 80s, occasionally employed a different management theory.[25] He once called an entire trading desk to an "impromptu performance review" on the desk's squawk-box. As seven or eight traders gathered around one or two seats, the entire trading floor was treated to Davis's "analysis" of their recent trading performance. As three of the traders recall the episode, it involved the word *fuck* repeated at louder and increasingly frequent intervals for about 15 minutes.

The trading desk in question got the message and pulled in their risk taking. So did the rest of the trading floor.

Based in Greenwich, Connecticut, at One Greenwich Plaza, right off the railroad station, the shop topped out at several hundred people by the mid-1990s. Though not the apparent gold factory that ILFC was, and it couldn't be said to have the consistent nine-figure profit generating capability of FP, but AIG Trading was a solid and consistent performer in its own right. Throughout the 1990s, it increased revenues at a double-digit growth rate and did so in a variety of different market environments, earning consistent and healthy 25 percent and 30 percent operating margins. Permanently the youngest brother in a family of superstars, company filings show that the unit more than doubled its operating income from 1992 to 1998, going to $123 million from $56 million.

If the business was working out exactly as the "plan" would have it—and it's not certain even now whether AIG Trading was Greenberg's diversification hedge in the capital markets against FP's complexity or Matthews's hunch they could do better in commodities and currency—the one constant was tension. Gary Davis and Howard Sosin had a pretty sharp difference of opinion on most everything that had to do with swaps, with Sosin arguing that Trading shouldn't be allowed to do anything in swaps and Davis arguing that Sosin was shutting him out of a lucrative market in his niche of energy, commodity, and currencies. Nor did Rubin and Davis try to conceal the disdain for the colleagues they took pains to refer to as "those bastards in Westport."

The feud became increasingly bitter. Ed Matthews described his job as "patrolling the borders" of the feud, preventing outright warfare. He failed often. In one memorable incident, he was on the phone with Sosin in the early 1990s laying out the origins of a deep beef Davis had with FP. In a moment that stuns Matthews to this day, Sosin said he would call up Davis and smooth it over "like brothers from the same family."

Getting up from his desk to get a cup of coffee and use the restroom, Matthews told his secretary that he would likely win the Nobel Peace Prize. Before he made it down the hall, however, his secretary came running after him with an emergency phone call from Davis. Picking it up, Davis began the conversation by screaming, "That son of a bitch Sosin!"

Matthews, who appreciated the hundreds of millions of dollars in income the two Drexel alumni brought to his life, kissed his notional Nobel Prize goodbye.

On another occasion, when telling CFO Howie Smith that he was going out to dinner that night with Sosin and Davis, he was advised not to go to a steakhouse. When Matthews asked why not, Smith said,

"Too many big knives in a steak place. A few drinks and either Sosin or Gary might be dead and you'll be a material witness. Go Italian."

■ ■ ■

AIG Trading worked out well for Davis, Klein, and Rubin in that they did what they loved and earned tens of millions of dollars each doing it, but Greenberg did not make the same mistake twice. His control over every aspect of their business was absolute, and, on occasion, he would remind them of it.

Walking into a meeting with Greenberg in 1997, Davis was presented with a copy of his proposed budget for the following year, including a salary chart and list of estimated bonus payments to his staff. Greenberg took his pencil and started asking him questions about computer costs, salary increases for support staff, and bonuses. After going through dozens of employees and being forced to explain in depth why people were compensated at certain levels, Davis asked when they were going to get to the "risk" part of the proceedings. Greenberg frowned and said, "This is the 'risk.' Your people are your assets—you underpay them, they leave and you lose, you overpay them and they won't work as hard anymore or they won't care about risk."

Driving back to Greenwich, Davis did the math in his head. He supposed there were two dozen other AIG subsidiaries that had more revenue and profits than his unit. He had spent a few hours with one of the most powerful men in the business world talking about software costs and what he pays secretaries and traders. He could not decide if this was the smartest thing he had ever encountered or the silliest.

As he arrived back at work, Davis found himself leaning toward "smartest" because he now was convinced that every single thing that happened at AIG, every last pencil or computer they bought, Greenberg saw. No one could ever do anything really stupid at AIG, he decided, because Hank would see it. Both he and Rubin had decided long ago that they were either favored sons whose progress he enjoyed monitoring or that Greenberg truly was some sort of other-worldly being that didn't sleep or eat and drink and simply monitored AIG's expenses and risks.

It wasn't idle speculation. On many occasions, Davis and Rubin had gotten called out of meetings, flagged down on vacations, interrupted in the middle of a big trade, and ordered to defend a certain position then on the books. The rub was that most every time it was the tail end of some big trade they were squaring away with a large customer and were in the process of selling. On a few occasions, they had made the mistake of attempting to reason with Greenberg, something to the effect of, "Hank, this is a $5 million position in yen futures/gold forwards/natural gas options. It's really liquid and pretty minimal in the scope of—"

"Hedge it, reinsure it, or there are consequences."

There was, of course, no use to discussing the matter further. The position was eliminated and life went on. They had stopped telling their friends and former Drexel colleagues about these episodes years prior. Few of them believed that a modern CEO could muster the interest to monitor a $5 million position in something like gold futures on a company with a $150 billion balance sheet.

To men who came from modern Wall Street, where traders spent decades without so much as a conversation with the firm's CEO, life with a boss like Greenberg was something that had to be seen before it could be believed. The money poured over the bow, hardened men like Gary Davis were converted, new alliances were struck with the likes of Savage and Udvar-Hazy, and it all, every day, reinforced to a marketplace that was becoming used to the cornerstones of business collapsing overnight just how very different AIG was.

You would pay more to own a piece of that company, and you would allow the man who ran that company his leeway. That was the formula that had worked for what was nearly a quarter-century at that point. As long as that was the state of play, AIG was going to be just fine.

Chapter 4

Changes

The golden era of Financial Products began with a series of meetings among the half-dozen remaining senior executives after the departure of Sosin and his team in late 1992. They were, as a few participants described it, meeting to figure out who might be the captain to go down with the ship. They had reason to be pessimistic: though there was a good core group of producers remaining, the founder of the unit had taken the leadership with him and the chief executive was unambiguously furious about how things played out.

There wasn't much campaigning for the job. "No one remembers the last chief of E. F. Hutton or PaineWebber before they went away," said one member of this group. "There was a chance that might have happened here."

The four—Joe Cassano, Tom Savage, Michael Hurst, and Kelly Kirkland—considered running AIGFP as a committee but scrapped the idea. Instead, they went with an 11-person committee and decided to vote on a president. Tom Savage won. Afterward, they were kind of laughing sheepishly about his "victory" when the question evolved into whether anyone really wanted to do lead AIGFP after what Sosin went through, in spite of the numbers he put up.

This was the question Savage had been asking himself since Sosin left. A mathematician by training—he had a Claremont PhD before he packed in his academic life—Savage decided to approach the question like a math problem: there was an equation with a variable to be solved for. He had come to realize that much of the tension of the past few years was avoidable. Greenberg had no real problem with Sosin's business plan, or certainly his results, but he clearly felt that he was being kept in the dark, like a mere investor in a hedge fund. The guy had built an incredible business and knew risk like no one else, and he felt that he was being treated as a nuisance. So, to Savage, it logically followed that if Greenberg was intellectually capable of being comfortable with having FP do what no one else was able or willing to do in finance, then the way to avoid the political insanity of the past five years was to make Greenberg an active partner: brief him, ask him for advice, spare none of the details, don't snow him.

AIG was publicly traded, thought Savage, but it was in every sense Greenberg's company—there just happened to be a stock price involved.

Greenberg shared none of Savage's conviction. At a winter retreat in 1993 at AIG's ski resort in Stowe, Vermont, he told Savage in no uncertain terms, "I'm not sure you have the buttons for this job," to which Savage replied, "Maybe Mr. Greenberg. Let me try, though."

The doubts weren't misplaced.

Savage had spent his first three years at FP abroad in London and Paris trading interest rate options, and was relatively unknown to AIG management. The way Greenberg and Matthews saw it, his management experience consisted of nothing but a small trading desk at Drexel a few years back. They did not like being asked to turn over this headache of a unit's keys to *another* academic. More importantly, they were worried that after a few years, Savage would get bored or desperate and start angling to take the triple-A rating and gin up some quick revenues.

But if he didn't have the longest managerial resume, they also acknowledged that he was a profitable and resourceful producer who appeared to understand a fair amount of what FP actually *did*. Savage was respected by Rackson and Sosin, yet had a laid-back, nonpolitical demeanor that earned him respect among the other 90-odd FP employees. Savage was open to most anything that made a buck, their allies were telling them, but you might have to work really hard to get someone who had more discipline when it came to taking risk.

With the full knowledge that they were taking a shot at someone unproven, they gave the then 44-year-old Duluth, Minnesota, native the job. At an offsite meeting not long after, at the Ritz Carlton in Dallas, Savage made his pitch to his assembled colleagues. "We can do even better," he said, arguing to colleagues, who had flown in from London, Paris, Tokyo, and Westport, that they had nothing to fear from AIG "if [we] honor the trust they placed in us."

■ ■ ■

In his first week, Savage began the process of taking the standard Tuesday risk-management meetings one step further. The meetings had been in place since Sosin and involved the general counsel, CFO, Ed, Hank, senior risk management, Financial Services leadership, and Savage. They were blunt—everything that could move up or down in value was discussed, even if there was no likelihood of its ever happening. No matter where Hank was in the world, or what he was doing, he made time for the meetings.

"I'd call him up after the meetings and took the approach of being direct and candid. I wouldn't glaze over anything, and then I'd shut up. Hank had things to say, and I'd listen. He knew a lot of things and had some good advice. He was pretty good at it."

So was Savage, apparently.

In his first three years at the helm, AIG's filings show that FP reported numbers of over $460 million in operating income; in the subsequent two, they cleared another $575 million. The equity option business was booming, guaranteed investment contracts were booming, the myriad currency arbitrage solutions for corporations were hot, and then there were the "only-in-Westport" transactions that defined AIGFP, like the Section 29 deals.

In brief, the Internal Revenue Service, at the behest of the Department of Energy, made the decision in the 1970s to offer a tax credit of up to $2 per barrel of oil and gas that had been extracted from nontraditional sources, such as coal seams. David Ackert, a former tax attorney who had been hired from Goldman's corporate finance department, suggested that if FP bought the land and structured a particular sort of lease to a company able to extract it, they could keep the $2 per barrel tax credit and earn a percentage of revenue from every barrel. Maps were consulted, geologists and other experts hired and above all, a comprehensive ruling from the IRS was sought (and obtained) that confirmed the tax benefits of the deal.

Given that this was FP, every barrel extracted had a buyer already contracted with—Savage had made clear to all that he loved the deal, but he wasn't looking forward to getting into the oil storage business.

It worked. They made about $850 million on this Section 29 deal, and were soon on to others. The biggest risk wasn't market based or even the vagaries of pulling the stuff out of the ground, it was that AIG Trading chief Gary Davis would somehow convince Hank and Ed, who after all had brought them in to be the resident commodity experts, to let AIG Trading take over the transactions. They raised hell, but Savage's constant communication with Greenberg, his bringing him into the loop on matters big and small, paid off big time. In a brief but meaningful phone call, Greenberg let Davis know that when a truly complicated thing came along down the pike, FP was probably going to be handling these sorts of things. Greenberg would tell anyone who would listen that he *loved* the Section 29 deals. That was exactly why FP was put together, as he saw it, and if he could redirect some internal flack away from them, he was happy to.

Natural resource deals would remain part of FP's DNA until the very end. They made a small fortune on what they called "spray and pray," where they took advantage of long-forgotten tax credits that were designed to foster the development of synthetic coal.[1] Designed to support the transformation of coal into the more energy-efficient liquid states or a solid that was less environmentally harmful, in reality it was a way to lock in a $24-per-ton tax credit when coal was fetching $21 per ton.

As much as Savage was willing to sponsor forays into things like oil and gas exploration, anything mortgage related left him cold. He took a literal view of the issue: any security backed by a house or building was

verboten. His colleagues saw it as a quirk of his personality, like the way
Barry Goldman liked a bowl of ice cream for breakfast. It was anything
but that. As a groundbreaking modeler in the mortgage departments at
First Boston and Drexel, he had come to see that all of mortgage trading
was just a way to make money until the next unanticipated blow up.
Time after time, the same thing happened: rates changed and entire
trading desks, whole fixed-income divisions were blown out of the
water because of one or two mortgage trading positions. Savage had a
litany of reasons why: hedges—if they were even available—always
underperformed because the securities were too leveraged to interest
rates. In turn, brokers and hedge funds, trying to squeeze every last dime
of profit out of a trade, used too much leverage in positioning the
bonds, so when the market reversed, they were always forced to sell in
a panic.

Savage saw his former specialty, modeling mortgages, as little more
than folly. The models the banks touted assumed that rates would move
in sequential, orderly patterns and that market prices would follow.
The opposite happened, of course, with panic, greed, and liquidity
flowing into or out of the market at a second's notice. Somehow *those*
inputs never seemed to make it into the models. Mortgage desk chiefs
across Wall Street, Savage recalled, had story upon story about trying to
discuss how the market worked, what the bonds were really made of,
and what they were supposed to do to the men who ran their firms. The
takeaway: despite assurances to the contrary, very few of the chief
executives and CFOs really knew what they were committing billions of
dollars of capital to.

There was no getting around that mortgages were here to stay as a
crucial feature of Wall Street, but Savage took comfort that Hank and
Ed allowed him to take a pass on the sector. Sosin had passed on every
mortgage deal he was shown as well, but being Sosin, he had a suitably
high-concept reason: FP had no information advantage. What could
anyone at FP know in mortgages that no one else knew? In the end, he
told everyone, they would *always* be long unanalyzable credit and
unquantifiable risk if they got involved with mortgages.

As Savage gained traction and grew into his job running FP, he took
comfort in the fact that FP had established a culture of passing on low-
hanging fruit-like mortgages. After all, as 1994 closed and another

excellent year was booked, Savage saw firsthand the cost of being wrong on mortgages: Kidder Peabody collapsed and Salomon Brothers lost nearly $400 million on mortgages alone. Every other investment bank's mortgage desk was bruised in some fashion, with Merrill—the most aggressive in trading with the soon-to-be-bankrupt Orange County— taking losses that pushed into the nine-figure range.

He was proud, truth be told. Savage reasoned that whenever he left, FP would surely have it in their DNA to stay away from bets on the American homeowner.

■ ■ ■

If there was a moment where Greenberg and the "new" FP fused, it was in February 1995. As the centuries-old British institution Barings Bank was liquidating after erstwhile trader Nick Leeson was found to have disguised $1.3 billion in futures trading losses, Hank Greenberg was making final preparations for a trip to Tokyo. When the offending positions were dumped en masse on the Tokyo exchange, its bench-mark Nikkei index sold off 900 points and gave a $10 million black eye to a long-standing options trade FP then had on. Savage immediately called Greenberg to brief him and to tell him that if the Nikkei con-tinued to fall—and no one really knew how much Barings was going to wind up having to sell—the trade could wind up costing even more. Savage didn't sugarcoat it, and Greenberg said he appreciated it.[2]

Upon arrival in Tokyo, Greenberg went straight to FP's offices and sat with trader Phil Lavers (who had inherited the position from a trader who had left) for three hours. They discussed the risks and possibilities of the trade and the direction of the Tokyo markets before he went on his way. Lavers told everyone he was flattered and it was a highpoint of his career; Greenberg shrugs when asked to recall it, saying it was a smart business thing to do and he had confidence in "Savage's man." As it turned out, Barings didn't sell much more, the market stabilized, and FP got out of it for a little more than a $10 million loss.

It is an unremarkable story that has probably occurred in 1,000 companies: Boss is briefed on a loss in the regional office before a scheduled trip to the regional office, Boss stops by, gets the measure of the situation, and leaves to tend to business. But Greenberg's visit somehow became a defining part of FP lore. In the years since 1995, FP personnel have made this the integral "Hank Greenberg Watched This Place Like a Hawk" story. In about a dozen interviews, the story was repeated with as many variations. In some, Lavers was shaking like a leaf until Greenberg came to the office and took over; in others, Greenberg has just come back from meetings with Japanese Ministry of Finance officials and, possessing inside scoop, tells Lavers what to do—and it works, natch. In another, Greenberg, furious at the prospect of a loss, flew to Tokyo to grill Lavers personally on the trade and left only after adjustments he ordered were made. That nothing like this happened is beside the point.

On the one hand, every big corporation likely has some handed-down story about a key executive that has gotten so worn from the telling that it bears little resemblance to what actually happened. On the other hand, it is clear that in the wake of the traumas surrounding the 2008 collapse, it offered a stark reminder that the CEO of AIG once closely scrutinized and understood FP enough to travel across the world to monitor it.

■ ■ ■

It may be safely said that the dot-com years and FP were ships passing in the night. At FP, the mounting frenzy of Internet riches and venture-capital dreams was viewed with a general sense of detached bemusement with dashes of incredulity and alarm thrown in. Jake DeSantis, a gifted options and equity-derivatives trader, and a few of his colleagues toyed around with the idea of perhaps shorting some of the more outrageously overvalued stocks before scratching the idea as wholly outside of the scope of what FP was all about.

Though they were creatures of the markets, the life and death of trading desks, funds and firms were matters for consideration and analysis, not for cause and worry. Most of FP hadn't even known they had had exposure in the Nikkei index in 1995. The summer of 1998 and its roiling markets were different. In front of their eyes, they were watching the landscape of the capital markets freeze in front of them. Currencies devalued, sovereign nations defaulted on their debt, and in minutes it all migrated to the trading desks that dealt with FP.

To be certain, they didn't live every second in the markets; their value as a unit was not something that could be punched up on a Bloomberg terminal, but they needed them nonetheless. The "capital lite" model of not having hundreds of millions of dollars at risk in market bets paid handsome dividends as the vicious circle of margin calls on levered investments that was devastating brokers and hedge funds in the summer of 1998 happened apart from them. Savage could not help but notice that the devastation of the mortgage market was at the center of everything.

Still, the removal of Westport only served to highlight the unreality of the financial world they were of, but not wholly in. They no longer caught stray chatter from trading desks about this rival that was getting nicked or that hedge fund suffering waves of redemptions. The front page of the *Wall Street Journal*'s "C" section, the first read for the finance world, ran story after story of hedge funds walloped by losses of 30 percent or more. In a world where Long Term Capital Management, the hedge fund that many Wall Street executives most readily analogized to FP, had been devastated by its absurd leverage—50 times (and higher) in numerous trades—some FP executives began to wonder if they had the only business model that could possibly work in a world like that.

Savage and his colleagues talked about it all the time: the leverage, the crowded trades full of competing trading desks, and hedge funds all betting on the same thing for declining returns and the volatility of capital flows. There were lessons to be had, and Savage wanted to make sure that his staff learned them. He never forgot, as he drove home to his family after a long day, that they were academic lessons in FP's case. They didn't do those things in Westport.

■ ■ ■

In the autumn of 1998, a 30-year-old graduate of the India Institute of Technology named Ram Sundaram took a good look around at what had become of his dream job and decided that someone or something was teaching him an object lesson.

Sundaram was a derivatives expert with Morgan Stanley Asset Management's (MSAM) Emerging Markets Group, which was a formal way of saying that he was a well-educated fireman. A specialist in the construction of what was then becoming known as structured products, Sundaram and his colleagues took the debt carving and slicing skills developed by people like Tom Savage earlier in the previous decade and expanded its application. For instance, instead of slicing up a mortgage loan into bits and pieces whose interest payments could be redirected into all sorts of baffling bonds, Ram and his colleagues would take standard bonds and add a derivative feature or something whose value was referenced to something else. It could be an index of interest rates, a basket of commodities, or put or call options that gave the holder the right to sell the bond at a certain price or buy a stock or commodity at another. They could do anything, it seemed, at least with enough hard work, some open-minded customers, and computers.

For a few years, they did. Sundaram was happily constructing derivatives for Morgan's mammoth Institutional Securities Group when bond chief Ken deRegt and a few others politely pulled him aside one day and told the hardworking associate that the firm could really use him in the Asset Management area, where they were making a big push, and if he could put on his propeller cap and figure out a way to deploy his ability to devise and structure asset-backed securities, well, he most assuredly would not be forgotten come bonus time.

What could he say but "Yes"? He loved Morgan and its collegial culture; he thought deRegt was an excellent guy, and if they needed him to lend a hand, he'd be happy to.

Hardworking, smart, and a true believer in the Morgan Stanley culture of cooperation across unit lines, Sundaram did just fine building a niche selling banks and insurance companies a variety of individually tailored asset-management products using derivatives and ABS. Unfortunately, his colleague down the hall who ran a fund called the Emerging Markets Debt Opportunities fund didn't do as well. As the growing currency and debt crisis unfolded in Asia, he was called in to help analyze the portfolio and see if there was anything that could be done to salvage value. The fund was heavily levered to Argentina and Russia and when events in Russia set off a global bond-market collapse waves of panicked selling and margin calls resulted in a complete loss of liquidity.[3] Brokerage after brokerage wouldn't make markets or, if they did, simply refused to buy at the indicative price. The fund was obliterated. Hundreds of millions of dollars of losses were sustained, its manager was summarily fired, and, in a desperate bid to somehow value what was left, Ram was brought in. In his office, which had become his bedroom as he worked around the clock, he pondered the past few weeks and realized that every assumption Wall Street had was absurdly wrong. Everything was correlated. It mattered little if it was generic Fannie Mae pass-throughs or derivatives referenced to Russian sovereign debt, panics didn't stay local for very long. The mortgage market was devastated; entire trading desks had been wiped out and were shutting down. That market's golden promises of noncorrelation failed in an epic fashion—it appeared that everything declined in price when there were no bids and no cash in the marketplace, complex structures be damned. Not that Emerging Markets were any better. Russia, India, and Argentina were thousands of miles apart and had totally different economic dynamics but collapsed just as readily in price as some impossible-to-even-conceptualize collateralized mortgage obligation.

The root of everything, in Sundaram's exhausted opinion, was the fallout from heavily levered dealers and hedge funds getting margin pulled from them. It was asinine to think Wall Street in this era wouldn't overcrowd trades again. The banks were now the biggest players in the market, with their infinite balance sheets, and manias were just part of the human landscape. Discipline and reason were out.

The way to survive the next one of these collapse debacles was to have what was known in trading desk jargon as *capacity* or the ability to avoid balance sheet dependency on short-term financing. Having a balance sheet was always nice but was no guarantee of health, since you could just as easily fill it up with junk. The billion-dollar-plus losses at Nomura, Credit Suisse First Boston, and Merrill Lynch proved that easily enough. Not that being smaller was any saving grace, since Goldman and Lehman had suffered painful losses too.[4]

Having longer-term financing in place insured that you wouldn't have to sell things the minute your counterparty to a repurchase trade got in trouble. In the way modern trading worked, you could be fine but if enough counterparties got in a spot, funding yourself could get either more difficult as people pulled in their horns or it could get more expensive, which would hurt your profitability. You would need *access* to balance sheet longer term—plenty of balance sheet, to have at your beck and call so that you could absorb blows, continue to trade as others faded away, and, if suited your purposes, to lease out. He decided right there that he would try to "lock up" capacity wherever his next job took him.

■ ■ ■

In the summer of 1998, Savage's second-in-command, Joe Cassano, approached him with a new moneymaking idea that two up-and-coming derivatives pros from J. P. Morgan had brought the New Products Group. As Savage recounts it, he was faintly bemused since Cassano appeared to have fallen in love with the transaction.

Called a BISTRO, short for a Broad Index Secured Trust Offering, Savage immediately recognized its outlines from his days on the mortgage desks of First Boston and Drexel, where he had worked on carving up the bonds backed by thousands of residential mortgages into the first collateralized mortgage obligations (CMOs). A bond made from another bond, it was met with some degrees of abject horror from bond-market veterans who decried its complexity and the sundry arcane structures that CMOs could be spun into; investors, smitten with the mortgage market's liquidity and their spread over treasuries, were grateful for a new way to capture extra yield with low risk and bought them hand over fist. They were now a cornerstone of the bond market's landscape. Taking many different shapes, they were now known as collateralized debt obligations (CDOs).[5]

In brief, loans J. P. Morgan had made to hundreds of its investment-grade corporate-lending clients were pooled and then carved up into $1,000 face value bonds. Instead of a corporation issuing a bond whose principal and interest were guaranteed out of its cash flows, these bonds had their principal and interest paid from the cash flows thrown off by the pooled loans. The thinking went, then as now, that the wide diversity of loans would ensure that even if one, or even a series, of loans went bad at once, the principal and interest would be paid.

The J. P. Morgan team's internal assessment of its risks led them to set aside about $700 million in reserve against possible losses for the initial deal. Getting the ratings agencies to see things J. P. Morgan's way proved easy enough, and a triple-A rating was put in place; regulators, in contrast to their compliant posture a decade later, proved a more significant challenge. They sought assurance that there would be strong guarantees in place to handle the balance of the $9 billion credit risk. If that were secured, the bank would have to keep much less cash in reserve, as banks traditionally had been made to hold 8 percent of the value of the collateral of these deals on its balance sheet as a reserve against losses.[6]

Enter Financial Products.

J. P. Morgan proposed that FP effectively guarantee the paper's triple-A rating, for which they would pay all of two basis points annually. The payment struck FP executives as initially low, but the deal was not as one-sided as it may have seemed since these loans were hand-selected to represent the bank's best and highest-rated corporate customers. From J. P. Morgan's perspective, they were paying $194 million annually to insure something that had a near zero probability of any losses, let alone anything material.[7]

After the first few passes, Savage really thought this was a good use of the AIG balance sheet—especially since it had almost no risk. A $9.7 billion deal that paid you two basis points annually to insure highly rated bank loans? These loans got paid before bondholders did; no company played games with their banks. Either it was the easiest $194 million annuity they had ever seen or Cassano had missed something really, really big. Savage couldn't decide which.

But this was FP, and risk management was the family business. Before they signed off, given the zero-sum nature of this deal (like most insurance, if a "claim" resulted from the contract, they would have an obligation to pay immediately), a Herculean effort would be made to assess the risk. The problem was trying to define risk in something like this.

Analysts at AIGFP, spearheaded by Cassano, spent hundreds of hours studying the structure of the deal and back-testing it against the most extreme market movements of the post–Second World War era: the crash of 1987, massive interest movements in 1994, market seizures in 1973–1974 and 1989, simulated defaults of large sections of the bond's collateral. In every case, the result was the same: the principal and interest was paid. Even as the crazy events of the summer of 1998 swirled around them as Russia defaulted and global markets collapsed, the loan collateral (and the companies they were made to) seemed to perform well.

At every step, Greenberg and Matthews were included in the analysis and process, lawyers from both FP and AIG were brought in, models that had other models attached to them were built and studied for hours on end, and always, in the end, the principal and interest on the loans would appear to get paid. Eventually, they said yes because they ran out of reasons to say no. Cassano, it emerged, hadn't missed anything that they could find.

Thus, did FP help launch the CDO swap business.

They would do several dozen more transactions over the next few years, and the fee would rise to about 11 basis points per billion dollars of collateral, although the amount of protection purchased would shrink, as the deals were smaller. According to Greenberg, Savage, and a host of other FP alumni, these deals were for capital relief purposes— freeing up bank balance sheets to make more loans or investments since they would have to hold hundreds of millions of dollars less in reserve against the possibility of default—and, more importantly, the banks on the other side of the deal were primarily European banks whose credit was implicitly backed by their respective countries.[8]

Each deal, though, was vetted for a few weeks prior to a decision's being rendered. The collateral—the bank's loans—was picked apart, the bank itself was studied from a credit perspective, and even the countries they were located within were given a careful going over. Germany, for example, where many of these deals were struck, was in the process of integrating the disastrous East German economy and was forced to spend billions to improve infrastructure, social services, and environ- mental safeguards, with no end then in sight. Its debt load was bal- looning, and if anything happened to a troubled regional bank, AIG didn't want to have to press its claims in bankruptcy court. So it reduced the number of transactions it did there. Everything was monitored in real time; there wasn't a market for this paper, so a team of analysts worked around the clock to formulate an opinion on the German economy's prospects over the coming decade.

Of the decision to enter the CDO swap business, Savage says, "Whatever else this [business] became later, it wasn't that way when we did it then. Every deal was pored over and we studied the fine points."

To this day, more importantly, this book of business appears to have performed quite well and was not the basis for the drama that emerged in the coming years—an ironic and misunderstood point since the CDO swaps done for capital relief were a vastly larger portfolio than the swaps done on asset-backed CDOs.

■ ■ ■

The Savage era worked because for all his seemingly easygoing ways, Savage worked tirelessly to get the entire set from AIG's corporate headquarters at 70 Pine Street on board with everything FP did and ensured that everyone had some intellectual and political stake in the unit's success. There were no longer any surprises; AIGFP's new Wilton headquarters might have been 90 minutes from southern Manhattan, but it was seen as a lot closer than Westport had ever been.

From 1999 to 2001, FP made $1.88 billion in operating income. A unit that Greenberg was 50/50 on shuttering in 1993 had become a core operating group at the company. So when Savage, whose wife had long since grown weary of the cold, sought to retire and move to Florida in 2001, Greenberg was stunned. A man who had long viewed retirement as a preposterous and inefficient social scheme, Greenberg used every trick at his disposal to keep Savage, but the last straw was the hassles in air travel after September 11. Everyone agreed that running FP was not something that could be done via telecommuting. A few last-ditch appeals were made, but the native Minnesotan's mind was set. He was done.

Greenberg would reflect of Savage's tenure, "He did a good job," which was high praise indeed, and the numbers seem to bear this out. More than a few Greenberg loyalists like to compare the Savage tenure to Sosin—something Greenberg does little to dissuade—but this is ultimately neither fair to Sosin (who also did a very good job, though Greenberg, it appears, would rather be shot than say so) nor Savage. Sosin tried to replicate the Rand Corporation of the 1960s, with the densest collection of brilliant financial minds who ever had access to a triple-A-rated balance sheet. He largely achieved it. Savage, a refugee from academia, had little interest in redefining what was capable of being done in finance and preferred hardworking people who were capable of solving the theoretically baffling on a daily basis.

Both approaches worked.

Before he left, in the mid-autumn of 2001, Savage called Howie Smith and told him that he wanted to go over the handful of candidates he had in mind to run the unit. Smith told him that the offer of his input was appreciated but that there was no need for it since a decision had been already made.

"We're going with Joe," said Smith.

There wasn't all that much to say, Savage recalls. Cassano had done well in running both the operations of the unit and heading up the New Products group. He could be abrasive, but he kept his temper in check. He had, insiders concluded, seen the Howard Sosin way, and he had seen the Tom Savage way, and it was broadly supposed that he would pick the latter as a management methodology.

Nor is it a stretch to imagine Greenberg thinking that as long as he had a smart, hardworking sort in that slot who respected him and the AIG legacy, well, that was all you needed. There developed a widespread perception that managing FP was very similar to being in charge of an elite military unit: with a clearly defined mission and parameters, close supervision from an experienced member of the ranks and enough operating latitude, positive results were nearly assured. There had, after all, been almost a decade since any material FP screw up. There was a new culture, a new level of cooperation.

Indeed, the initial meeting between Matthews and Greenberg and Cassano discussing his looming appointment drilled home this very point. "You've seen what happened to Howard; you've done pretty well under Tom. You do recognize the difference, don't you?" asked Greenberg.

Cassano assured them that he did. They really didn't have anything more to say. Pressed on the issue years later, Greenberg acknowledges that Cassano seemed to have a grasp of what FP was really supposed to be about fused with the experience of running its operations and a key revenue center, the New Products Group. Unsaid was that in the 14 years of FP's existence, many men had gotten very rich doing this work and were, it seemed, happy enough in its system. If they went and brought in an outsider who had visions of a volume-driven shop, or turning it into a hedge fund, then they might have to relive the Sosin nightmare all over. This is why the perception of Cassano having no interest in doing things differently or independently was probably his biggest asset in getting the job. It is less clear if any of the bigger producers at FP had any interest in the job.

Discussing Cassano years later with Greenberg and Matthews, Howie Smith recalled a meeting with Cassano and Sosin at the end of 1992 in a conference room at 70 Pine Street.

"We were fighting back and forth over the swaps valuation nonsense, and Cassano had begun the meeting sitting next to Sosin at the top of the table and was arguing FP's position with passion and emotion. He really, really backed Sosin—he was honestly loyal, a tribal guy. No matter how ridiculous the position, he backed and supported Howard to the hilt. Well there comes a point when Sosin just stops pressing his case and says nothing, he just gives up and looks down at the paper in front of him."

"Everybody knows he's gone at this point. Within minutes of that, Cassano is down by me on the AIG side and is nodding at us like he has been thinking what I'm saying has been true all along, like he wasn't suggesting I was an idiot 15 minutes before. Sosin is sitting there all alone. Cassano is a survivor. He fought his fight, saw the result and wanted to live again to work at FP."

■ ■ ■

Starting out on Wall Street in the late 1970s, Cassano would have none of the advantages that many others had: no summer internships at Merrill Lynch, an uncle who worked with a senator or the mayor, athletic glory, or the right high school and college. He was the son of a police officer who went to Brooklyn College on financial aid and graduated with a political science degree. There was no prospect of talking himself onto a trading floor job so he took a series of back-office jobs in Wall Street firms and wound up at Drexel in 1980. By dint of hard work and curiosity, he was given the job of setting up the control systems and processing the trades of a brilliant new trader named Howard Sosin, a man who spoke in mathematics and was greatly stretching the firm's back-office capabilities. It didn't matter: Cassano threw himself into the task of understanding what Sosin was doing and getting him the support he needed, helping to build his operation into the moneymaker it became.

Though Wall Street is brimming with legions of young men and women with burning desires to do anything to succeed, Cassano's plan to get ahead, according to those who worked with him and knew him, was simple: he worked harder. There was no question he didn't ask and no process or system he didn't stay late to master. In his free time, he taught himself the basics of accounting and risk management. To a man like Sosin, who was aware enough to recall that Wall Street's back-office and operational failures had shut down entire trading floors for a day at a time as late as the 1970s, Cassano was invaluable.

In an atmosphere of people who happily worked 12-hour days, Cassano worked 14 to 16 hours, sometimes more. A former colleague describes Cassano's early years there as "Part work, but mostly study. He studied risk management, he reverse engineered swaps in his free time, and gradually mastered everything that FP did."

Colleagues began to notice that Cassano wasn't just concerned with the life cycle of a trade—its processing, the transfer of payments and the proper accounting—but was increasingly interested in why Sosin and his colleagues were doing what he did.

The harder, rougher edges of Cassano's personality were evident from the first day at FP on Madison Avenue. Some thought it an affectation, a *faux* Brooklyn tough guy thing but there was no one from FP who doesn't have "a Joe story." One veteran recalled a furious episode over free-weights that weren't returned to their racks in the Wilton gym, others recall being screamed at over the most basic slights—accidentally explaining the basics of a deal or forgetting to include small details of a trade. There was an arbitrary and capricious nature to it all: a gold trader who regularly produced enough revenue to get paid over $2 million annually was dressed down in front of everyone over closing out a profitable trade too early, and an information technology (IT) employee was publicly hectored for a year over the tone of an email.

The contrast between the Sosin/Savage regimes was obvious, and perhaps intentional. There was an irony to it: FP was full of aggressive self-starters who needed no prodding to fly overseas for a night to seal a transaction or to work 18 hours straight to ensure that some pending deal was well hedged. Nor, given the flat organizational hierarchy, was there much angling for power or bids for prestige. A first-year hire could earn $5 million, no questions asked, if the production warranted it and 15-year veterans were not sure of their formal title. FP, culturally, was in some senses akin to an elite military unit like the SEALs or the British Special Air Service; a commander had to guide, direct, and formulate the correct missions, but presumably wouldn't have much concern over motivation and discipline.

Cassano didn't see life that way. A thorough, publicly administered screaming remained, to his way of thinking, an efficient means of communicating and motivation. Because Cassano had a work ethic and drive to succeed second to none, the occasional verbal whipping was just another thing, along with the endless days, that came to define life at FP.

There was another side, though, one that has been less remarked upon, and that is Cassano's generosity. The loss of a loved one, sickness, and personal tumult were all met with unusual graciousness and warmth. Jake DeSantis's wife was stricken with a rare form of brain tumor, and when he went to inform Cassano that he was going to resign or at least go on extended unpaid leave, Cassano refused to hear of it. He kept DeSantis on with full pay and benefits. He didn't just do it for his biggest producers but the administrative and support staff as well. It extended to gray areas like divorces or relocations as well—weeks and even months were given to employees without any loss in income or benefits. Similarly, there was a practical side to Cassano. He knew that a good producer having a difficult year would likely rebound so in a good year he often gave these staffers a little more year-end bonus than they might deserve to keep them from looking for other jobs.

Cassano shelved his fighter image around Greenberg, who had had to fight for his life and knew much more clearly what not having much really meant. For Greenberg, Cassano was a matter-of-fact corporate unit chief, concerned with making numbers and staying on the boss's good side. He liked his work ethic and really liked that he seemed to have no desire for a life apart from running AIGFP.

Many of his colleagues would later call Cassano a bully but argued that his most abrasive conduct occurred after Greenberg left, which is to say that every schoolyard fighter knew that there is always the one kid who not only knows how to fight, but likes it. Cassano, the cop's kid from Brooklyn, understood odds as well as anyone on Wall Street and had seen firsthand that crossing Hank Greenberg was a bet that rarely paid off.

■ ■ ■

On November 12, 1999, then President Clinton put his signature on the repeal of the Glass–Steagall Act, ending about 65 years' worth of separation between investment banking and commercial banking.

The statement of the legislation's prime mover, Texas Senator Phil Gramm, summed up the view of a bipartisan consensus in an America where subprime home loans were not yet 5 percent of the mortgage market:

> We are here today to repeal Glass–Steagall because we have learned that government is not the answer. We have learned that freedom and competition are the answers. We have learned that we promote economic growth and we promote stability by having competition and freedom.

In truth, Glass–Steagall had been incrementally reduced in scope since the 1980s as one market after another was opened to commercial banks. Still, through the mid-1990s, investment banks had dominated the trading and raising of capital. With one stroke of the pen, that was changed, and banks, with their oceans of customer deposits, were allowed into the previously forbidden world of investment banking. Few, very few, pointed out the incongruity of allowing commercial banks, which are chartered and run to limit risk into the world of investment banks, which are chartered and run to seek out and broker risk. The only question after the ink dried was what the five major investment banks could do to compete against the incredible funding advantage banks had over them.

In retrospect, it was obvious. Merrill Lynch, Goldman Sachs, Morgan Stanley, Lehman Brothers, and Bear Stearns competed by adding amounts of leverage onto their balance sheets that bordered on the surreal. When the market heated up between 2005 and 2008, each of the investment banks ran between 30 and 40 times their equity capital. When Merrill Lynch ran at 40 times leverage, a 2.5 percent decline in the value of their asset base wiped out the firm's equity.

The annual reports of these firms revealed $4.1 trillion in debt on their balance sheets at the end of 2007.

More narrowly, the dismantling of Glass-Steagall ensured that money-center banks could vertically integrate mortgages into the cornerstone of their business model. The casual observer, from the space of a few years removed, might be forgiven for thinking that banks used their newfound freedoms to become mortgage businesses with a sideline in consumer and commercial banking. This is unfair, of course. Banks became giant investment pools, relentlessly gathering capital to seek out any opportunity to exploit their funding advantage in a low-interest-rate environment with longer-term, higher-yielding assets. Mortgages were just the way they were able to express this wish in the greatest size and in the shortest amount of time.

They also made some loans on the side. Increasingly, however, those too were a part of a broader capital markets strategy. At a Citigroup or Bank of America, a customer would get a mortgage online or at a retail branch—often as part of a suite of debt-related services, including credit cards and home-equity lines—all of which would be commingled with hundreds of thousands of their other customers, carved up, and sold off into the capital markets in $1,000 face-value bonds. The same would be done with corporate loans.

After the mortgage, credit card, and home equity line debt was in the secondary marketplace, any number of the bank's mortgage-trading desks within their exponentially expanding securities units (whose capital was bolstered by the checking and savings accounts of the customers they sold the original mortgage to)—with trading portfolios at each individual desk that often ran into the billions of dollars—might wind up buying a slice of the original loan. As icing on the cake, these desks used only a portion of the capital required, opting to use a series of complicated overnight loans with other banks and brokers to raise the cash. It was, in finance parlance, a capital-efficient maneuver, as it allowed their capital to be used elsewhere to generate returns while simultaneously spreading the risk around. The idea wasn't half bad until everyone realized that risk wasn't dispersed after all, and everyone had similar exposures. With most everyone funding themselves identically via overnight loans, all it took to create a waterfall of selling was a few key players to begin to exit the market or cut back on lending.

Investment banks have come and gone for as long as there have been assets to speculate on. New York's financial district is full of their solemn reminders, their names written prominently on marble only to fade as few even can recall the likes and power of what was A. G. Becker or Kuhn Loeb.

Not so banks. Allowing commercial banks to marry their disproportionate funding advantages to the capital markets and the modern era's fetish for quarterly earnings growth was something sharply more dangerous than the old P. J. O'Rourke line about giving teenage boys whiskey and car keys.[9] It allowed the cornerstones of the Western world's financial system to internally concentrate risk to a level never before seen.

And when desperation struck in the middle of 2008, the safety valves of the marketplace—the large commercial banks and their balance sheets—were welded to the floor of the sinking ship desperate for rescue themselves.

Chapter 5

The Dirt Below

More than six years later, the letter from AIG still rankles David Schiff.

It was a sharply worded letter to the editor of *The Economist* in London, responding to a quote the publication used from the February 2004 edition of his newsletter, where Schiff pointed out that AIG liberally used an ever-changing group of descriptive yardsticks to hype their quarterly releases, regardless of whether it was reflective of what the company's actual earnings were.

Written by Steve Rautenberg, AIG's global chief of communications, it begins with "Once again, *The Economist* is full of Schiff" before dismissing him as "an insurance stock speculator" who writes for "a small newsletter" and that the *Economist* article is merely "a rewrite" of his own. In a hectoring and sharp tone, Rautenberg then accuses the magazine of "collaborating" with a critic to damage the company.[1]

More than the cheap shots directed toward him, Schiff was astounded by the surpassing arrogance of the letter. AIG was accusing

The Economist of pretty severe levels of malpractice and threw in a little conspiratorial supposition as an aside. To start with, *The Economist* is something of the Bible for the transAtlantic set, so picking a running battle with them seemed foolish in the extreme. He was a one-man band writing out of his apartment on the West Side of Manhattan using wit and logic; AIG, one of the world's most important corporations, happily rose to the fight and used personal attacks. For a company that was arguably one of the globe's most important, it reeked of churlish bitterness and vendetta—the complete opposite of how public relations was traditionally practiced. It was the least sensical approach imaginable. It also redefined the phrase, "The lady doth protest too much."

In another sense, however, it seemed to perfectly sum up the company's response to his decade-plus investigation into how AIG really operated.

■ ■ ■

A character who could only have emerged from a certain kind of New York City milieu in the second half of the 20th century, David Schiff was perhaps the least likely insurance detective you could imagine. An upper-middle-class product of a tony Manhattan prep school, he was admitted to Duke University only to drop out after a semester, claiming to his baffled corporate lawyer father that, "It was a waste of time. All anyone cared about was going to fraternity parties."

Most kids from that background take time off, "discover themselves," and head back to school. Not Schiff. He kicked around lower Manhattan's New School for a few years and eventually went to work at his uncle's insurance brokerage and, though he found the work beyond dreary, became utterly fascinated with insurance. This natural curiosity soon branched out to investments and business. He worked hard, he asked questions, and went on sales calls. At night, he taught himself to go over the small details of the often mammoth and always obtuse financial filings of large insurance companies. This all-night traipsing through documents eventually led him to set up a small investment partnership to take advantage of various mispricings he was convinced were ripe for profits. He wound up running, and then selling, an insurance company. If lower Manhattan's legion of investors and traders had a document-driven polymath, Schiff was it.

After doing some freelance investigative reporting for *Barron's* on some preposterous doings he had uncovered, in 1989 he branched out into writing his own newsletter. Written in a breezy and often wry style, his accessible approach ran the risk of minimizing just how deadly serious he was as every issue launched another assault on the confusing, the oily, the baffling, and the hidden secrets of the insurance industry. In that he was the only person doing this, he had many, many targets from which to pick.

Over time, Schiff looked at nearly everything AIG would have preferred stayed ignored.

"AIG was what everyone in insurance sooner or later got around to talking about, and once they got around to them, pretty soon the subject of Hank came up. Plus, I had spent hours wandering around lower Manhattan and I fell in love with their building [at 70 Pine Street.] It was impossible not to resent them and it was impossible not to admire AIG."

"Everybody talked about them," Schiff added, "but no one really looked into them."

With his first AIG article in the December 1993 issue, "Swaps and Derivatives: AIG Hits Hyperspace," Schiff made several arguments that had been lost in the coverage of Sosin's departure from AIGFP and his handsome compensation package. One was that the investment trading business is entirely different than the insurance business and that for a company with a 16 price-to-earnings (P/E) multiple—it was soon to climb steadily for nearly a decade—investors were still treating AIG like a pure insurance play. If they factored in that 15.5 percent of AIG's operating income came from capital markets, its stock would get the sort of lower multiple that riskier enterprises, like Salomon Brothers and J. P. Morgan, received.

Much of his work didn't make it out of the narrow confines of his analyst/hedge fund/industry executive readership, but that was beside the point. He was writing what no else thought about or, more likely, dared.

Schiff hit his stride in 1996 when he wrote three long investigations of a 1987 reinsurance deal AIG put together called Coral Re.[2] For approximately $60 million the company created, with the help of

Goldman Sachs, a maddeningly complex circular series of transactions wrapped around an entity domiciled in Barbados, allowing it to take on a billion dollars of insurance risk without appearing to do so. There was also the issue of its "accredited investors," a squad of Standard & Poor's (S&P) 500 CEOs who didn't put up a penny of capital (Sanwa bank fronted them the dough) and managed to bank between $25,000 and $45,000 for their "shares" each year in Coral Re. Nor did Schiff miss that the Molson Companies, Canada's giant brewer, bought into the deal in 1991, making the fact that Marshall Cohen, its CEO, joined the AIG board in 1992 all the more telling.

It wasn't that most international insurance companies didn't do something like this—they did, and frequently it was much more gratuitous—it was that AIG, virtually alone among insurers, had no real *need* to do it. This sort of penny ante trick-the-investors-and-regulators business was totally superfluous. Unlike its competitors, it had massive and profitable (and diverse) insurance operations that threw off acres of cash. Unlike its competitors, who as often as not were helmed by the men that Greenberg railed against, AIG had an honest-to-goodness visionary at its helm. These maneuvers, Schiff supposed, couldn't have added more than a few cents to earnings per share, but they were "cheap" earnings that were both one-off and dangerous. It was as if an exceptionally rich person went out of their way to regularly trick a harried cashier at the checkout counter into using the wrong coupon to save a few dollars. There was the thrill of the thing, of course, and the savings are perhaps real enough, but eventually there is a cost attached to such efforts. More broadly, when the rich person is nailed, the reckoning is either ugly, embarrassing, or both. Eventually, they would be caught, he supposed, and then what? What else would come out in the wash when lawyers got a hold of long-buried deals?

If there is a theme to Schiff's work—beyond a debt to the noir sensibilities of Raymond Chandler—it's that AIG had an affinity for doing things and not feeling the need to disclose them. There was much profit to be had, for instance, mining IRS documents to trace the links between AIG and its directors. In June 2003, Schiff wrote about the $36.5 million the C. V. Starr Foundation—where Greenberg was the Chairman—gave the Museum of Natural History between 1999 and 2001. Coincidentally, an AIG "independent" director, Ellen

Futter—who had just accepted an invitation to the board—was the president of the museum where Greenberg was also a trustee.[3]

AIG disclosed none of this in its proxy.

In comparison to the absurdities that were surfacing about the "governance" approach of many boards of directors in the dot-com era—or the complicity of Wall Street's brokerages in ginning up investor enthusiasm for various corporate client excesses—it was small potatoes, but it spoke volumes in its own fashion. That was the way business was done in the time of the founding of AIG, and that was the way it continued to be done under Greenberg. An argument can be made that some of this was organic. The C. V. Starr Foundation was tasked with funding various charities and museums are indeed places worthy of being funded, and there was little prompting needed for a career diplomat and board member like Richard Holbrooke and Hank Greenberg to intersect at someplace like the Council of Foreign Relations, or former U.S. Trade Representative Carla Hills and Greenberg at the U.S.-China Business Council.

In fact, the notion that the AIG board would be anything *but* interconnected with Greenberg on many levels suggests a level of naïveté. As a CEO who oversaw the affairs of the company with a keen eye to detail, he needed a board that represented the many facets of AIG: AIG as the Asian-American success story, AIG as the pillar of the New York business community, AIG as the financial powerhouse, AIG as the projector of U.S. soft power. In turn, that required AIG to support the directors in their public pursuits, whether it was think tanks or personal and civic charities.

To Greenberg, this was how enterprises developed stature and scope, how they expressed their views and pressed their interests. A sudden evangelical fervor for the opposite—total disclosure and separation of the interests of the company and its board—was some idiotic passing mania that contributed precisely nothing to the success of a business.

Like it or not, running a global multinational company like AIG meant that the composition of its board was a selling point. When senior AIG managers, or even Greenberg himself, called on senior foreign officials to secure lucrative contracts, its board, with former senior trade-negotiator Carla Hills, or chief U.S. diplomatic fixer Holbrooke, or (later on) the Secretary of Defense William Cohen, was often viewed as reassuring to foreign Trade and Finance ministry officials who saw these "experienced hands" as a sign that they were dealing with a company that "knew how things worked."

That this also meant that the board was essentially a reinforcement mechanism for how Hank Greenberg conducted business and saw the world was precisely Schiff's point. There was no one who could say to senior staff "No!" and make it stick; things (as Schiff supposed) would have to get to a crisis point for the board to act. What would constitute "a crisis point" for AIG was anybody's guess.

Much like it is said that generals fight "the previous war" from an intellectual or planning point of view, AIG's board represented "the previous global economy." They were representative of a world where the projection of American economic power and financial prowess was reassuring or bracing, where AIG was the only firm operating in the forgotten, forbidden, or dark corners of the world.

So Schiff and the small underground of AIG skeptics continued to pick apart aspects of its affairs though in every sense it seemed to many to be a fool's errand. In 1997, AIG earned $2.47 billion in operating income; in 2003, it was $9.3 billion. While every quarter seemed to introduce a new measurement of earnings—generally accepted accounting principles (GAAP) or non-GAAP, "core," or excluding "one-time" charges (such as the World Trade Center or more standard claims like hurricanes)—by any measure it seemed that every quarter the company beat estimates.

The insurance-financial colossus of AIG obliterated the few short sellers who bet against the company and the horde of sell-side analysts happily fell into line and put a constellation of recommendations that were all variations on a theme of "Buy." There was, it appeared, no marginal utility in doubting AIG or Greenberg whatsoever.

This march of triumph would provide little comfort to Greenberg. His success in building diversified and complementary insurance and financial earnings streams that were correlated—but not necessarily connected—had put him in a position of great responsibility. AIG was held the world over and was considered a "safe-haven" for investors. As the markets corrected after the dot-com bubble burst in March of 2000, AIG's share price was bid up on the view that it was a repository of steady and predictable earnings. For much of 2000 and 2001, the company sported a 30 to 40 times P/E, making it a growth stock par excellence.

This was no paper crown.

In the 21st century, being the CEO of a growth stock was a designation unlike any other in the capital markets. Your stock stayed well bid when others in your sector sold off; the bad news or ill omens that forced the stock prices of your bitter rivals ever lower affected you half so much. Even if a full-bore contraction took place when things turned back around, your company's share price was the first to inflate.[4] All this CEO had to do was continue to grow: revenues were good, earnings were better.

The flip side of being a growth stock was being a company that had engendered deep-seated investor disappointment. Growth stock investors didn't rotate out of a stock, they abandoned it, resulting in the unrestrained selling of shares—it took very little time in globally integrated securities markets to go from overvalued to undervalued—and a board that would likely decide that a change of leadership was needed. The growth stock CEOs club was not one that you could voluntarily leave, save for feet first.[5]

In Greenberg's case, all he had to do to justify the continued faith of investors and analysts was grow earnings at about 15 percent annually in an industry where bottom-line growth of 5 percent was considered healthy. His investors no longer seemed to care about his skepticism of certain lines of the insurance business nor his distaste for paying up for acquisitions—those attributes are for building enterprises and are prized by value investors—who, it need hardly be said, often refuse to pay up for shares.

Being a growth *insurance* company was a whole other challenge.

The details of running an insurance company—reserves against claims, liquidity, underwriting discipline, an aversion to risk—all come into conflict with the pressures of growth stock status. An insurance man at his core, Greenberg did not seek the easy path to goosing earnings in the short term, by underreserving and writing insurance coverage on anything and everything in a grab for premiums. He chose growth, but the path and the methods to growth would be on his terms.

He had, in a sense, already been on that path since August of 1998 when he bought Eli Broad's SunAmerica for $18 billion. The deal was unusual in that the Los Angeles–based retirement annuities marketer was growing so fast that AIG exchanged 0.855 of its shares for each one of SunAmerica's. Though there was an obvious appeal to having a large retirement planning franchise as the Baby Boomer generation entered its 50s, there was no getting around the fact a slower-growing property and casualty company bought a faster-growing company whose success was almost entirely driven by the bull-market in equities. Indeed, in the conference call announcing the deal, Greenberg noted that SunAmerica had had 30 straight quarters of growth, and was fortunate that none of the analysts on the phone did the math and figured out that the last time SunAmerica didn't grow was in the middle of the 1990–1991 recession. No one asked the intemperate question or made the coldly logical inference that AIG was paying a 26 percent premium for an enterprise that appeared to slow down in anything other than a bull market.

Greenberg's situation in 2000–2001 left him little cover. The company was so big and in so many sectors of the market that there was no "natural" target left for them. So, in a move that was rare for him, he did what other CEOs did in this dilemma: he bought other companies simply because that's where the growth was.

Operationally, this is always trouble as a company like AIG was forced to buy things it had probably decided to pass on in earlier days for decent reasons, but which now were being considered only because the target company had proven it could "grow" its net income. There were, however, some fair stock market arguments for buying growth this way. The first was AIG's high-flying, richly valued stock. The peculiarities of Wall Street's "math" ensured that, for example, when AIG bought Hartford Steam Boiler in the fall of 2000, it bought a company whose stock was trading at a P/E of 20 times 2001's (estimated) earnings. Whatever the merits of the company, the deal was immediately a boon to the company's bottom-line since its own P/E was about 36 at the time. Investors cared not a whit that there was another $1.2 billion of its stock out in the market since the deal immediately added around 5 percent to its bottom line for the next year.

In May 2001, while Prudential PLC was trying to salvage its previously announced $26 billion deal with Houston's American General (its share price was dropping, leaving the American General investors stuck with being acquired by a company whose value was declining daily), AIG swooped in and bid $23 billion for the life insurer, finance company, and retirement services combination. It was applauded as vintage Greenberg: decisively opportune and deeply strategic. A key global competitor struggled to close a carefully planned deal so in one fell swoop AIG moved to bolster key aspects of its long-term strategy. Outside of arbitrage desks and the cynics' lairs, no one really noticed that with a P/E of 32 purchasing a P/E of 18, it was very difficult for this to be a bad deal in the short run.

And if the cynics mentioned to each other on the phone or in emails that this was all some sort of earnings arbitrage gambit, there were probably fewer still who noted that since the summer of 1998, AIG had used $42 billion in stock to purchase its newest operating units. Earnings were growing faster than the shares that were issued to pay for these premium deals, but so was the balance sheet. The 1997 10-K lists $139.5 billion in liabilities for the year prior to the SunAmerica deal; the 2002 10-K lists $438 billion.[6] The balance sheet of the company in three short years had been radically transformed.

There was no meeting where Greenberg was directed to grow the business in this manner, no directive to accomplish this goal or that one. Of course, no one told the tiger where to stalk his prey. What Greenberg did was innate and biological, although, seen from some distance, it was every bit about his survival as well.

Motives aside, these would be the last "happy," unquestioned, and event-free days of Greenberg's reign at AIG.

■ ■ ■

Starting in 2002, AIG's share price began a slide that it would never really recover from, dropping from just under $80 in early 2002 to the low $50s in September 2002.

This drove Greenberg positively mad. With zero concern for appearances, he called the chief of the New York Stock Exchange (NYSE) on which AIG's shares traded and hectored chief executive Dick Grasso about what he viewed was the very poor handling of AIG's shares by Spear, Leeds & Kellogg, the specialists assigned to the stock. Greenberg's frequent calls and his threats to delist AIG and take it to the Nasdaq became a regular[7] and challenging feature of Grasso's life. AIG was too prominent an issuer to ignore and risk losing, so Grasso spent perhaps more time appeasing Greenberg than any other CEO on the exchange. His calls, in fact, became so commonplace a feature of

Grasso's life that the issue of whether Grasso forced the specialists to treat AIG's stock differently than other listed companies became part of the formal SEC investigation of the NYSE in 2004. Complicating matters even more so was Greenberg's place on the NYSE compensation committee that awarded him his infamous $139.5 million pay and retirement package.[8]

Greenberg was not shy about telling anyone who walked into his office that AIG's shares were sharply undervalued. Even if they were, his options were very limited. At a two-year low share price of $44.47 in the first quarter of 2003 an attempt to return AIG to privately held status—since the company was in effect run as a partnership—via leveraged buyout would have cost at least $116 billion and more likely would have been around $130 billion. That was a little too steep for a business that already carried over $75 billion in various debt liabilities.[9]

He confided to his inner circle that they would tough it out. The year 2004 looked promising in many ways, Greenberg allowed, and often enough solutions to headaches like a stock price presented themselves in due course.

This would prove to be a spectacularly inaccurate sentiment.

■ ■ ■

The beginning of the end for what was the greatness of the old AIG—and most definitely for the reign of Hank Greenberg—came around December 1998 when a pair of up-against-the-wall executives from an Indianapolis-based wireless device company called Brightpoint reached out to officials at the National Union Fire Insurance Company for some help.

The Brightpoint duo, corporate controller John Delaney and risk management chief Timothy Harcharik, sought a hand because one of their units had booked larger than expected losses: A previously announced $13 to $18 million loss had grown to $29 million, and if reported as such there would be hell to pay. This being the dot-com era, lying to make one's numbers was not entirely frowned upon.

This is where AIG's National Union Fire came in handy. It turned out that over time within this longstanding subsidiary had developed something called the "LMU," short for Loss Mitigation Unit. A more accurate term might have been the "APTG," or accounting parlor trick group.

Here's how it worked: Brightpoint, to get out of its deeper-than-bargained-for hole, paid AIG about $15 million in monthly "premium" for "retroactive" coverage for an imaginary loss. AIG in turn paid out $11.9 million in fictitious "claims." All of this sleight-of-hand allowed Brightpoint to claim the $11.9 million as an "Insurance Receivable," thus reducing the loss to the previous range.

Brightpoint's gain from contracting out with AIG was not imaginary; the fake insurance allowed them to overstate earnings by 61 percent. Absent moral considerations, a company that was presumably trying to protect its battered $6 share price might have run this level of risk, but for a company with a then $90 share price who made all of $3.1 million in "premiums," it was preposterous. It was worse than the "round trip of cash" that the Securities and Exchange Commission (SEC) claimed,[10] as it appeared the LMU may have been a business line—helping companies falsify their financial statements—that AIG's National Union was deeply involved in.

We can say this because David Schiff, when looking at AIG's web site in December 2004 noticed that the Loss Mitigation Unit's services were still offered, even after the authorities had begun proceedings. The site included three examples of how its "insurance" product—the site's quote marks are on words like "premium," "funding mechanism" and "uninsured settlement," implying they are euphemisms—can help companies deal with "obstacles posed by large-scale liabilities."

AIG's LMU was a large "FU" to the spirit of accounting standards and insurance practices. Though many brokers and insurance companies have actively helped clients rejigger earnings so the best face could be put on today's crummy news or a better one for tomorrow's, that AIG's corporate web site continued to actively promote this was reckless.

The settlement discussions with the SEC were basic. With absolutely no realistic bargaining position, AIG's general counsel's office agreed to the first number that was proposed: a $10 million penalty.

It was almost a lot more. Ernie Patrikis, AIG's general counsel, had ordered staff from Sullivan & Cromwell to prepare documents to meet the SEC's subpoena. Unfortunately, a junior lawyer misplaced a marketing document an AIG staff accountant had written in 1997 explaining the LMU's services for AIG executives. As the investigation was wrapping up, the document was found and turned over to the SEC. The SEC staff was furious, accusing AIG of covering up "marketing materials" until the end of the investigation, delivered another subpoena, held more depositions, and threatened a whole new set of charges. A former SEC lawyer described the just-discovered document as "a smoking gun" since it referred to the LMU's efforts as providing "income statement smoothing."

Eventually, a senior partner at Sullivan & Cromwell defused the matter when he wrote the SEC's New York office a letter taking full responsibility for the mix up.

The entire episode rattled the board and for the first time, Greenberg's explanation for the affair was challenged by board members unhappy to have AIG caught up in tawdry accounting games. Though it happened dozens of levels below him, involved a sum of money that was insignificant, and America's premier law firm admitted their culpability in almost making matters worse, the SEC complaint was a black eye.

Greenberg seethed at what he saw was the lack of proportion shown by the SEC and to an extent, his board, who expressed their displeasure to him in no uncertain terms.

In the coming months he would likely yearn for a return to the board's "lack of proportion" in the Brightpoint matter.

■■■

In the late 1980s, the Japanese economic "miracle" collapsed, and its commercial banking system, the engine of its decades-long ascent out of the post-Second World War rubble, began what would amount to a slow-motion incineration. In a series of concentric calamities, years' worth of strategic business errors met macroeconomic reverses—unemployment spiked, a frenzied and futile expansion into the U.S. capital markets, low gross domestic product (GDP) growth and above all, massive loans in support of their own real estate bubble—and sent the once seemingly invincible Japanese economy into an extended recession. By the mid-1990s many of the formerly powerful global banks were bloated husks, known derisively as *ghost banks*.

With government stimulus programs effecting little real improvement, the previously unthinkable soon became the necessary and regulators sought foreign investors or consolidation within the sector as the last, best hope to salvage the banks. The problem became attracting buyers when their balance sheets were full of disastrous real estate loans.

AIGFP's Tokyo office had a solution. Executives there had devised a way to move the busted loans off bank balance sheet's into an AIG owned special-purpose entity (SPE), or a "corporation" that existed only on paper and whose only "asset" were billions of dollars of essentially worthless loans. The bank got a balance sheet that was no longer radioactive, and AIG got a handsome fee and (through an additional series of accounting moves) managed to return the risk of the SPE—its "assets"—to the bank.

Thus, was born something called Contributed Guaranteed Alternative Investment Trusts, soon to be thankfully shortened to C-GAITs.

The Bank of Japan (their Federal Reserve) and the Ministry of Finance fully approved of this gambit.[11] FP chief Tom Savage told Greenberg about the success of the transactions, and Greenberg replied, "Let's see if we can do something like that here."[12]

Actually, they had. For the previous three years, FP had been doing a version of it for fellow insurance companies under a fellow named Lucien Burnett. A former Bankers Trust executive, Burnett helped insurance companies obtain capital relief so they could invest surplus capital in stocks and bonds. The deals Burnett worked were called GAITs and were considered plain vanilla: in return for a fee, the insurance company bought notes from FP that saved them hundreds of millions of dollars annually in capital charges.

They were different from the deals done in Japan in some very key aspects. FP created SPEs that took some longer-dated assets (not always busted loans) and used some counterparty cash to purchase something like a Vanguard index mutual fund that generally provided an S&P 500 level of return. FP would take in the dividends and profit appreciation of the Vanguard fund and have it taxed at a lower rate. Moreover, they consolidated the transaction onto their balance sheet for the duration of the transaction. Their accountants and lawyers had no qualms with the insurance company's freeing up some capital and AIG's returns being taxed at a lower rate. It was a line of business that was profitable—though

FP alumni note that it was not spectacularly so, perhaps $3 million per deal—and had been in effect since the mid-1990s.

Around the winter of 2001, an FP consultant named Gary Gorton, a Yale School of Management professor, suggested that the insurance transactions could be modified to address one of the pressing needs for banks, which was balance sheet relief. Many banks, whose balance sheets were full of bad loans to dot-coms, corporate fraudsters, and their own venture capital and private-equity investment losses, would presumably appreciate the opportunity to present a cleaner appearance. Naturally, transactions such as these have to be tweaked for a U.S. corporate customer since it was unlikely that legal contortions that had "saving face" as a guiding principle would have passed muster even in early 2001. It's not even clear that the deal would have passed any formal muster internally at AIG.

Chuck Lucas, AIG's chief market risk manager, told the then-departing Tom Savage that, "I know what you're trying to do with the deal, but to get [regulators] to sign off, you'll have to consolidate this onto the balance sheet." His words usually carried extra weight, since he had been the New York Fed's head of International Capital Markets and had direct, open-door access to Greenberg.

The deal itself was run out of Cassano's new transactions group and he was intimately involved with its execution, according to former colleagues.

Howie Smith recalls matters differently. He says that after being assured from Cassano that it was a variation on the GAITs deals and there was only "a bell and whistle" that would be different. Smith, who said he recalled how even the smallest unexamined possible contingencies at FP could wind up being monumental headaches, told Cassano that if that was the case he wanted another auditor to look at it, which led to the introduction of Ernst & Young into the equation.

Under accounting rules, the SPEs, or holding companies created to "own" assets a bank, insurance company, or broker wanted to be rid of, had to be an independent third party (AIG) with capital invested into the SPE and bearing the risks and rewards from its valuation. In other words, if it went up or down in value, AIG was the only company that stood to profit or lose. Since this was no longer a capital relief situation, the risk-averse AIGFP was unwilling to consolidate the transaction onto their balance sheets since it involved "improving" the appearances of a customer's balance sheet.

Of all the banks AIGFP shopped this idea to, only PNC bit. FP proposed setting up an SPE that would own the crummy loans as well as some cash that the counterparty had put into it. The cash would be used to buy a 30-year zero-coupon note equal to the amount of crummy loans and cash in the SPE—and due AIG. AIG would contribute 3 percent of the SPE's value in cash and then turn around and buy highly rated bonds and keep the interest as a dividend. The agreement also allowed for AIG to keep 75 basis points (0.75 percent) of the assets as a fee.

As a marketing tool, they had a letter from Ernst & Young that broadly suggested that C-GAITs were congruent with accounting standards. The problem was that it didn't touch upon all of the features in C-GAITs.[13] According to the SEC complaint, AIG's issuance of the zero-coupon note was a violation of accounting provisions that prohibited a return of investor capital in an active SPE. Eventually, the accountants caught on and informed AIG that the zero coupon was problematic, but AIG continued to market these deals to potential clients without mentioning the possible accounting risk.

PNC went ahead and proceeded to offload $762 million in three separate C-GAITs deals between the end of June and the end of November 2001, allowing it to report a net income 52 percent higher than it would have ordinarily.

For its part, AIG booked $39.21 million in fees and continued to pitch deals to insurance companies and banks using this structure. Before the last of the three transactions closed in late November, the Federal Reserve had written PNC and raised serious concerns about their moving the liabilities off balance sheet. By the end of January, the deals were put back on PNC's balance sheet and a massive accounting restatement was in the works. Several months later, the SEC subpoenas went out. Soon after that came the Department of Justice subpoenas for violations of the antifraud statutes.

The difference between AIG and the rest of the world's corporations when it came to dealing with a regulator would never be starker. PNC appears to have folded its cards the minute the Fed raised questions in late October 2001. It signed a cease-and-desist order in

November 2002 and paid a $115 million fine in the summer of 2003. The 15- or 16-month turnaround from subpoena receipt to complaint to settlement is a remarkably compressed timeframe by SEC standards and proof that PNC sought to do anything it could to put the episode behind it.

AIG took a different tack.

The company complied with the SEC and Department of Justice (DoJ) document requests but mounted a vigorous defense, hiring Baker & Botts, who proceeded to argue to Greenberg and the general counsel's office that they could win a trial in court. This was good enough for Greenberg, who gave every indication that he was willing to fight this. Though the lawyers no doubt had marshaled any number of arguments that made sense to his ears, Greenberg and the defenders of the deal at FP were failing to realize that the collapse of Enron in late 2001 had changed everything.

The SEC, humiliated at having missed a host of obvious corporate frauds that cost shareholders hundreds of billions of dollars, was on the warpath in a desperate bid to salvage its tattered reputation. The DoJ was riding high as it prepared to prosecute dozens of corporate wrongdoers in some of the highest-profile trials in history.[14] In contrast, AIG was defending off-balance-sheet financing designed to mask a bank's massive losses at a time when most every business-press-reading American knew the names of the various trusts Enron had employed. It was not a strong hand to play, and the only question was how badly it would end up for AIG.

The answer? Very, very badly.

Unlike Greenberg, Patrikis and his staff in the general counsel's office were under no illusions whatsoever about the PNC deals. An internal AIG assessment of the deals at the time noted that it was "a deal that was on balance much, much worse than it initially appeared." Another senior AIG executive involved in cleaning up the mess described it as "intellectually indefensible." For all of the awesome intellectual firepower at FP, they had failed to draw a distinction between run-of-the-mill capital relief that the GAITs transactions had given insurance companies and the "accounting-driven" transactions that sought (as the goal of its client) to fundamentally alter the perception of its financial statements. FP also misunderstood the schism between insurance regulators and bank regulators. The latter are often based in state capitols and seek to guarantee that there is a margin of safety for policyholders to ensure that all valid claims presented are met; the former are often federal and have wide-ranging powers to influence the bank's operations.

The conclusion was obvious and time-tested: put up a good defense, and then seek to settle on the best terms they could. But, in this instance, there was no stopping the regulators once they were on the warpath.

Even AIG's press releases aroused the ire of the SEC and the DoJ. On October 4, 2004, the SEC and DoJ put out a statement warning that AIG's previous press releases underplayed the depth and the full scope of the investigation.

That was the least of Ernie Patrikis's problems, however. Every time he got close to inking a settlement, a story popped up in the national press about how much trouble AIG was in, knocking another billion off of its market capitalization. It was an old game, to be certain, but a cruelly efficient one: if the general counsel or CEO had cold feet about signing a deal, the leaks served to focus the AIG board's mind on settling.

An October 18, 2004, a *BusinessWeek* story drove home this point.[15] Full of juicy one-sided leaks describing AIG's alleged failures to produce this document or that—and how hard and aggressive the SEC attorneys were playing "the game"—it was probably the most pro-SEC piece of reporting in years. To combat this, Patrikis filed a detailed complaint with the SEC's inspector general demanding an inquiry into how the media had access to details of the discovery AIG had provided. Several weeks later, he received a form letter thanking him for his efforts but declining to pursue the matter.

Seven weeks later, Patrikis had his deal.

AIG paid a tad over $126 million—$80 million in penalties plus $46 million to a PNC investor restitution fund—and it agreed to a series of procedural changes including setting up a transaction review committee and hiring a chief compliance officer. In a twist most often seen in low-level narcotics cases, the DoJ's press release announcing the settlement noted that federal prosecutors had agreed to "a deferred prosecution" pending AIG's full compliance with terms of the agreement. In other words, if AIGFP kept its nose clean through January 2006, no one would be indicted.

Most AIG employees, investors, and research analysts likely missed the deferred prosecution news or focused on the size of the settlement, and were happy to put it all behind them. Patrikis and his staff didn't share that return-to-business-as-usual sentiment. They knew fully that the DoJ was prepared to move on indictments if they didn't get everything they sought. There was no assurance that if the DoJ went to court against AIG they would have won, but that wasn't really the point. It would have cost tens of millions of dollars in legal costs, and the publicity alone might have shaved another few billion dollars in market cap. There was the larger issue that many in the general counsel's office worried that the group in Wilton—most especially the 18th floor of corporate headquarters at 70 Pine Street, where Greenberg worked—were missing: no deal should ever be done that carries with it the risk that one day you will have to litigate it in front of a jury. "We think we can win this in the courtroom" could *never* be a rationale for a transaction.

Investors were drawing their own conclusions and beginning to discount the company's profit growth, as evidenced in the declining share price. Few investors doubted that management had failed to grow the enterprise, but few could argue that at least some of the growth was apparently coming from business that was, at the very least, questionable.

Also drawing its own conclusions about the matter was the board of directors. They noticed an unpleasant trend in settlement size between those who had set out to mislead their investors—AIG's clients—and those who helped them do so, namely AIG. In both cases, AIG paid measurably greater fines and settlements than did their clients. This may or may not have been an appropriate regulatory outcome or even legally just, but it was a very clear signal that the direction of enforcement in 2005 was going to be skewed toward those who aided and abetted in misleading investors about corporate financial health.

There was also the issue of the drama involved in each case. Prosecutors may have crossed lines in demanding changes in how press releases are issued, but the board wasn't there to launch a noble quest to reign in prosecutorial abuses. They were in a fight, a brutal one, and there was little to suggest that it was going to end.

As one very pronounced pro-Greenberg board member said of this period, "Everywhere we looked, it was worse. No one thought that Brightpoint and PNC were the only deals that were [problematic]. The company was making money but we weren't sure where the next headache might come from. The risks seemed to just build and build."

The company was still making plenty of money. As the last quarter of the year began, with operating income up 22 percent to $12.6 billion year to date, there wasn't much that could be criticized on that front. But if the risks continued to build, the rewards were not. Investors sat on their hands, and the stock spent the year hovering in the mid-$60s, closing down about 2 percent.

The pro–Hank Greenberg board took little solace in the fact that he had made Joe Cassano sign the settlement agreement (a de facto admission of guilt) and pay the fine out of FP's working capital. This alone was its own mini-drama. When Greenberg told Cassano that he wanted him to pay the full penalty, Cassano replied, "Fuck you!" Greenberg held his ground, and Cassano's FP paid every cent. (Years later, FP executives appear entirely comfortable with their unit's role in perpetuating the PNC fraud, but remained astounded that Greenberg put up with this level of disrespect.)[16]

Greenberg's assurances that he knew nothing about the deals or had not been involved in them in any fashion were immaterial to the board; the concern was why these baldly illegal deals were happening at all. AIG was a huge and complex company, but so were a number of AIG's competitors, such as Travelers, and none of them seemed to be running afoul of the most basic aspects of securities law.

They were sticking with Hank because there was no one else they thought could do a better job at the present time. He had his loyalists on the board, and his AIG colleagues, Martin Sullivan, Donald Kanak and Edmund Tse, would seen as likely to stand by him until the very end of time, but as a group, the board had reached their limit.

There would be no more tolerance of protracted federal regulatory and criminal investigations. Hank Greenberg had broadened and expanded C. V. Starr's work beyond anyone's dreams because he was able to shape and control the tiniest details of operations and policy. It was now abundantly clear to his board members that Greenberg—whom they still saw as an honest man—could not control the far-flung businesses of AIG's 100,000-employee empire the way that he once had.

This last sentiment is arguably unfair. Greenberg still struck fear and admiration in most every employee who met him. The culture of AIG—which he had largely shaped—managed to willingly get a level of work and initiative out of even the lowest-ranking employee that was replicated nowhere else in the insurance industry. Where he was demonstrably losing his grasp was in the quest to bolster earnings via the use of ethically marginal financing techniques. He may not have approved of individual transactions that violated the letter of the law, but he definitely structured a culture where failing to meet earnings bore grave consequences.

In a mature industry, where only AIG's triple-A rating distinguished it from a pack of insurance and finance competitors—many of whom had their own variation of an FP unit—the ability to do unique transactions that were proprietary and lucrative was fast diminishing. Hundreds of separate hedge and private-equity funds stood at the ready to snap up senior FP talent and there was no trade or few transactions that the major brokerages weren't trying to compete against them.

The way around this was to push into ever-grayer shadowlands between finance and insurance where regulatory oversight was non-existent and the law vague. But, as they had just learned, just because regulators didn't keep an eye on things in a new market didn't mean that anything goes.

At FP in Wilton, there was a resigned air about the PNC settlement. The prevailing view was that "it happened, they did it, they paid for it, it is over." There was no apparent public reflection or reconsideration of the deals other than the acknowledgment, in private among groups of colleagues, that they had been totally absurd propositions. As a senior manager said, "That's what you get for doing accounting-driven deals. I'm really not sure how Joe thought he was going to get away with it."

So back to work it was.

■ ■ ■

Questioned about PNC six years after the fact, a half-dozen of the unit's more senior producers share a primary memory of the episode: no one was fired. There were no sudden departures or even unexpected "retirements"; no one was reassigned to another unit. A 200-person unit that nearly had executives indicted and whose actions led to a nine-figure fine and a loss of corporate prestige was left entirely alone.

Put simply, there is nowhere else in corporate America where anything like that series of events could have transpired without sweeping changes occurring in its wake.

A few of FP's longest serving members, as well as some alumni, recalled that Howard Sosin was run out of the company on a rail for losing a couple of hundred million dollars in one transaction. Under Joe Cassano, there had now been a criminal investigation, $126 million in fines and more adverse publicity than the company had ever received. Yet he reported to work and continued to build the portfolio out, never mentioning it again. Actually, as Savage departed for retirement in Florida, Cassano consolidated his power and began to rule FP in a fashion that in short order would be unchecked and broadly unquestioned.

It is safe to conclude that the absence of a material lesson from the PNC deal was the lesson Joe Cassano took to heart.

Chapter 6

War by Another Name

As with any large company, rumors were a fact of life at AIG. The main question being whispered in AIG's downtown Manhattan headquarters as 2005 dawned was: when is Greenberg going to retire and who is on the short list to be his successor?

Relentless regulatory investigation at AIG in 2004–2005 turned hushed whispers into open conversation among the middle and senior ranks of management about Greenberg's possibly being out of touch, too old, a step behind. In the boardroom, these whispers centered on the phrase *succession plan*. AIG's succession plan was simplicity itself to Greenberg: he would run it until he didn't want to. As it so happened, he was indeed contemplating relinquishing the CEO slot and taking the chairman's post to ensure a smooth two- to three-year "break-in period." The few people he had mentioned this to, board member and close friend Frank Zarb in particular, took that to mean that Greenberg was leaning toward picking Martin Sullivan, the head of American International Underwriters, its massive property and casualty unit, as opposed to Donald Kanak, its chief operating officer.

Sullivan was a brilliant insurance executive who had worked at AIG since he was 17, but he knew virtually nothing about capital markets or finance. Kanak was the polar opposite: a polished and sophisticated Oxford and Harvard Law grad, he had run AIG's Asian units and was married to the daughter of the former speaker of Japan's parliament.

Kanak would likely get up to speed quickly, but it was Sullivan who had been groomed by Greenberg for more than a decade. Institutional investors and analysts would love Kanak, as he would remind them of the men who ran their own firms. The AIG rank-and-file loved Martin— like a pop star, he was universally known by his first name throughout the company—for his unassuming ways and would go through walls for him. Greenberg, it was broadly supposed, would place a premium on having a CEO with Sullivan's fierce loyalty to AIG (and him) as a primary asset to that of Kanak's brilliance and polish.

(Greenberg had two sons, Jeffrey and Evan, who had distinguished themselves in a variety of AIG posts and were widely speculated to be the frontrunners to succeed their father. Both left the company in frustration and took CEO posts with rival insurers.)

Regardless, Greenberg knew that whatever he did, it was a lock that the board would go along. Whoever it was, that man would be successful if he mirrored Greenberg's decisions and management style. There was some paper listing successors and the like in the event of an emergency, but that was just tripe to keep the good-governance busybodies happy. In this, as in many other things, he would decide what was best for AIG, and, he strongly suspected, he would be right.

For now, though, he wanted to run AIG—as he made very clear to the few brave enough to inquire. The whole thing frankly pissed him off, and he seemed to enjoy cutting short idiot analysts who never tired of asking.

For the first time, this wasn't good enough for the board and they tried to gently let him know. Men who owed Greenberg much, like Frank Zarb and Richard Holbrooke, or someone who had abiding respect for the man and his legacy, like Carla Hills, let it be known one way or another that there should be a concrete schedule with a designated successor. He would play a huge role in the company, keep the chairman's title, with a full roster of perks, but someone else needed to be ready to take over.

But if the Brightpoint and PNC issues could be said to have been a brightly painted red line pointing Greenberg out of 70 Pine Street—even if he hadn't had any direct oversight or even awareness of the deals—his fate was all but sealed in late January 2005 when it was announced that independent members of the board of directors at first WorldCom and then Enron would pay settlements out-of-pocket to dismiss class-action claims. Amounting to around 20 percent of their net worth (outside of fixed retirement plans and primary residences), it was an instant shock to other corporate boards. If something happened at some regional office and metastasized into a nine-figure loss and they couldn't be proven to have taken all due haste to stop it, if someone ignored them and the board didn't follow up, there was now legal precedent that could be used against them.

Serving on any corporate board has long been the career equivalent of dessert, a way to enjoy private-sector pay and perks while maintaining an intellectual engagement with the events of the day. The concept of a binding legal duty to an abstraction like a shareholder base was one thing, but it was another thing to get your life rerouted financially because of a mistaken decision in some board meeting. Interviews with three former members of the board serving at this time made clear that at that moment the board became a whole lot less resolved to fight for Hank Greenberg.

Privately, as details emerged over the Enron settlement, there were other unpleasant similarities for the board to ponder, including the high-profile nature of the CEO, the massive and widely distributed shareholder base, the red flags raised earlier over smaller regulatory matters, the multiple personal and economic connections between the company and board members. It was asinine to analogize Hank Greenberg with Ken Lay and Bernie Ebbers, both of whom argued that they had no idea what was happening operationally at their companies. Hank watched over AIG's operations like a hawk. That was the problem, according to board members. He was honest—if inclined to always see things his way—and smart, qualities that the slick CEOs of the other troubled companies often were not.

But AIG was huge and getting larger every day, and it was involved in a diversity of businesses that even a full-time board member couldn't track. Greenberg insisted that he was never more engaged with the company, and no one kept a busier schedule, but maybe, just maybe, that was the reason they had an overseer from the federal government stationed in headquarters.

A former board member had a checklist he used to keep track of just how big AIG was. Just on Wall Street, it owned more government bonds than most primary dealers in Treasury securities. In size of paper owned, it dominated the mortgage market more than anyone save for Fannie Mae and Freddie Mac. It was the largest player in retirement planning, and, when the board member could remember it, whatever it was that FP was doing was bringing in billions of dollars. The board member would then repeat the exercise, adjusting for AIG's presence in foreign markets. Once that was done, they would do the same for domestic insurance and then repeat it for foreign insurance. They were exposed to everyone and everything, the board member concluded, and made money, it would appear, anytime anyone bought or sold nearly anything.

When the board member repeated this to Greenberg, he smiled a knowing smile.

"Well, you know what they say about owning the toll roads. . . ."

The board member, despite an open admiration for Greenberg, wasn't so sure. They were so big that they would have no idea what was really going on, and they would be easy fodder for a halfway-skilled trial attorney. Greenberg's response? The board member was wrong, per Hank, but yes, the trial lawyers were absolutely out of control and AIG should increase the amount they gave to get tort reform passed since it was desperately needed.

The resignation was submitted in due course. This was most assuredly not where the board member was heading with the conversation, but then they hadn't supposed that Hank was going to agree to major changes.

AIG's directors earned between $90,000 and $160,000 in 2005, and many of them were decidedly affluent, if not rich, from a host of other sources. A look at AIG's 2005 proxy shows that the board's work consisted largely of serving on other boards, "consulting," and various other socially sanctioned influence peddling. Spitzer's suing them would have ruined this gravy train. All the more reason to not fork over 20 percent of their life's work because of some insane combination of screw-ups in the corporate hinterlands, Greenberg's combativeness, and a legal regime that put board members firmly at risk for things they had never been told about.

If it came to it, Hank was going to go. It was not a difficult decision.

■ ■ ■

Insurance companies get paid to provide security for the things that you worry about but can never fully see coming. What no one at AIG saw coming was Eliot Spitzer, and there was no insurance against him. A man whose ambition could hardly be contained in the New York State attorney general's post, he had largely transcended his job with a series of high-profile salvos against Wall Street firms and their business practices.

Spitzer's assault against Wall Street's biggest brokers in the wake of the dot-com collapse for their massively abusive, conflict-of-interest-ridden research recommendations clearly resonated with a public shocked not only by what was uncovered, but also by the Justice Department and Securities and Exchange Commission's (SEC's) cluelessness—or seeming lack of interest—in what was even going on.

It is difficult to understate what Spitzer and his small staff of modestly compensated state attorneys had accomplished in a few years against some of the richest firms in the world. His campaign had defrocked a series of once-lionized research analysts as charlatans, forced a wholesale shift in Wall Street's business practices, and secured a $1.4 billion settlement.

Equally difficult to understate was the public reaction to him. In a highly partisan, post-Lewinsky age, Spitzer's desire to force account-ability on Wall Street harkened back to the Athenian ideals of public service. People from Milwaukee to Modesto sensed that he had waged a solitary campaign against the biggest local employers in his state and that had he not prevailed, he faced near certain ruin. As a product of New York's finest prep schools, its Jewish community, and Princeton and Harvard Law, Spitzer also showed true courage in running up against most of the world he came from when he went after Wall Street. Politically speaking, there was the prospect of alienating much of the newly acquired Wall Street financial muscle in the Democratic party's fund-raising base. But Spitzer had won going away.

The wages of victory were immense. To start with, there was bipartisan adulation and (more importantly) a media treatment that had no analogue. The *New Yorker,* the *New York Times,* the *Washington Post,* and the major television networks gave him extended national exposure and, soon enough, an implicitly uncritical approach to his future pronouncements.

Spitzer began to proceed like a man with a mandate to do the difficult work of cleaning up American business practices. In an age where American economic power was most evident as the location of, and biggest player in, a global marketplace and clearinghouse for capital at risk, it was assumed that he would correct the excesses of the traders and the fund managers that had rocketed from being rich to ultra-wealthy. It was the perfect moment for an evolution from attorney general to protector-in-chief.

He had little competition. The guardians were all down or against the ropes. Industry regulators like the SEC had earned widespread scorn over missing or being late to every ugly scandal over the previous decade; the federal prosecutors and FBI were never that much better than the SEC and were now heavily geared toward antiterror activities in the wake of September 11 and the run-up to the Iraq war.

The media, the traditional watchdogs of both corporate and political power, was in a full-bore collapse of its generations-long business model. Readership dropped sharply, and in turn ad revenues gave way. It wasn't long before investigative or enterprise reporting work was trimmed. There wasn't much chance, in other words, that a reporter or a federal prosecutor looking for corporate shenanigans was going to beat Spitzer to the punch.

With a mandate in popular opinion that had few rivals, the campaigns began in short order.

■ ■ ■

First was the practice of late trading and mutual-fund timing in 2003. Bank of America alone would pay $625 million to settle charges it actively sought to let hedge funds enter late orders to buy and sell its mutual funds after the close of trading. He also forced a hedge fund run by Edward Stern—a member of the billionaire Stern family, one of the

New York metro area's most prominent business families—to pay $40 million, a settlement that did nothing to harm his credentials as a populist.

The next stop was the New York Stock Exchange, where he sued its chairman and CEO Richard Grasso for being excessively compensated as the head of a nonprofit.[1] The suit proved to be monumentally embarrassing for the roster of Wall Street and corporate CEOs who rubber-stamped what was a package valued at a minimum of $139.5 million. It proved fatal to Grasso and his group of long-standing colleagues, who eventually resigned under the weight of the ceaseless disclosures and media reports. Even the most jaded New York business insider was astounded at the turnaround. Barely two years prior, Grasso was nationally lauded as a hero for his mighty labors to reopen the exchange in the wake of the devastation in lower Manhattan after the September 11 attacks; he was now alternately a butt of jokes or a poster boy for cronyism and captured regulation.

Shortly thereafter, he launched investigations into and then prosecuted Marsh & McLennan, Willis Group Holdings, and Aon for various bid-rigging schemes that dated back to the late 1990s.

It was with the insurance investigations that Spitzer evolved from a legal crusader into a moralist. In one incident, as negotiations began and then broke down with Marsh—headed by one Jeffrey Greenberg, Hank's eldest son—he very publicly stated, "That management is not one that I will talk with. It is not one that I will negotiate with."[2]

There is, of course, precedent for an attorney general in refusing to negotiate with a corporation's management, but those are instances where the company is obviously a front for organized crime. The implication for the business and legal communities, who read Spitzer's confident statement in a press conference, was that in his eyes, there was little practical difference between the Gambino family and the world's largest insurance broker. A more shrewd take is that in making a statement like that, which had little precedent in recent memory, was that Spitzer was telegraphing to New York's legal and business communities that he would not really negotiate, at least in substance. He didn't have to. The attorney general's demands would be met or he would be willing to consider ever more extreme action.

The message was received.

The takeaway for Marsh's senior leadership and corporate board was that they needed to (1) somehow get Jeff Greenberg out of there and (2) immediately replace him with someone who was demonstrably acceptable to the attorney general, who could otherwise (3) indict the company.[3] To be clear, he never threatened or even implied that he would indict Marsh, but his demand that Marsh meet his staffing requirements suggests, at the very least, that something was monumentally wrong with that company.

To wit: Greenberg was summarily retired in October, Spitzer's former boss at the New York district attorney's office was plucked from running Marsh's Kroll unit, and an $850 million settlement was announced. Shareholders could begin to breathe again, having seen their stock drop $8.44 when the suit was filed, taking $4.43 billion in market capitalization with it.

There is a cruel irony, as underneath all of the brinksmanship, Spitzer's office had what appeared to be (at the time) a very good case. Marsh's "contingent commission" activities, even though they had long been customary in the insurance industry, seemed to the eye to be a complex series of collusions between it and erstwhile competitors to keep the prices of various commercial insurance lines high enough to be profitable for all the insurance companies. But the story of wrongdoing and the mechanics of building and winning a case that was much more complex than had been initially reported was a distant second in the public eye—to the media, the story *was* Spitzer and his back-room negotiations and threats.

■ ■ ■

AIG's response to what was becoming Spitzer's permanent investigation into the insurance industry was to try to mount an intellectual challenge to what many in the New York business community saw as an "anti-business" bent to the attorney general's efforts. In the main, this is a valid approach; the way AIG went about it was evocative of the Keystone Kops. Through a concentric series of screw-ups and miscommunications, AIG somehow wound up attempting to pay prominent financial and political commentators up to $25,000 for publishing op-eds critical of Spitzer.

The Washington, D.C.–based Qorvis Communications, hired by AIG in early October 2004 to provide public relations advice, was behind the scheme.[4] At some point in the following few weeks, this evolved into Qorvis's use of a booking agency to solicit sympathetic speakers via email to sway public opinion, according to the *Wall Street Journal*. Within hours of AIG general counsel Ernie Patrikis's finding out about the scheme, Qorvis was fired. Regardless, AIG looked alternately deceitful and inept when the matter surfaced.[5]

There would be no consequences for Spitzer's ordering leadership changes in private enterprises. After the wealth destruction of the dot-com era collapses and more Wall Street scandals than could be tracked, the voting public seemed grateful for an attorney general who wasn't awed by his opponents' money or prestige.[6] From the perspective of the media in the fall of 2004 and winter of 2005, the proof was over-whelming: it was impossible to keep up with the indictments and guilty pleas, and even if it couldn't be seen, reporters knew that wholesale business shifts at not only Marsh but other major insurers (a pair of midlevel executives at AIG also pled to bid-rigging charges) were being put into place. It was difficult to argue that Spitzer's sustained legal efforts, which appeared to have just as much in common with military strategy as they did the writ of law, were anything other than a success. Indeed, the dollar volume of his settlements forced his friends and foes alike to concede that he got results.[7]

With the Marsh matter settled on the last day of January 2005, there was hardly time to reflect for Spitzer and his investor protection bureau. A rapidly evolving series of events would proceed to be one of the defining cases of his career.

On February 8, reinsurance giant Gen Re—under investigation by the SEC and federal prosecutors in Virginia for potential abuses for sales of finite reinsurance to a struggling malpractice insurer called Reciprocal of America—presented the SEC with the results of an internal investigation that showed AIG as a link in a chain of dubious deals that purported to transfer risk, but in the end, merely served to dress up financial results.[8]

The next day, February 9, the attorney general sent AIG a sub-poena. The day after that, the SEC—with whom they were working closely and quite effectively—sent its own. On February 11, Spitzer's office sent Greenberg himself a subpoena. Spitzer was making clear that the investigation was taking an unusual tack. There would be no starting with staff accountants or midlevel executives and building a case upward over a period of months, document by document, one deposition at a time.

It did not take a battle-tested courtroom watcher to discern the attorney general's theory of the case: AIG's CEO was at the very center of something that was very big and really wrong. Whatever the case became, it would be a referendum on a company and the man who built it and made little distinction between the corporation and himself.

■ ■ ■

The transaction that launched a thousand subpoenas was actually more than five years old. On October 26, 2000, AIG announced its third-quarter earnings. The level of reserves available is always one of the most important barometers for an insurance company's strength, but AIG reported a $59 million decline in general insurance reserves. About $6.06 was shaved off the then $99 stock price, and the damage was done.

Greenberg was fairly well brassed off. AIG then had $24.5 billion in reserves and having to lose market cap because a few Wall Street lemmings were fretting about a decline of less than 1 percent of their reserves made him ill. It was, he thought, a dubious concern since the company had made exceptionally clear that its TransAtlantic unit had experienced an increase in catastrophe claims in the third quarter of 2000. Nonetheless, analysts (at that point in time) called the tune. It was how a nonproblem, to Greenberg, became self-fulfilling: because a 30-something-year-old analyst, who had been looking at insurance companies for maybe five years, said AIG had a reserves problem, the people who controlled AIG stock price thought Hank was underreserving. Until the next quarter when another person looked at the number in a spreadsheet and wrote that AIG was now adequately reserved, at which point all was forgotten.

By October 31, 2000, the stock price had returned to the $99 level, but Greenberg picked up the phone and called the Gen Re CEO Ron Ferguson anyway, to discuss doing something about this headache. It's at this point that—to use a British term—the spanner went into the works and things became wholly screwed up. This is also the point where accounts begin to vary wildly.

Here's what actually happened: A series of deeply complex deals were struck in order for AIG to get a $500 million loan from Gen Re that was disguised as a reserve against possible claims. The pair of analysts who were so worried about a $59 million drop in reserves, were going to have all their concerns addressed and fall in love with AIG's stock all over again because it now had *plenty* of reserves.

From Gen Re's position, the $500 million loan was designed to appear as if it was paying $500 million in insurance premiums to AIG to reinsure an equal amount of "risk." For this several month "deal," Gen Re would get $5.2 million from AIG.

It was all nonsense; there was no risk, so there was no risk transfer. If AIG got $500 million to reinsure that amount of risk, then it had no risk, according to both legal and accounting standards. Phony legal language, accounting, and documentation bounced across subsidiaries on two continents. One thing that was real, however, was the cover note to the underwriting file at Gen Re that mandated (per its CEO's orders) that only a few people were allowed to even see the file.

For his part, Hank Greenberg has argued loudly that he ordered a transaction happen—just not the one that *did*. Per his arguments, the October 31 phone call to Ron Ferguson was to order a legitimate deal involving the purchase of a loss portfolio. This is exactly what it sounds like: a portfolio of loss obligations that have already been incurred and are slated to be paid in the future. AIG was seeking to have Gen Re locate a $500 million portfolio of them that they would reinsure. In return for a premium of perhaps $475 million or so, AIG would pay the claims as they came due.[9] Of course, with their cash and earnings generating ability, they would take the premium amount and salt it away into reserves.

Gen Re, according to testimony, had a dozen people working full bore for 13 days on this deal for AIG. On the two week anniversary of Greenberg's phone call, a Gen Re employee named Chris Garand first raised the prospect of a no-risk deal as a possible solution to a very real problem Gen Re was having at the time—they couldn't find a portfolio that met AIGs needs. According to Greenberg's legal filings, none of his lawyers, accountants, and colleagues advised him that an attempt to purchase a loan-loss portfolio had evolved into a riskless transaction. Quite the opposite: he had ordered up a certain kind of deal, was told that it was being handled, and met all accounting and legal scrutiny.

There is another card Greenberg has played in his defense: no one has produced documents or testified that Greenberg (or Howie Smith) told or wrote an email to anyone that what they really wanted was a riskless transaction. The thrust of the future legal battle would be an attempt to stitch together the threads of the bad deal's genesis (Gen Re, two weeks after), its communication to AIG (about two weeks after that, to its head of reinsurance, Chris Milton) and, eventually, to Greenberg. The first two threads exist; the third, connecting Greenberg's approval or awareness of the dubious nature of the transaction, does not seem to in the thousands of pages of documents and transcripts the trial has generated.

If Greenberg's defense is true—that he had no idea any of this occurred—there is a likely explanation for how he could have missed it. AIG's culture, especially at the upper ranks, was remarkably loyal to him (arguably blindly so) and he generally reciprocated. If the head of his reinsurance unit said he understood what was required of a transaction and was going to take care of something, then Greenberg believed to his core that it would be taken care of. You did not get to be the head of a business unit at AIG without executing to Greenberg's standards and being fully congruent with how he conducted business. Ordering something and then being told of its satisfactory completion was not a desirable outcome, but rather, what was expected.

One element of Greenberg's defense—a minor one, to be sure— also rings true: his high level of activity and his management style. All people who discuss Greenberg and his tenure at AIG eventually mention the beehive of his office. People came and went, orders were delivered—often in under one minute—and more people flow in and more orders are laid out. Among them flitted Greenberg's two receptionists, delivering papers and messages, telling him who was waiting for him on the phone and why they couldn't hail who he was seeking to call, and the occasional waiter or two, with some herbal tea or water.

It was common for a division chief, earning well into seven figures, to be sitting in a chair next to the CFO as Greenberg sat behind his desk on the phone listening to someone from Tokyo while carrying on (possibly) related conversations with the division chief and CFO. Often, these conversations were truly material as to corporate strategy and direction. He would give a directive and expect that it would wind its way down the food chain to the person responsible for carrying it out, at which point the matter was closed. If there needed to be an update—often there didn't need to be since Greenberg is big on results, not process—it would be scheduled weeks later, at which point the whole episode would be repeated.

When Greenberg got it in his mind that he needed specific details or market intelligence, he would then call down many ranks and find the person responsible for what he was looking for. (In the Gen Re case, there was a very tightly closed information loop: Greenberg, Chris Milton, and a bare handful of others.)

None of this is unique in the life of the modern CEO, but there are likely few CEOs who embraced the instinctive, rapid-decision style of management more.[10] There is an excellent chance that Greenberg gave the Gen Re issues—which cost him his job, his honor, his status and, perhaps, over \$1 billion in personal wealth—all of five minutes of consideration. An anecdote from his time serving as the chairman of a Council of Foreign Relations panel analyzing terror financing in 2002, in the wake of the September 11 attacks illustrates this point.

In the course of interviewing dozens of regulators, financial authorities, and various national security officials and analyzing thousands of pages of documents, it became clear to the project codirectors, Lee Wolosky (prior to becoming Greenberg's lawyer) and Will Wechsler, that Saudi Arabian cash was playing a vital role in funding a host of terror-oriented entities, in the United States as well as the Middle East.[11] The point of the visit was twofold: to give a heads up to Greenberg in that the Saudis were putting a full-court press behind the scenes to minimize the report and to tell Greenberg that AIG stood an excellent chance of losing business—possibly a lot of it—in Saudi Arabia and other countries if the report was released as Wolosky and Wechsler had drafted it.

As Wechsler tried to lay out some of the report's revelations and their likely blowback scenarios, he noticed that Greenberg was looking off into the distance as his secretaries presented him with message after message and another group of executives was (loudly) being ushered in.

Greenberg shrugged and cut off Wechsler's reasoned analysis midsentence.

"Do it," he said with a nod. He sat down, picked up the phone, and waved the group of executives in. On the way out, and safely out of earshot, Wechsler told his friend and former colleague Wolosky, "I never even got to what he's going to lose. Possibly, it's a lot. The Saudis will make him pay." A decision about what was easily hundreds of millions of dollars' worth of annual revenue, which was irreversible and could potentially reverberate throughout an entire volatile region, was struck in three minutes without a public relations person, executive, or lawyer near the room. Another issue loomed that they hardly even touched on: Greenberg's relationship with the Bush administration was profoundly threatened with the report's release because of its critical tone toward the Saudis, a nation that President Bush maintained was disposed to U.S. interests. (The report drew a very different conclusion of the Saudi Arabian leadership.)[12]

Wechsler, recounting the tale, is not sure nearly a decade on if Greenberg even listened to his argument. For his part, the Saudis were furious with Greenberg and accused him of being part of a "Zionist conspiracy"; it is difficult to imagine that Saudi Arabia's many friends in the diplomatic corps and its alumni community did not make life difficult for Greenberg and AIG's interests in the following years.

Greenberg's management style inarguably served him well as AIG's head count grew, but it also was a recipe for missing signals and seemingly minor details that would later become major ones.

The deal highlights an epic failure of risk management and control in AIG. Someone should have raised concerns before the deals were signed. They either didn't see anything wrong (which is scarily inept) or never saw the deal at all (which is poor management). At a minimum, Greenberg's failure to put in place a level of oversight or control to prevent such a preposterous scheme from getting under way is damning.

■ ■ ■

Ernie Patrikis didn't waste time sitting around waiting for someone in the attorney general's office to tell him what was in the deal and why they did it. He launched his own inquiry that left him more stunned than the PNC deal had. There was, he would tell colleagues, simply no way they could possibly defend this transaction. No way.

In late February, the newest addition to AIG's media relations team, Chris Winans, a long-time insurance industry analyst, author, and former *Wall Street Journal* editor and reporter, was in Greenberg's office discussing how to treat the Gen Re issue in the media, where, quite predictably, they were being pilloried.

Winans, on the job for perhaps 10 days, had worked mightily to staunch the rivers of critical ink sluicing toward 70 Pine Street daily. He had had Theo Francis and Leslie Schism of the *Journal*, the pair of veteran reporters then covering AIG, in for a background talk to hear from Hank's mouth how they were handling things, how good things really were, how this was all such terribly small beer.

It didn't work. The Gen Re story, as the saying went, had "legs," which pissed off Hank off to no end.

"You clear time out of my schedule to talk to these stupid reporters and they print this crap?"

Winans didn't have time to go over the fact that just because the reporters talked to you didn't mean they were going to make you happy. The much more important issue at hand was that these stories all contained aspects of the Gen Re deal that were remarkably one-sided. There *were* facts in those stories, but they were skewed so much against AIG that they could have only come from one place: Spitzer's office. The subpoenas were all of two weeks old to Greenberg and AIG, and he was leaking production from Gen Re's federal case from Virginia. Spitzer hadn't even filed a complaint yet.

Winans could not comprehend a defense that they could possibly muster. A background meeting between Hank and a pair of reporters at AIG in those times involved corporate legal, public relations, and countless others. He could talk to reporters on deep background about the case, maybe feed them a tidbit of what he was able to pick up in meetings with the general counsel's office—but leak evidence that they were producing in a vital court case? He would be summarily fired for even privately suggesting such a thing if Patrikis caught wind of it.

Spitzer was going to win, Winans thought, because he was willing to do what no one else in his position would even consider. What else was he doing? What wouldn't he do? Was there anything? He didn't think so.

Hank never stopped telling anyone who would listen that Spitzer was doing this for some always unnamed "political motives," but now Winans wasn't so sure. Maybe it had zero to do with politics. This was about power and about destruction. If you were willing to break that many rules to get unfavorable newspaper stories about your enemies printed, your goal wasn't really to obtain a favorable judgment for the people of the state of New York, it was to demonstrate to others that you had the power and nerve to do this. If you had to lay waste to livelihoods or even a company, then so be it.

Now reporters at the *New York Times*, *Wall Street Journal*, *New York Post*, and *Bloomberg News* had decided they had ignored AIG for too long. Its complexity, the earnings, and fear of Hank all conspired for AIG to be granted a multiyear pass that no one else had. It was open season, however, and the media was both pissed and embarrassed. What Spitzer couldn't do to them, the media would.

■ ■ ■

Five years later, more than a few AIG board members profess to having known all along that Spitzer's office would eventually turn up on AIG's doorstep. The combination of its massive financial operations, increasingly complex accounting for transactions that were difficult for all but a select few to understand, its universal exposure to every stripe of insurance product—these were siren songs to an aggressive regulator. There would be, as one long-serving board member put it, no "promising away" Eliot Spitzer; no $15 million fine and the promise to create oversight boards. AIG was going to be a very different company in short order, if the recent past was any guide.

The reaction of the AIG board was swift. They didn't wait around for Hank and his staff to engage with the attorney general in the standard legal Kabuki of a formal response and production. Prodded by then Greenberg loyalists Frank Zarb and Bernie Aidenoff, they started leaning heavily on Dick Beattie of Simpson Thatcher, one of the long-standing wise men of the New York corporate defense bar whom they had hired a few months after the PNC settlement, to advise them.

Beattie's role was evolving from the solely legal to the strategic. For the legal mechanics, the board hired Paul, Weiss, Rifkind, Garrison & Wharton—Spitzer's old firm—but for what they should do, how they should handle both the fine and broader points for the storm brewing, they wanted Beattie and his colleague Jamie Gambel to give them advice about changing AIG.

From a legal standpoint, key allies of his on the board were no longer certain that they had the same legal interests that Greenberg did. Actually, if they were looking for strategic input, the shift was not merely legal. They wanted to go in a different direction, and they wanted to do it in a way that would make a statement.

A fighter to his core, Greenberg would not take this lightly. But for the time being, he would have to run AIG while it was under legal assault from a man who had done more to change the corporate landscape in New York—and America—than anyone over the past 100 years.

Proof, if any was needed, to Greenberg's mind of what a good company can do that isn't under corporate assault was seen in the annual earnings of more than $11 billion that were released on February 9, 2005. During the conference call, in response to a question from an analyst about the risks from the regulatory environment, he replied, "When you begin to look at foot faults and make them into a murder charge, then you have gone too far." Greenberg also took the time to announce that its regulatory problems would soon be behind it.

Spitzer, speaking at a Goldman Sachs dinner that night, interrupted his prepared remarks to fire back at Greenberg, "Hank Greenberg should be very, very careful talking about foot faults. Too many foot faults and you lose the match. But more importantly, these are not just foot faults."

The following Monday, the investing public voted with their wallets and sent AIG's stock down more than $2 to $71. Subpoenas were the smoke, and where there was smoke, there was fire. Even if these investors weren't taking into account the preliminary nature of the investigation, trouble was brewing, that much was clear. As of mid-February 2005, who had fought Spitzer and won? What firm the size of AIG had avoided paying large fines and the attendant huge declines in market cap?

From his plane, en route to Europe, Greenberg ordered an AIG trader named Keith Duffy to buy 250,000 shares near the market's close of 4 PM. When Duffy balked out of a fear of violating provisions governing corporate stock buy-backs, Greenberg overruled him and told him to place the order. The NYSE specialist assigned to AIG's stock, himself a frequent target of Greenberg's wrath, refused to handle the order.

It would later emerge that Greenberg had ordered stock purchases on February 3 and then again on the 22nd to support the price of the stock. Even though Greenberg was renowned for going way down the organization chart for the bottom line answer to a marketplace question, calling a trader to strategize over pushing the stock price up was unusual even for him and a difficult issue to rationalize for those who had to defend him. Coming as it did a few short years after the dot-com bubble, it was the sort of thing that in the public's eye came exceptionally close to manipulation, even though there was no suggestion that the purchases on the 3rd or the 22nd were made at the end of the day.[13]

When the trades became public the following month, they merely reinforced a view that Greenberg—despite his continuing excellence in managing an enterprise that rivaled few others globally in its complexity—was fundamentally stuck in 1975 from a governance perspective.

By the middle of March, Greenberg's word was no longer enough. The board rapidly transitioned from reviewing Gen Re, to another series of offshore reinsurance deals Spitzer had expressed concern about to ordering a review of the way in which AIG conducted business. Several board members argued that a review was an important step in getting a handle on what the attorney general was concerned about; others thought it was a necessary precursor to mounting a defense for the inevitable suit.

As Paul Weiss's lawyers consulted with hundreds of employees, the Greenberg divorce became all but final as he is excluded from executive and board discussions of the report. On March 11, prior to a series of board meetings, Greenberg and his legal team—Lee Wolosky and David Boies of Boies, Schiller, Flexner—held a meeting with general counsel Ernie Patrikis to discuss the status of legal issues, where Patrikis told them that the board and Hank Greenberg now have separate legal interests.

Chief executives that have different legal status from their boards are not usually long for the corner office. All that remained was the formal request for his resignation. Boies Schiller's lawyers began drawing up a retirement package for Greenberg: $1.2 million a year in pay for consulting, the use of corporate jets, office space, his two secretaries, and other corporate benefits such as medical and life insurance.

As the series of board meetings got under way, Wolosky was stuck in the office of a traveling AIG executive, watching lawyers from Paul Weiss and Simpson Thatcher scurry to and fro. Told that he would be summoned when Greenberg was needed, he wound up waiting all day and left at 6 PM, no longer needed, like his client.

Two days later, in an all-day conference at Beattie's office at Simpson Thatcher office on Lexington Avenue, the outside directors—the majority of the board, save for the then four AIG executives on it—the options were hashed out. It was easy: there were none. Greenberg had to step down. As long as he was running the company, no matter what surfaced, he would fight. Greenberg was willing to fight the SEC, and he was, most of all, begging to fight back against Spitzer. With Hank, they had a multiyear war of annihilation against an obsessed attorney general, market cap declines and a media circus; with Hank on the sidelines, they could settle and go back to earning money.

Greenberg, who was on the phone from his 100-foot boat at the Ocean Reef Club in the Florida Keys, was furious at the board for having caved to a McCarthyite political witch hunt, for submitting to the judgment of lawyers over tested businessmen, and most of all for such a brutal display of disloyalty.

Greenberg had been exceedingly generous to them all. Frank Zarb? AIG gave the big money for Hofstra University's Zarb school of Business? Bernie Aidenoff? A 45-year friend who had a lovely six-figure consulting income from AIG for sitting on FP's board and some special projects. Holbrooke? He'd helped that guy more than he could count in ways big and small and had been weighing an investment in his private-equity shop. The list went on and on. The phone calls that opened doors, the donations, the recommendations, the prestige of AIG's name and power and when it mattered—how many of them had traded on their AIG board memberships to get jobs consulting or other board jobs—and when he needed them, they made sure to throw him overboard. To Greenberg, people who couldn't spell the word *insurance* were now making decisions for the most powerful financial company on earth.[14]

On March 14, 2005, Greenberg resigned agreeing to a role as a nonexecutive chairman with Martin Sullivan, a long-standing Greenberg ally, to take over as chief executive. There was a sizable minority who had pulled for Donald Kanak, the head of Asian operations, but the combination of Kanak's wife's long-standing reluctance to relocate to New York and Sullivan's personal popularity within the company's management ranks and the board conspired against him. Howie Smith, the CFO, was fired when he refused to cooperate with the investigation.[15]

For a nightmare scenario it was a passable resolution, according to Greenberg. He would help oversee a transition of Sullivan, who had, all could agree, done a fine job running American International Underwriters, AIG's property and casualty arm. The plan was to watch his every move for three years and get him up to speed on the financial side where Ed Matthews could be a big help.[16]

For the board it reaffirmed what had become its unofficial policy: Despite deep professional and personal bonds to Greenberg, the Brightpoint and PNC problems precluded them from putting up a fight in his defense.

In the third week of March came one of the most ridiculous aspects of the affair when lawyers from Paul Weiss accused lawyers from Boies Schiller, who were securing documents from the Bermuda offices of Starr International—Greenberg wasn't giving up his role as chairman of the company—of stealing and destroying documents that belonged to AIG. Actually, they did more than this: they called Eliot Spitzer who was on a ski trip in Vail and described in detail how Greenberg's lawyers were destroying evidence. There is no more clear admission of guilt than destroyed evidence, and paired with the linkage to Greenberg and Smith on the Gen Re deal and the enormous power wielded over AIG's destiny and health with the two related entities, C. V. Starr and Starr International, Spitzer had what he needed.

The message Spitzer delivered the board, after some back and forth, was unmistakable: either Greenberg was completely gone by Monday with no affiliation with the company, or he indicted AIG. If they had any doubt, they were welcome to try their luck. To emphasize his point, he mentioned that with Greenberg still there, "You have serious criminal exposure."

Interviews with AIG corporate leadership and board members at the time indicate some confusion over the word *you*. The AIG side took it to mean the company's board was in trouble while Spitzer and his loyalists say it meant liability to the company. Regardless, Greenberg was gone, forbidden from coming near AIG's office and security guards were posted all around AIG's offices in Bermuda to guard remaining files.

It is difficult to know where to begin, but this much is clear: Spitzer was given bad information from the start. C. V. Starr had long been an important broker of specialty insurance lines that did mutually profitable business with AIG and if it was an unusual structure—and it was certainly the only structure of its kind in the financial and insurance realm—it was an unusual structure that had sat in place for over 30 years, fully disclosed and accounted for without setting off any fainting spells among regulators.

C. V. Starr shared the same offices with AIG in Bermuda but was an entirely separate legal and commercial entity of which Greenberg was chairman. Given the virtually certain legal action to come, and the wide-ranging subpoenas from the attorney general, it made sense for his lawyers to secure documents dealing with specialty insurance transactions done offshore. Paul Weiss's lawyers should have known that; AIG's staff should have made that clear. Regardless, an extensive SEC investigation launched into what Spitzer called "The Document Caper," focusing on Boise Schiller's lawyers, showed no wrongdoing on their part.[17]

More broadly, Spitzer threatened to indict AIG over a series of transactions that would later be taken to amount to some fraction of 1 percent of its book value. Assuming complete guilt and ill intent, the dismissal and indictments of Smith and Greenberg would have been warranted; the forced and immediate bankruptcy of AIG with the attendant collapse of its then $900 billion balance sheet would have been a different affair.

AIG's collapse in 2008 took the wealth and credibility of the U.S. government to the very limit of its operating ability, in order to stave off what was uniformly assumed to be a looming global economic calamity. An attorney general fed incomplete information from his former firm was indicating that he was happy to threaten the same to win a dispute over governance and offshore reinsurance accounting issues centering around two executives who had already vacated their jobs. It takes little ingenuity to imagine what a calamity the unprompted and forced bankruptcy of AIG would have been. An unhedged capital marketplace, with massive exposure to a triple-A-rated company, millions of policyholders in 130 countries and over 90,000 people would have been the thin end of the attorney general's wedge.

Did the attorney general fully understand the utter mayhem that would be unleashed if AIG suddenly collapsed? It's not certain and, at any rate, it probably misses the point. States attorneys general have many tools at their disposal to carry out what they define as the people's business; forcing the bankruptcy of massive corporations is rarely one of them.

■ ■ ■

Ed Matthews, a colleague of Martin Sullivan's for more than 30 years, pushed through a meeting with Martin at the end of March 2005. Sullivan's life was a whirlwind of meetings and phone calls to key customers and clients, and he wanted to reschedule but Matthews insisted. He felt strongly that Sullivan needed to know the hard truth about the finance unit at AIG—the weak players, the strong managers, and the real risks he wasn't going to see or hear about from his staff.

"Look, Martin, you're taking this over now and you'll need to know a few things. . . ." Thus, kicked off what Matthews described as the longest time he had ever talked without pausing. At the end of two hours, he had given Sullivan the lay of the land like no one else could or would, the things he had learned the hard way, with no details or faults spared; there were risks in abundance throughout AIG and according to Matthews he was given every last one of them.

Be tough on Cassano and FP. He'll bitch plenty but in the end will respect you for it. Look out for Win Neuger at AIG Global Investments and his burgeoning hedge fund empire. Go to cash if you think its best and worry about the loss of profits later. Protect capital at all costs. Listen to yourself, not Wall Street.

"You have any questions?" Matthews asked, reasoning that there had to be a few, as he wasn't sure if had said something and Sullivan had missed it.

"No, Ed. That about does it. You've been a huge help, really. Thanks."

With that, he shook his hand and never talked to Ed Matthews again.

On his way out of Sullivan's office, Ed Matthews looked down and saw the legal pad Sullivan had made a show of taking out for note-taking purposes. It was completely blank.

■ ■ ■

On the night of March 13, Chris Winans, Martin Sullivan, Ernie Patrikis, and others were holed up in a spare conference room going over issues that might surface in the analyst conference call the following morning, where Sullivan would formally become the face of AIG to Wall Street.

Hank Greenberg, strolling by the office, walks in and interrupts the planning. Staring at Patrikis, he points at him and snarls, "It's your fault, Ernie. All yours, every last bit of it. You brought in the outside lawyers, you allowed them to run amok. This company is run by lawyers now, Ernie, and it's your fucking fault!" With that, he turned around and stormed out. The group, who were staring at their feet, shuffled in their seats awkwardly before resuming about one minute later.

Conference calls with analysts were scripted affairs where for 45 minutes Martin Sullivan, or almost any other senior executive, often sounded like they had been born and bred for the CEO post. There was an importance to this since analysts and investors placed a great premium on the tone and depth with which questions were answered.[18] A bad conference call, where answers were fumbled or executives stumped, could prove devastating to a company's share price in the short term and its perception in the long term.

Sullivan, who had been an inside operator for every day of his 35 years at AIG, was now the face of a wounded franchise. So in order to refine his communication skills in advance of the annual meeting, Sullivan began a crash course in public speaking with Dick Beattie and the AIG board's outside public relations counsel, George Sard from Sard Verbinnen & Co. at Beattie's office.

Sullivan was picking up on the facts well enough and was adept at discussing the legal maelstrom they found themselves in but in referring to Greenberg, he would, despite his adviser's gentle chiding, always call him Mr. Greenberg. Finally, Sard had heard enough.

"Martin," he said in a cool, flat voice. "You are the duly elected chief executive of one of the world's largest and most important corporations. You do not call your colleagues 'Mr.' in a formal setting. It is beneath you and makes you seem weak. The employees and shareholders are relying on you to sound in control and authoritative."

Sullivan agreed, and they proceeded to walk through additional staged questions and answers on a slew of subjects. Sure enough, Sullivan tripped up again and referred to "Mr. Greenberg."

"Jesus Christ, Martin," said Beattie, throwing his arms up. "Really, what's wrong with you? Don't you get it?"

In a soft voice, Sullivan looked both Sard and Beattie in the eye and told them, "I have always called him 'Mr. Greenberg.' It's hard for me not to."

Beattie, a tactician first and foremost, conceded defeat and went on to other concerns.

Sard, however, was struck by both the issue and Sullivan's acknowledgment. He had worked with CEOs of large and small companies for more than 25 years and they all had one thing in common: they wanted to put their own mark on a company. Yet here was a situation where the company's guiding light was leaving and the next CEO had to urgently signal a break from the past, and they still couldn't get him to call his former boss by his first name.

It wasn't habit that made Sullivan do this, Sard thought, it was belief.

If that was the case, then there really wasn't much chance that he would do much differently elsewhere either. And if that was true, Sard would recall later to his colleagues, Sullivan had better be good. Really, really good.

■ ■ ■

If the board had had enough, the ratings agencies were long since past that point.

On March 31, Standard & Poor's cut the AAA rating to AA+. On its "watch list" since March 15, their thinking was fairly straightforward: the cascade of flawed deals that ran in a line from Brightpoint to Gen Re—and, it would emerge, names of other deals like CAPCO, Union Excess, and Nan Shan—was enough to cast doubts about their long-standing admiration of AIG profits. Ratings analysts read newspapers, too, and if every year brought another few deals that were dubious, then pretty soon their AIG cash-flow models and net income projections were likely overstating things as well. If you back out enough cash and profits, pretty soon the (growing) liabilities and risks to the business seem a little large for a triple-A-rated company.

They never would write anything so blunt, of course, with the official release noting dryly that "Our opinion of AIG had changed in large part due to the company's involvement in a number of questionable financial transactions, and reflected our revised assessment of AIG's management, internal controls, corporate governance and culture."

The timing could not have been worse for AIG.

In reality, their business was healthy enough and the profits were still eye-opening and would grow. But with the Paul Weiss internal review going full-bore and a new CEO and chief financial officer (CFO) installed, they were in a Catch-22. They could not truthfully say that all the weak spots had been identified and bad practices eliminated; they couldn't be sure when the review would even be done. Without a handle on what they had to charge off (and almost certainly pay fines for), their financial position was what anyone said it was. Sullivan and Steve Bensinger, the former treasurer and the new CFO, could not defend the credit rating until they could sign off on and certify the new financials. They wouldn't be in a position to legally do that until every last problem was identified and remedies put into place, including a charge against earnings if necessary. Defending their triple-A rating, simply because that was what Hank would have done, was no longer an option. In passing up a fight with S&P, AIG was sending a message that they were trying to follow the letter of the law and set a new tone.[19]

Several AIG senior managers from that period argue that even if Bensinger and Sullivan could have been able to certify the company's financials, the growing number of purportedly dubious deals—or what they had been told were dubious at the time—prevented an honest defense of the triple-A.

Interviews point to a sense among the middle- and upper-management ranks that a few quarters of earnings after the internal review was done would be enough to show the ratings agencies what they needed to see and that the triple-A would be restored. Indeed, when it didn't happen, chatter around the water cooler and hallways often turned to how an ethically revitalized AIG posted tens of billions of dollars of operating income in 2006 and somehow wasn't rewarded with an upgrade.

Senior management saw it differently. Quietly, very quietly, they began to plan for life without a triple-A. In addition to booking outsized profits and remaking the company's practices—something that they would have done either way—getting the triple-A back would require a whole lot of medicine that few were in the mood for. There would be a redirection of free cash flow, for instance, toward paying down debt and balance sheet constriction, cost cutting, capping potential dividend growth and limited (if any) buybacks. After the gut-wrenching months of late 2004 and 2005, when their industry and company were under assault, this would be taking away the punchbowl in a big fashion.

Bensinger and a handful of other colleagues, starting in early 2006, began to scrutinize AIG for sources of "excess capital" and for ways to "leverage the balance sheet" in the hunt for easy carry-trade profits in what seemed like an attractive interest rate environment.

Hank Greenberg might eternally be "Mr. Greenberg" to Martin Sullivan and his colleagues atop AIG, but Mr. Greenberg's precious and hard-won triple-A rating would forever be relegated to a past full of things that no longer worked in modern times.

■ ■ ■

At FP, the world that Howard Sosin built was now gone.

The downgrade brought immediate repercussions in the form of $1.2 billion in collateral calls, there was an air of frustrated resignation to the loss of the triple-A. More than anyone else at AIG, their operating ability had just been changed.

When his colleagues gamely protested to him that there *had* to be something he could do, Joe Cassano was circumspect, if typically blunt.

"What the fuck can I do? I didn't do any of these deals—that was Hank and Howie. We're boxed in here. We can still do OK and that's what matters."

And "OK" they were, for the time being.

Chapter 7

The Kids Are Alright

W hen the downgrade came, it was decision time for one man.

In his offices on Manhattan's West 54th Street, a professional Doubting Thomas named Jim Chanos had spent the previous two years doing what he described as "brutal" work into the reality of AIG's financial state of affairs. After hundreds of man-hours doing what could fairly be described as a forensic reconstruction of one of the world's largest companies, he was even more confused than when he started.

For many men, the prospect of working that much on something for that long and having little certainty of an answer would be demoralizing. For Jim Chanos, this was good news: he was a short-seller who made money borrowing stock and selling it on the open market on the view that it would decline in value. Thus, his profit was the difference between where he sold the shares and where he eventually bought them back and delivered them back to the lender.[1]

Looking for what couldn't be readily explained had made Jim Chanos a very rich man, but the more he and his staff looked at AIG, the more he couldn't figure how they did it, quarter after quarter, year after year.

■ ■ ■

Chanos had sprung into the popular imagination when Bethany McLean, a *Fortune* magazine reporter with a Wall Street background and a love of writing about corporate wrongdoing, wrote an article in March 2001 about a company whose earnings were difficult to trace. Everybody and their grandmother seemingly owned shares, and the media lionized its executives, but she couldn't get a handle on where this magic came from.

The company was Enron.

There wasn't much of an effect when her article came out in the spring of 2001.[2] Around Labor Day, though, after CEO Jeff Skilling left and the *Wall Street Journal* started writing a series of articles looking at a group of off-balance-sheet transactions involving hundreds of millions of dollars of debt it had not disclosed, the article looked mighty prescient indeed. Chanos, it would be revealed, played a central role as McLean's source in the *Fortune* story. He was aided by a pair of *Journal* reporters, John Emshwiller and Rebecca Smith, whose reporting actually led to the ratings downgrades that forced Enron into bankruptcy.

Enron was Chanos's most public triumph, but not his first. He had found a measure of fame (or notoriety, as his legion of detractors would have it) as a 24-year-old junior analyst in 1982 covering the insurance sector for Gilford Securities, a small brokerage. Well-regarded insurer Baldwin United had evolved from a sleepy piano company to a financial conglomerate after merging with a mutual fund and using massive amounts of borrowing to get into, among other things, mortgage insurance. Chanos, based on state insurance filings that said it was dipping into reserves to get cash, issued a "Sell" rating. No one listened, and the stock doubled. So Chanos doubled down, fleshing out his accounting and cash-flow arguments in more detail and advising clients to sell the stock short. His trading desk lost clients, others scoffed, Baldwin United threatened to sue, and a rival analyst publicly sneered.

Then, on Christmas Eve in 1982, insurance regulators seized the company because it was, per Chanos's arguments, dipping into policyholder reserves for desperately needed cash.

The life of a Wall Street skeptic was not unbridled blessing. A few years later, given a chance to manage money at Deutsche Bank Asset Management, Chanos was unceremoniously dumped from his job when a *Wall Street Journal* article portrayed him and other short-sellers as spreading rumors and using sneaky tactics to get information on companies.[3] So the Wisconsin native launched his own fund, named Kynikos, Greek for *cynic*.

Unlike other short-sellers, he didn't get too wrapped up in executives, their ability to operate, industries, product success or failure, or even a company's competitive position. He reasoned that good companies can have bad executives and vice versa, and betting on a drop in a stock's price because you think you know more about a product or market cycle in industry wasn't how he wanted to spend his days. Instead, he and his analysts tracked cash flows and return on capital. Chanos wanted to bet against companies whose finances were dependent on manias or fads. Betting against Drexel's clients, for example, in the late 1980s—especially the ones involved in real estate—was obvious. The companies had no cash flow other than what Drexel's junk-bond desk could raise for them. When Drexel went, most of these companies couldn't get additional financing and withered away.

Chanos's reasoning behind it was simple. If a company could not consistently earn a rate of return above its cost to borrow money—if it earned 4 percent on the capital it borrowed but paid out 6 percent to its lenders—that company would eventually have an existential crisis. Executives and their plans came and went, but companies that couldn't generate cash without borrowing it all faded away sooner or later. Companies that were dependent on demonstrably short-term trends like certain kinds of federal contracts or fads for their cash flow were also welcome opportunities.

Using return on capital as a benchmark also allowed Kynikos analysts to reduce complex and opaque companies down to a few simple questions: Is this company able to stand alone without aid from the markets? Or is it in a cash flow spiral and cannot exist apart from capital raising or loans?

If the answer to the former was "yes," then there was an excellent place to begin researching Kynikos's next short.

■ ■ ■

Chanos had had his eye on AIG for some time. When the insurer was downgraded in March, he ordered a full review of its financials from his staff. If Chanos had some differences in operating style from other short-sellers, temperamentally he was no different from them: an avowed skeptic and financial freethinker, he believed very little in the way of official explanation. At bottom, he did not believe for a second that rating agency concern over the Brightpoint and PNC transactions were the sole reasons for AIG's downgrade.

He began to push his staff harder. He sent spreadsheets back for more work and asked that they pull more files from state insurance commission offices on its operating subsidiaries. On a balance sheet that pushed $1 trillion, a mere $136 million in fines for two bad deals should not shake a ratings agency's faith; he became convinced they were seeing something.[4] That Kynikos's analysts could not move back up the numbers line and reconstruct the earnings with any precision was frustrating, but telling.

AIG was all of Jim Chanos's concerns in the world circa 2005 wrapped up in one. A company earning 15 percent return on equity when its competitors were happy for 5 percent or 6 percent in a market that was both mature and competitive. Huge exposure to real estate. Large and growing private equity and hedge fund units. A black box unit of their very own at FP. Lots and lots of room for accounting judgment calls between U.S. and foreign units and, crucially, a make-your-numbers culture.

Two threads of Chanos's bear fleshing out here. The first is that Chanos had long been skeptical of the explosive growth of hedge and private-equity funds, both in absolute terms and the size of the assets they control. This is to say that he was skeptical of the fact that by 2003 institutional sources of capital—union pension funds, wealthy family trusts, endowments, and the corporate working capital of places like AIG—were happily funneling billions of dollars to anything calling itself a hedge fund. Though he could hardly decry the concept of hedge funds, Chanos was very worried about the fact that he was seeing an exponentially growing amount of capital allocated to highly levered strategies in the bond market. Borrowing 6, 8, and 10 times their equity capital, these new funds would buy various asset- and mortgage-backed-type securities. As long as the market went up, they made outsized returns. The minute it went down, they would be wiped out. A hardened cynic, Chanos cared less about the inevitable and violent deaths of these funds than about the whiplash effect, as the institutions that staked them sought to recoup their losses by redeeming investments in other, better-managed hedge funds, setting off a circular series of redemptions—and selling—as the hedge funds that *didn't* do stupid things with their money (like his, he supposed) were forced to raise cash to return capital.

Chanos also had developed some defined views of the boom in private-equity (PE) transactions that grew larger and splashier every day. On good days he was amused at their declarations that they added value to corporations. He would often wonder aloud if investment bankers, which was what all PE managers started out as, had ever added managerial or operational value to anything. It was a very good question: many (if not all) companies taken private were saddled with massive debt loads and had their remaining cash flows often redirected to the PE fund coffers as "dividends." On bad days he saw it as a combination of a mania and a plain scam.

AIG was certainly heavily levered to the explosion in hedge and PE funds and the operating income was becoming material to the corporate bottom line. In 2003 it was $227 million; by 2004 it was $515 million. There was virtually no disclosure as to where these funds were invested but a few quick phone calls revealed that they had exposure to all the name-brand, "star" alternative asset managers. At its 25 percent to 50 percent growth rate, it was difficult to imagine it leaving anything other than an ugly crater when it burst. This unit wasn't the only one due for a pasting when the cycle shifted: quarterly Securities and Exchange Commission (SEC) and state insurance filings showed that with north of $400 billion in stocks and bonds, AIG's balance sheet and income statements were going to look very different after a correction.

Where Chanos and his team began to feel like they were making some headway was when they discovered page 54 of the first quarter's

10-Q filing detailing the almost $1.2 billion in collateral postings required with the ratings downgrade to AA+. None of the dozens of analysts who had written about this ever mentioned the collateral calls, nor had management; the filing just mentioned the number. It was a big question mark, and no one knew anything about it.

Chanos and a few analysts pounded on the fund's sources in the big investment banks, analyzed rival insurance companies, and looked for other examples of collateral calls in AIG filings—yet kept coming up empty. Their market sources told them that as far as they could see, none of AIG's trading desks were making some epic one-way trade that had gone against them. In the absence of information, common sense would have to do.

Collateral calls, as every short-seller knew all too well, only came into play when a trade went against you. But they knew AIG's trading desks weren't making a big bet. If it wasn't a trade, then it had to be some sort of insurance or private counterparty credit agreement that wasn't easily observed. AIG, in other words, was renting out its balance sheet. This changed everything. The market was whiter than white hot, every fool with a few million dollars in Manhattan was making money in the market and AIG was still having to post more than a billion dollars in collateral for a one-notch downgrade? As well as they knew collateral calls, Kynikos knew ratings downgrades. They rarely stopped at just one.

For men who did nothing but look for failure and fraud to earn a living, the collateral call issue also opened up a philosophical door they hadn't even pondered. They expected that AIG's recent regulatory track record might bring to light more ugly deals, or alternately, when AIG was forced to play by the letter of the law, margins would get squeezed. They also thought that with enough work, they would find some crummy insurance scam at a small subsidiary that could pose a looming threat. They had not remotely conceived of AIG's being happy to become a way station for all comers to express some sort of off-balance-sheet bet on God only knew what.

If that was considered a good use of capital to AIG management, and if that was what was passing through their risk-management controls—and Kynikos's analysts could imagine no other reason for the collateral calls after the March downgrade—then AIG had better be pricing the cost of renting out its balance sheet to cover risks from additional downgrades when this bull market finally ended. Chanos doubted they were.[5]

Regardless, Chanos had seen enough. In the spring of 2005, his fund's trading desk began selling short what would amount to about 750,000 shares of AIG. He had no idea what AIG was really up to, but he knew there was a secret in there and that it couldn't be good.

He hadn't meant to do it, but in becoming one of the few short-sellers to bet against AIG in this time frame, Chanos had filled in an important missing link in his housing thesis short. AIG was clearly using its balance sheet and credit rating to support some sort of volatile capital markets boondoggle. He knew other companies like mortgage origi-nators were doing stupid things, but he hadn't seen proof of the "smart money" set doing something so fundamentally dangerous. It fit in nicely with the short-seller's holy grail of dangerous and unsustainable behav-ior that Kynikos's analysts had uncovered in the credit and housing markets. Over the previous two years, they had found:

- A subsidiary of the venerable Lehman Brothers happily providing loans to all comers that required no documents so the firm could make them into bonds.
- Countrywide Financial Corporation had telephone scripts for its army of loan personnel that permitted them to loan up to $500,000 that day to people whose credit worthiness was rated C− by their own system (its second-worst score) and extending loans to appli-cants who were delinquent on other home loans within the past year.
- The investment banks provided the data that the ratings agencies used to rate the pools of mortgage-backed securities and other securitized products triple-A. There was no credit work involved— at any level—and ratings could be delivered within the hour. They were also the ratings agency's biggest customers, paying them hundreds of millions of dollars annually.
- Businesses like Ambac and MBIA had "evolved" past their longtime businesses of insuring municipal bonds and thrown themselves headlong into the "wrapping" of a fair amount of the collateralized debt obligation (CDO) product, then exploding into the marketplace

with a triple-A rating. They were using their balance sheet—at that time, both sported triple-A ratings—to guarantee that this river of new paper would remain triple-A, no matter what happened to its underlying collateral and in the face of any downgrades. They were doing this for about 10 basis points per $1 million of CDOs insured, or $100,000.

The American financial firmament, Chanos would tell colleagues and investors, appeared to have lost its collective mind.

■ ■ ■

Had they been aware of Chanos's furious efforts to understand their business, it is doubtful that AIG's new management would have much cared. Greenberg had made quick work of short-sellers in the past; with his earnings growth and with their legal headaches receding, their own numbers were looking none too shabby. But the earnings, however fantastic the numbers were, miss the point of the AIG management mind-set.

Looking at the 2005 10-K, filed nearly a year to the day after Sullivan assumed control of AIG, AIG's management and lawyers structured their world much the same as if it were 1970 all over again, and AIG was emerging from the combination of Mr. Starr's hodge-podge of businesses. The $24.9 billion in real estate loans were "heavily collateralized," and the $20.4 billion in real estate–related receivables were "well diversified." Above all, "AA+-rated" meant competence and prudence. They were the risk management keywords for a world based on trust and faith—in the ratings agencies, in securitization and the liquidity of a global marketplace with thoroughly diversified risks, in Fannie Mae and Freddie Mac as trusted stewards of an orderly mortgage market, and the Federal Reserve in maintaining a low-interest-rate policy for so long (and then again when it began the protracted series of rate increases.) This wasn't the childlike trust based on simplistic notion of a shared vision of right and wrong, but the trust in a market of rational actors with interconnected self-interests. No one would do the things that might force them to veer off course because there was simply too much money to be made.

The world Jim Chanos had uncovered didn't exist, because no one at AIG had ever conceived of its even applying to them. Greenberg's ruthless management of risk and his quest for diversification and his acquisitions hadn't made them lazy; people still worked insane hours and earned more in a career in AIG than anywhere else in the insurance industry. It did, however, make them feel impervious.

■■■

As 2005 progressed, Hank Greenberg plotted his next moves from the office of Boies Schiller on Lexington Avenue. It had been the most miserable months of his life; fighting in the frozen Korean waste or against the Germans wasn't half as bad. It was open season on him in the press where he had become both a corporate villain and laughingstock. After 45-plus years of building AIG his career was being reduced every day into some scandal narrative. The most galling was that every time he read his name in print, it was prefaced by some variation of the phrase "disgraced former CEO of AIG."

For David Boies, Lee Wolosky, and the growing "Team Green-berg," reporter hyperbole was the least of their troubles. Generations of legal precedent were going out the door on a daily basis, but no one cared enough to write about that; in contrast, it seemed to make the media happy. On April 10, Eliot Spitzer, in an interview with ABC's George Stephanopoulos, felt secure enough to engage in a freeform riff with the TV newsman: "The evidence is overwhelming that these were transactions created for the purpose of deceiving the market. We call that fraud. It is deceptive. It is wrong. It is illegal. . . . We have powerful evidence . . . it could be criminal."[6]

There is, of course, a long-standing and notable tradition of lawyer bluffing, posturing, and gamesmanship—in a courtroom, after a suit has been filed or an indictment handed down. In Boies's Armonk home, in Wolosky's house in Scarsdale, and Greenberg's apartment in Manhattan, there was utter disbelief. The most powerful attorney general in America was simply cutting out the annoying and tedious business of mustering evidence and filing suit, and pronounced Greenberg guilty of something that was in all likelihood criminal.

Nick Gravante, a Boies partner and a 20-year veteran of white-collar criminal trials, summed up the Greenberg camp's side when he said, "No one had ever seen anything like it. Truly surreal. No one called [Spitzer] on it. There were so many legal, ethical, and professional problems with what he did there that you can't easily start in any one place."

Soon, Gravante and his colleagues would have much richer examples of Spitzer's legal philosophy to ponder.

Greenberg, after he had blown his stack and vented at Wolosky and Boies, got down to the business of trying to do—*something*. His wife, Corrine, had tried to reimpose some aspects of AIG life upon him, and by default the Boies lawyers, such as his rigid diet of fish, fruit, and vegetables. It was appreciated by Hank (much less so by the Boies staff), but it was cosmetic. His entire life was gone.

In return for building one of the greatest wealth creation machines the world had seen, he was, as he saw it, chased from the building like a young clerk caught running a bookkeeping scam. He was forbidden to take personal possessions like wartime letters from his mothers and clothing; Starr International Company was forbidden to get valuable art it owned. C. V. Starr & Co. was having its employees and customers poached.

It would get worse. On May 9, according to documents produced later at trial, AIG would give Spitzer's staffers access to the internal review the Paul Weiss law firm had conducted. It would take more than six months of nonstop, very expensive litigation for a judge to finally order a copy produced to Greenberg.

On the 25th of May, while at a Starr International Co. board meeting in Dublin, Spitzer informed David Zornow, a personal friend of his at the big New York law firm Skadden, Arps, Meagher & Flom that he was going to have Greenberg arrested when he returned to the United States. As it so happened, Skadden was where Ken Bialkin, one of Greenberg's criminal defense attorneys, worked and Zornow, partner-to-partner, mentioned this to Bialkin, who dropped everything that he was doing and contacted Lee Wolosky.

Wolosky gave the phone to Greenberg and, as he recalls, notes that it was one of the few times he was ever to see the man truly shaken. He quickly regained his composure and gave the phone back to Wolosky, who was also at a loss for words.

The next day they got good news and bad news. The good news was that like much else the attorney general said, there was little chance of its actually coming to pass, but that was because Spitzer had decided to file a civil complaint that claimed Greenberg and former CFO Howie Smith participated in numerous fraudulent transactions.

On the 31st, AIG restated earnings and took a $4 billion charge, amounting to about 10 percent of the net income between 2000 and 2005. At AIG headquarters at 70 Pine Street, the new CFO, Bensinger, and Martin Sullivan breathed a sigh of relief, happy to be able to sign off on financials. The first step in putting the Greenberg era behind them was done.

For Greenberg, he too felt something akin to relief. The battle lines were drawn. He religiously insisted on his innocence and aggressively began to fund a legal and public relations campaign to fight AIG and Spitzer without remorse. On Greenberg's behalf, Boies Schiller launched a legal battle that had little analogue in recent history among the litigation-obsessed New York business community. They fought AIG and the attorney general's office on every motion and claim; every courtroom declaration was met and objected to. There were surely valid legal reasons for much of this, but in total it mired legal proceedings down into the courtroom equivalent of the Western Front's remorseless trench warfare. Word got out among the New York Bar that this was a legal rivalry that had to be seen to be believed. If they could not muster even basic courtroom civility, the lawyers from both firms sniped at each other behind closed doors to reporters and other lawyers.

All of which made Hank Greenberg very happy. He would build out C. V. Starr's specialty businesses and, using a Rolodex that may have had no peer globally, he would get Howie and Ed back in the saddle and build out the business. Every day, he woke up and happily spent millions to make AIG and the attorney general pay and then went to work and took some business from AIG here and there.

He was once again at war. He had survived everything that the monsters of the 20th century, in their lust to kill and dominate, had thrown at him, and he had done so in far worse conditions than an Art Deco building in Midtown East. He would win again, and he would bear the price with ease. The men he had helped reach the pinnacle of the business world were now being made to face the fact their former boss' campaign against them would never cease and would cost them dearly.

The rank-and-file, the men and women who worked long hours and who never would get the brass ring of a SICO or C. V. Starr equity stake, well, that was harder for him to think about. He loved and respected those people, but, well, there was a cost to be borne when you were led by the weak and the unprincipled.

■ ■ ■

Martin Sullivan followed the age-old playbook of chief executives who take over a company in hot water to a T: he went retail. He got on one of the company's Gulfstream jets or into cars, and he met hundreds of employees in dozens of offices and shook their hands. He had drinks with managers still tightly wound from the authoritarian style of Greenberg, and he demanded that other senior officers at least try to do the same. Results mattered now more than ever, but he had to get people relaxed again, he told board members, reasoning that in what was essentially a partnership the events of the past few months were like a family that had experienced a death or a trauma.

AIG, Sullivan recognized, worked well because it didn't have the ridiculous political problems that other companies had. There was one CEO, the operating committee was the same, and there was never any nonsense about hostile takeovers and the like. The men who built it still helped it, 50 years later. Prudential, AIG executives supposed, spent millions building a brand as "The Rock" but would never build a company as unchanging and solidly successful as AIG.

A salesman to his core, Sullivan understood that AIG's people needed to feel that their management "got it." To do that, they needed a break from the Greenberg style. So he smiled a lot, he clapped shoulders, and he made small talk. He knew that people had to process what had happened.

Sullivan also knew what AIG needed most of all was a win. A clear, unambiguous reference point that showed all comers that when people talked about earnings in the insurance and finance industries, they would still be the first and the last word. He knew that Greenberg could never be forgotten, but that life would return to something like normal if they could show the world that AIG wasn't going away.

At every office, in every subsidiary during Sullivan's whistle-stop of the world of AIG, he pulled aside senior management and shut the door. He asked them to pull out all the stops—to stay later and come in early, dig deeper for more prospects, to watch costs, whatever it took to increase their numbers. It was not a terribly necessary move as every senior manager had much of his net worth in AIGs shares, but the fact that it came face to face drove home the point.

When Sullivan stopped up to AIG Financial Products in April 2005, it was the same routine. Meet people, shake some hands, smile a lot, hear some diplomatically worded updates, and pull the top guy aside. Sullivan knew Cassano was a Greenberg/Matthews man, more out of a practical sense of his corporate survival than anything else. Sullivan, who knew Cassano only in passing and knew even less about his business, was hopeful of a good relationship since his newly named Capital Markets group—of which FP was a key cog—made over $1 billion in operating income in 2004. He told board members that he suspected that being left alone would sit well with Cassano.

Cassano, as a man who prided himself as being steeped in risk vs. reward calculations, appreciated the elegant simplicity of the Greenberg/ Matthews value proposition: make your numbers and you are left alone. Sullivan, whom he knew much less well, was viewed with suspicion. Cassano told friends that he didn't anticipate problems from Sullivan, whom no one had ever seen ask a probing financial question, but that the unknown was always a concern.

Sullivan, not wanting to come across as unmindful of FP's numbers in 2004, gave Cassano a very brief version of his canned speech about good earnings and what that would do for morale and public perception, told him to keep his eyes open for anything that might add some immediate heft to the bottom line. Cassano, in relating the story to others later, noted how he had bitten his tongue and said something noncommittal, to the effect of, "Sure, Martin. We certainly will."

Like the good soldier, Cassano quickly got back to work. He had earned almost $12 million in salary and bonus in 2004, and had no interest in starting off the Sullivan era with any hassles. And with Sullivan out of his hair, he doubted there was going to be many headaches from Steve Bensinger, the new CFO. As far as he could see, there weren't many political speed bumps on the internal horizon. There was little interest, it would seem, in having him reprise the Tom Savage role to Sullivan's Hank Greenberg, eternally working the CEO into every calculation.

No one on Wall Street knew of Martin Sullivan's barnstorming tour or would have conceivably cared. All they knew was that in late April of 2005, AIG started returning the phone calls of most of the bigger mortgage desks on Wall Street and saying "yes" when asked if they were interested in writing credit–default swaps on CDOs.

■ ■ ■

The man saying yes was an amiable senior marketer named Alan Frost. An engineering major at Penn and a hard worker, Frost joined the firm during the Sosin era from the world of mortgages and worked his way up from what one of the FP founders called "at best a junior marketer" position to what would become the more infamous seat in financial history.

Frost had been hunting around for a business line to really put a stamp on and generate some solid revenue for FP. In 2004, though, that was getting harder and harder to do. Many hedge funds had morphed from their traditional niche of short-term, rapid trading into asset-based finance, acting as lenders and advisers; banks and brokerages still brought FP ideas, but as often as not kept the best ideas to do for themselves.

Frost saw opportunity in the wrapping of CDOs, providing the assurance to investors in the most securely structured pieces (*tranches*, in Wall Street vernacular) that they would remain triple-A-rated. The attractions were many: it had, of course, been a profitable business under Tom Savage and one that Cassano had personally overseen the entrance into (albeit one that was based on guaranteeing highly rated corporate loans, which in Europe at least, had little chance of going under). Yale business professor Gary Gorton, who had been consulting with FP since the Savage regime, had already built the analytical platform at great expense in time and little modification would be required. Savage, though a fondly remembered fellow, was gone and with him the antimortgage obsession that was his hallmark. Unlike a typical FP deal that could take months or even a year to hammer out, these could close in weeks since they were only doing the top-rated sections of hand-picked deals. They called the stop-tier sections "super-senior" tranches.

They would get nine basis points per deal, paid annually. As long as Gorton's models continued to indicate less than 1 percent loss scenarios, then they were fine. There had of course been headlines about mortgage pools downgraded in the prior few years, but those were all related to consistently abusive subprime mobile-home lenders like Conseco. FP, as the Street's brokers assured Frost, would only consider insuring loans that were prime, to borrowers who worked hard and did what was needed to be done to pay off loans. Quietly, Frost noted that while FP hadn't ever done much with mortgages, it wasn't like they were speculating in stocks since—as Gorton's models demonstrated *ad infinitum*—not only was the American homeowner religious about getting home payments in the mail, but FP was "attaching" its obligation at the most senior point in the bond. In other words, everything could go pretty damn wrong and FP would still get paid without having to pay anything out.

If Gorton's models were right, and 1929 didn't play out again, then they could easily have an eight-figure annual annuity on their hands, for many years to come. Frost began to speak to Cassano about the pos-sibilities in this business.

Cassano, who genuinely liked Frost—his colleagues describe the marketer as positively religious in his efforts to stay on Cassano's good side—weighed the evidence carefully. Every one of the CDO swap deals they had done since 1998's J. P. Morgan Broad Index Secured Trust Offering (BISTRO) deal was working out fine. A tweak here or there perhaps, but there was no way he (or anyone else) had lost sleep over the credit risk from the more than 200 CDO deals they had been involved in.

In mid-2004 Cassano gave his approval and it passed Trade Review. When it became clear that not only would headquarters appreciate a little boost, but brokers near and far were lined up to do business with FP, they were happy to deliver.

For the first time in its history, FP was in a feedback loop where the breakdown of any one part of the loop would leave them with no recourse and no way out. It was forced to do a type of business that was commercial, where its intellectual firepower and independence mattered little and its balance sheet ruled supreme.[7] Frost was secure that they were insuring the best kind of CDOs because the models—built in part on ratings agency credit ratings—told him there was little chance of credit loss; the investment banks, in turn, thought it was the best kind of collateral because the ratings agencies, using the information they got from the investment banks, told them their models thought this was the best sort of collateral.

For the first time ever, hope—namely, that others got their business assumptions correct—was a big component of FP strategy. The business model that Greenberg and Matthews had signed off on with Sosin, and which Savage had so ably picked up and furthered, was officially dead.

■ ■ ■

The men who were in effect writing hundreds of millions of dollars a week in insurance throughout the summer of 2005 appear to have missed a key CDO market development. As recently as 2002–2003, the CDO market had undergone some substantial stresses. In the years leading up to the September 11 attacks, billions of dollars' worth of manufactured housing and airplane lease–backed bonds were put into CDOs. After 9/11, when the airline industry was devastated as travel dropped off, and Conseco's Green Tree Finance unit filed bankruptcy protection, many CDOs were downgraded or dropped sharply in price.[8] In fact, most every CDO with asset-backed security (ABS) collateral had some of this paper in its collateral because ratings agencies forced CDO issuers to have a diversity of collateral in every deal.

According to Tom Adams, a former executive at AMBAC and FGIC, ratings agencies got lucky and were able to cite circumstances, namely terrorism and fraud, rather than shoddy ratings work, for the losses and downgrades in the CDOs where all this paper wound up.

When the CDO market slowed down, bankers sprang to the rescue.

"Bankers needed the market restarted because ABS trading and issuance was a huge part of their bottom line and ratings agencies lost millions of dollars in fees, so when bankers proposed eliminating collateral diversity requirements," said Adams, "there was no one willing to say no. It was the perfect rug for everything to be swept under."[9]

It was an excellent solution. Ratings analysts hadn't missed Green Tree's transparent borrower fraud and the thousands of reports of abusive lending and accounting, and bankers hadn't slopped together billions of dollars' worth of CDOs only for the sake of some fees. It was instead the fault of collateral diversity.

Starting in late 2003 and early 2004, CDO managers put together deals that were densely backed with mortgage-backed securities (MBSs) or ABSs, and in whatever proportion they wished. This spurred on a new development in consumer finance: Lending for the sake of securitization. Because of the massive demand from CDO managers who could put together whatever deal they wished, lenders were highly incentivized to sell loans at the highest yield possible (thus making the CDO they went into that much more profitable.)[10]

For FP's Frost and Cassano, it was easy to do commercially oriented business like writing swaps on CDOs—they are quick, easy, and a ready source of cash to boot—but it required maintaining an eternal vigilance for key shifts in the characteristics of the market. Every $50,000 a year insurance underwriting trainee knew that.

Al Frost, who earned several million dollars a year, apparently never learned that lesson.

■■■

In the winter of 2005 a series of reports that were otherwise highly forgettable came across the desk of a man named Win Neuger. The chief investment officer of AIG, who ran a far-flung and ever expanding enterprise called AIG Global Investment Corp., Neuger received many such reports that were designed to catch areas where profits were growing slowly or where troubles were percolating. In this case the reports were spot on, having flagged an area whose profit growth had indeed been positively glacial.

It was AIG's then $48 billion securities lending program.

Known as the AIG Global Securities Lending program, and managed by various Neuger charges within the AIG Global Investment Management Corporation, it had failed utterly to participate in the carry trade, the greatest *easy* moneymaking trade of the past decade, maybe longer. As has been noted, highly rated institutions could borrow much more cheaply than many market players; at a time of low interest rates, this is quite a boon. They can then turn around and earn easy cash buying bonds that pay a higher rate and pocketing the difference between the two.

Securities lending is an absurdly easy business for a company like AIG to be in. With its life insurance subsidiaries taking policyholder cash and investing it in high-grade corporate bonds, it made sense to lend those bonds out to hedge funds and other brokers who had need of them, either to turn around and lend them out to their own clients or use the paper themselves. In return for the use of the bond for up to six months, the borrower gave AIG cash plus another 2 percent security as a safety measure. In turn, AIG's portfolio managers would turn around and purchase highly rated—and very liquid—floating-rate Fannie Mae and Freddie Mac securities. At the end of the loan period, all the cash would be returned to the borrower and AIG would take the bond back, splitting whatever profits came from the loan 50/50 with the life insurance company.

There were a lot of moving parts in deals like this, but the over-arching goal of it all was simple enough: balance. In this case, that meant precisely matching the amount of the assets to the amount of the liabilities.[11]

This was a long-running Wall Street business, if a very low-margined one. From 1999 to 2004, AIG's program made about two basis-points profit on its growing portfolio. Greenberg had started it as a way of generating some excess return from the tens of billions of dollars in corporate debt that were literally sitting around in life insurance company portfolios.[12]

It showed up on Neuger's report, and caught his eye, because it was *designed* to be low profit. That it could be, at any time or under any market conditions, substantively profitable was seen by generations of financial executives as absurd. Neuger was not so sure about that.

There is no greater difference between the Sullivan and Greenberg era's at AIG than Neuger's securities lending program.

Greenberg was at his most Greenberg-like in ensuring its management as a plain vanilla enterprise. One story: in 2000, AIG took a $10 million loss in the portfolio when a small position in some barely investment-grade telecom bonds blew up.

In the words of then CFO Howard Smith, "Greenberg hit the roof. He called the poor bastards in who were managing it then and screamed for half an hour and wouldn't put the men out of their misery and fire them, keeping them in their jobs until the cash we had to inject in was restored over a year or so. Maybe they quit or died afterward, but Greenberg checked up on the poor SOBs weekly from then on and wouldn't let them forget it."[13]

Win Neuger had a much better idea. With interest rates low and the liquidity of the bond market at an all-time high as cash poured into it from the four corners of the earth, AIG would not have to settle for leaving tens of millions of dollars on the table anymore as a sop to Greenberg's safety demands. They could buy triple-A-rated ABSs with the same duration and earn a much juicier yield.

When safety concerns were raised about the idea—though many of his colleagues acknowledged to Neuger that it was as tempting as all get out—he replied that he wasn't seeing a whole lot of defaults in any marketplace, let alone the ABS market. Moreover, its liquidity was deep, spreads between bid and offer were tight and, in case anybody hadn't noticed, the company could use the money.

The risk issue wouldn't go away, however. A few quietly suggested to Neuger that this sort of thing had been tried in the past at other companies and had led to a blowup every time. This was even aggressive even for Hank, who was obsessed with profits. Neuger heard the concerns and addressed them calmly, arguing that Greenberg was no longer here, and that things would probably be changing a little. They had cause to believe him. Neuger had pulled off no small amount of change in the 13 years he had been at AIG.

Tasked with taking a witch's brew of fiefdoms and units picked up in AIG's diverse mergers and cobbling it all together into a global, integrated asset management unit that could reliably produce profits in good markets and bad, he had succeeded.

His colleagues, who had once joked about taking bets on his likely date of departure, now saw him book more than a half-billion dollars of operating income in 2004. With $6.1 million in compensation that year, and every paper full of the hedge fund riches being had all around him in Manhattan—almost all of which were being driven by the two areas he was striving mightily to take advantage of: the low-interest-rate environment and securitized products—it was probably easy for Neuger to look at the future and to be an optimist.

He was so confident that change was going to come that by the end of 2005, Neuger was talking about something he called "Ten Cubed," a comprehensive plan to get the asset management unit up to the $1 billion in operating income mark. Getting the $50 billion in bonds they had in-house that were earning bank savings account levels of profits to pull their fair share was at the center of this.

Neuger pressed his case to his peers, and if there were objections, they were a well-kept secret. Fixed-income chief Richard Scott, CFO Steve Bensinger, and chief risk officer Kevin McGinn all took a look at the issue Neuger laid before them and consented. The risk management staff was especially helpful, ginning up a compelling analysis of how little default risk there had been historically in this sector and just what it would take for things to become worrisome. No one who looked at the presentation thought the bond market was likely to take a turn down that road. Win, they all agreed, knew what he was doing.

There was a problem. The primary investors in AIG Global Securities Lending (the formal name of the unit running the program) had agreed to let their corporate bonds be managed in an ultra conservative, low-return fashion. Neuger was proposing a massive restructuring of this agreement. There was another problem. All of the securities lending investors were AIG subsidiaries.

So in December 2005, they eliminated the following sentence in the prospectus they had used to describe and market the GSL to the insurance subs:

> The Investment Policy is intended to preserve principal value and maintain a high degree of liquidity while providing current income, and to enhance the safety of funds and investments through the establishment of interest rate exposure restrictions and limitations on investments in derivatives.

That none of AIG's life insurance companies were told about this shift appears not to have been much of a concern. Neuger and his staff were free to turn a sleepy backwater whose profits, if they could even be called that, lagged comically behind the rest of his unit into something that would be special.

It became clearer every day to AIG veterans that things were indeed going to be different under Martin Sullivan.

Just in case anyone didn't get the message, Neuger liked to let slip within earshot of any naysayers and worrywarts that, "If they didn't want to be on this bus, now was a good time to get off."

One man, as it turns out, was very much contemplating getting off the bus, and throwing Neuger and a few of the crowd who always seemed to be nodding in mindless agreement at everything he said along with him under its wheels. The man was Michael Rieger, a senior portfolio manager at AIG GIC who would oversee up to $50 billion worth of asset- and mortgage-backed securities. Blunt and opinionated, he was not easy to work with and, presumably, would have been fired long before had he not been very, very good at his job.[14]

Rieger thought this was the stupidest idea he had encountered in his professional career. Nothing, in fact, had prepared him for a plan that so massively failed to account for even the basics of how the bond-trading business operated. It was, he would tell colleagues, so spectacularly stupid, so completely against what Greenberg would have ever allowed, that it was almost certainly going to get picked off at the general counsel's level, if not by risk management. (He had no idea, of course, that risk management and the general counsel's office were integral to its getting underway.)

It was surprising, he would tell colleagues, since Neuger had done some smart things. There had to be something he was missing. No one would do something like this. No one. He would, he confided to one colleague, give Neuger some time to clarify this before he said something.

■ ■ ■

In the middle of the summer of 2005, Fred Geissinger, a consumer finance veteran who was the head of AIG's American General Finance unit, which among other things, issued mortgages to "less than prime" or "nontraditional borrowers," had begun to pick up on some of the most absurd stories he had ever heard in his more than 35 years in the business.

It seemed that customers were telling Geissinger's branch managers that American General was the only place they were being asked for things like a W-2 or proof of assets. The remarks were not complementary. The biggest names in the business—Ameriquest, Countrywide, Golden West and others—were taking an open mind to what exactly constituted jobs and income. He was even hearing that his name brand rivals weren't hung up on even getting things like driver's licenses nailed down. Calls to longtime colleagues and industry friends revealed stories that were probably just chatter, but hearing about illegal immigrants, without a document or a word of English, qualifying for loans took his breath away. He had lived through everything since the early 1970s and thought he had seen every scam, cycle, and promotion there was out there.

The Evansville, Indiana–based Geissinger was a rock-ribbed Republican who was pro growth and pro subprime and had a contract that incentivized him to expand his unit's output and profits. But this was too much if even half of it was true. He ran a series of reports and studied his own unit's borrowers—people who wouldn't have been approved for a loan the decade prior were getting more than he had ever supposed was possible. Delinquencies were increasing, if slightly, and loan production industry-wide was hitting levels that appeared to indicate every American adult was borrowing, refinancing, or taking equity out of their home.

It wasn't hard. That July, just as FP reached its zenith in guaranteeing CDOs, Geissinger consulted with his key managers and told them they were getting out of subprime. They would honor whatever loans they had agreed to provide, and then they would do not a penny more. No one had a beef with him. He called out to New York and told his bosses that they were stopping subprime mortgage issuance because there were some things happening in the industry that really worried him and he wasn't willing to use shareholder money to keep up on this merry-go-round.

If anyone had a problem, from Bill Dooley, the Financial Services boss, to Bensinger the CFO to Martin Sullivan, Geissinger never heard a word of it. They shrugged, accepted his decision, and moved on. It was a good year after all, and if a unit chief had to make a tough call, well, it would either work or it wouldn't.

Geissinger, a loyal company man, never thought to call or email the likes of a Win Neuger or Joe Cassano. Those guys were in the annual report, on the conference calls, and ran key units; they briefed the board and were the face of AIG to the world. He couldn't imagine they would have much interest or time to discuss consumer finance trends with a colleague from Indiana.

AIG didn't have that kind of culture. Greenberg had set each unit up to be almost totally autonomous. The only thing that bound it all together was Greenberg and his command of every last detail—Geissinger would tell colleagues that there was no way that exiting subprime mortgage origination wouldn't have resulted in a three-hour grilling from Greenberg who would've wanted to know everything he saw and thought on the issue—but now he was gone and things were different.

■ ■ ■

After losing (or not winning—he waffles between the two terms) the race to be the CEO of Citigroup in the wake of the retirement and departure of Sandy Weill, Robert Willumstad had it in the back of his mind that he might be hearing from his old friend and colleague Frank Zarb.

A Long Island man like himself, the two became friendly over the years, most especially with Willumstad running the Commercial Credit unit of what eventually became Citigroup and Zarb running Smith Barney. Willumstad stayed put and rose to second in command of the Citigroup colossus before resigning in 2005. Zarb's career eventually took him out of the orbit of Sandy Weill, and into the realm of Hank Greenberg, who put him on the board of AIG.

Interested in running a financial services business after having run Citi's mammoth consumer banking franchise—where in effect he ran a corporation-within-a-corporation that made $10.9 billion in net income his last year—Willumstad figured Zarb might have an insight into where a search might be emerging. Zarb had an ear to the ground, and knew loads of people in New York and Washington and, well, was just an all around handy sort to have as a friend. So when Frank Zarb called in November of 2005 with an interesting offer, it was not unexpected. When that interesting offer was to join AIG's board, however, Willumstad *was* surprised.

Disposing with the "*Gee, Frank, I'm flattered to be considered*" bit, Willumstad said he was not really inclined to do it but that he'd have a meeting and talk about it with him the following week. He prided himself on being reflective and deliberate, and so he took the time and tried to think about the AIG board offer logically. He knew AIG well enough from his spell running Travelers. Their property and casualty units were top shelf; the 2005 earnings had been superior, all things considered.

But it struck him that AIG was similar to Citi—a legendary CEO leaving under a regulatory cloud, a generation of executives used to doing things "the Sandy way" or "the Hank way." Changing a place like that and getting it to do a different kind of business was never going to be easy. The politics alone, he thought, could be fatal.

There were a few other matters that dominated his thinking even more than the risk from entrenched thinking: AIG was furiously preparing an accounting restatement and was under SEC investigation. Being a board member at the time of a major regulatory inquiry was hard enough, but at a place that had been run by a once-in-a-lifetime personality who would always be identified with the place, while lawyers, prosecutors, and regulators kicked over stones looking and hoping for wrongdoing—that was going to be a new kind of hard. Walking onto a board that had signed off on an incomplete investigation or hadn't taken the charges necessary to put past sins behind could be fatal for a guy like him.

Things were also different now. Board members were being sued not for the occasionally illegal act, but for things they *didn't* do. He supposed that it was part of the new legal landscape, a tool in the class-action arsenal. Becoming a pelt for a trial lawyer was a real concern.

He would, of course, take the meeting with Zarb, but mostly to get a clearer sense of what had really happened with Greenberg. AIG was a prestige assignment, but he'd had plenty of prestige on Citi's board. And if AIG really was cutting corners as a business platform in an age where Eliot Spitzer was a folk hero, he'd find a polite way of letting his old friend know just how busy he was.

Willumstad wanted to build and expand a company of his own. He'd learned a lot about building and managing assets and had developed his own way of looking at value. Maybe some insight into how a place like AIG really ran could be helpful; maybe it was a complete waste of time. Time, though, was the one thing he had a good amount of for the first time since the mid-1960s.

The following week, during his meeting with Zarb at his office at Hellman & Friedman on New York's Park Avenue, Willumstad got the pitch.

"Turning things around." "Excellent core businesses." "Good people." And, of course, some version of the corporate recruiting chestnut, "We could use you to take AIG in a new direction." A long talk showing that if nothing else Zarb, notwithstanding what Greenberg said about him, truly cared about the company.

Board commitment was good because he had seen his fair share of directors who viewed their directorships as God-given rights for having reached a certain age and stage in life, and, ego-wise it was always nice to hear kind things from old friends. However, 90,000-employee companies don't turn around at the board level, nor do they change directions because a majority of directors pass a vote demanding it.

"OK, Frank, I'll buy that. I will. But what about the restatement, and what about the AG and the SEC? Where are you with settling?" Not that he expected to, but had he heard anything about a protracted fight with the regulators, he was planning on ending the meeting there.

Zarb had saved what he probably imagined was the best for last. "We're close and it's on track, from what I see. Talk to Dick Beattie over at Simpson Thatcher and he can give you specifics."

Beattie and his partner Jamie Gambel were blunt. AIG was on track to settle with the SEC and AG's office for over $1.5 billion to put to rest everything related to improper accounting, the Gen Re matter and bid-rigging charges, as well as to correct some other accounting matters. The settlement number might work even higher. Everything imaginable was in there. Big time remediation steps were being taken. Management cooperated fully. Hell, Martin had even set the tone—he had senior executives drop their work and focus full time on it.

He believed the pair from Simpson Thatcher. They had worked in and around AIG for over a year now and had met with every regulator involved. What he heard had, in fact, changed his mind. The legal problems were going to be behind the company, there was a change in tone at the top, and, most of all, the franchise was going to be preserved. He could learn some things, steer the company into some safer waters, and field offers from elsewhere. At least that was a plan that sounded workable. And the earnings were looking like something else entirely. An AIG with a clean slate and no restrictions on it was a formidable thing indeed.

He called Frank Zarb and told him he'd join the board.

■ ■ ■

Willumstad was indeed learning something. To start with, he had had no idea about the systems issues.

No one—not Zarb, not the Simpson Thatcher lawyers—had ever said a word about the fact that AIG had a massive internal control (for want of a better word) problem. The better word, perhaps, to frame what Willumstad came across was systems integration, boiling down to an inability to get up-to-the-minute numbers for every one of AIG's far-flung units and, more importantly, to integrate those numbers into reports that senior managers could act on.

There was one thing that distanced a CEO from the rest of the world: the art and science of data management. Nothing made reporters' or investors' eyes glaze over more readily; all they cared about was revenues or income or the internal drama of the moment. Though a CEO cared about those things, too, a *good* CEO was obsessed about managing the torrents of operational information a corporation like Citi or AIG kicked up. A credit-default swap struck with a wealthy Swiss family could have lasting implications for the Citi trading desk, even if they had found a counterparty in Los Angeles and were simply acting as a middleman. From his office, he could see the entire DNA of the trade: the cash-flow implications, possible legal risk, and the worth of the customers to the trading desk franchise. On a moment's notice, he knew Citi's cash balances and liability profile and could reconcile both of them to make an informed judgment on any major issue.

He had a growing suspicion that Greenberg could do all of that, too, but in his mind.

These weren't the gripes of a lifetime operations and administration nerd, though he was one; it got to the heart of how a global financial company assessed its risk and competitive position on a daily basis. The fact that the AIG board was obsessed over strategy, Willumstad recalls, was probably an attempt to compensate for not being able to drill into the fine points of its complex risk positions. Expecting to be hit with briefings and reams of paperwork on the minutiae of things such as its private-equity investments abroad, the cash position that week, and stress tests of its key liabilities, he instead received memos on strategy, possible expansion scenarios, and updates on plans struck long ago. There was *some* talk about numbers, but it was broad and related to previously stated goals. The audit and finance committees dug down a little more into the debits and credits, but this was nothing—*nothing*—like Citi, where after multiple hours (even days) of detailed briefings on cash, corporate liquidity, and liability-management issues, the board would be begging to talk just a little strategy.

This wasn't an advertising conglomerate; this was AIG, with its $679 billion in financial assets balance sheet in 2005. They owned a bank. They had a massive investment portfolio in a dozen different currencies. Instead, they got presentations he considered a mere primer for a man who had been in lending and markets for 40 years.

He flashed back to the daily reports sitting on his computer at Citi: "Here is our exposure to sovereign banks. . . . Here is what we own in Brazil. . . ."

Regardless, the systems problem was massive and didn't look like it was amenable to having money or even managerial skill deployed against it. There were, Willumstad saw, simply too many reporting entities, too many complicated ownership structures. AIG was just too big.

It wasn't that AIG didn't have good people, good processes, and a strong desire to do what was necessary to manage the business well. They did, and in spades. Nor did AIG scrimp on training or spending on the latest software, hardware, and the small army of consultants that always came with them. But what AIG was—its shape and structure— now came back to haunt them. There were over 4,000 separate legal entities that AIG owned, partially owned, advised, or otherwise were required to have their economic activity accounted for in the company's quarterly filings.

Good intentions aside, AIG was not up to the task.

The symptoms were many. Releasing the earnings on the last possible day before they would be in violation of SEC rules, Willumstad (in addition to several other former senior executives) said that the last few days prior to the filing deadline were mayhem in its purest sense.

"Within five business days before the quarter's close, we could go to the board at Citi and tell them within one penny where earnings would be," recalled Willumstad. "I had heard of companies where you wouldn't know until the night before what earnings were—I had not thought AIG would be [one of them.]"

Unlike other companies that opened or closed offshore subsidiaries based on expediency, it would appear that AIG used all of theirs on an ongoing basis. That meant AIG lawyers and accountants had to scrutinize the legal and accounting aspects of 4,000 different entities and then begin a process of consolidating their books into various national, regional, and ultimately company-wide ledgers. Certainly a whale of a task, but one other companies managed to perform. They also managed the unwieldy process of simultaneously handling the individual legal and regulatory filings and disclosures these thousands of operating companies, entities, and shells were also required to file in multiple languages and jurisdictions.

Where the burden became nearly unworkable was the fact that this was insurance accounting. AIG was not a manufacturing concern that wrote down (depreciated) the value of its plant and equipment a set amount every quarter, so the books of its far-flung subsidiaries often required individual managerial judgments on the adequacy of reserves for potential losses shipping wheat on the Baltic or insuring a strip mall in Alabama. Going further down this line, every set of books raised its own set of questions about investments, hedges, contested or unpaid claims, and so on. This doesn't even address the topic of reinsurance, the most arcane subset of insurance accounting.

The distinct culture of AIG contributed to this. The large number of "lifers" (those who had never worked in any other company) in key roles thought it was entirely acceptable and standard to have earnings moving around by large amounts several days before the corporate filing date. Those managers who had worked at other places, especially those in corporate communications, were astounded.

No one said anything at the board level because AIG worked where it mattered: the earnings release. As one supervisor said, "We knew it was crazy, but our job wasn't to worry about that; it was to ensure that good numbers came out."

It was a problem that generated its own good years; the massive earnings-generation power of its various businesses would eliminate any real need to worry about this. In bad years, the trouble spots were clear enough to management.

But Willumstad knew something that the lifers and loyalists did not: there were bad years and then there were *bad* years. When disaster hit, when you had operations in an economy abroad that was collapsing, when your models broke down was the time when your systems mattered most. You knew where every penny was and what you couldn't lay your hands on.

There were some valid arguments people could make about what Sandy had built at Citi; that was for sure, Willumstad would acknowledge to friends. But Sandy saw from the start that the only way to pull off his financial supermarket concept was to have the best analytical software in the world. If they could look into a problem like no one else, if they could see a problem before a rival did, they would succeed like no one else. Having great systems did not translate into making great decisions. To Willumstad's mind, evidence the first of that was Citi and the self-inflicted mayhem it wrought in its capital markets absurdities. Nor did the absence of effective operations systems prevent generally superior decision making, as Greenberg's tenure proved.

Regardless, AIG had to strain mightily—too mightily—to get senior management an accurate accounting of its affairs. The question in Willumstad's mind was *when*, not *if*, AIG would hit the rocks.

But the AIG board of 2006 had been dropping everything for a while and putting out fires, big ones, and were as run down and stressed out as everyone else. It was not, in other words, readily apparent that anyone would have taken him too seriously if he had decided to make the computer systems issue the centerpiece of his tenure. They were, in Willumstad's opinion, doing the best they could to fix the problem.

A corollary to being "a systems guy" was being results oriented. If the way AIG measured and assessed itself was really disappointing to Willumstad, what the company was doing with what it had was pretty damn spectacular. The 2005 results included over $108 billion in revenues and almost $15.2 billion in operating income. All the more so, he thought, since the company had been put through a regulatory and media meat grinder.

When they got the internal processes working just right, he thought, this was going to take off.

■ ■ ■

This sentiment and others like it were getting traction throughout the AIG empire. Greenberg and his lieutenants had controlled everything for so long that a life imagined without them was corporate heresy. The circumstances of Greenberg's departure engendered much sympathy for him as a man and leader; his conduct afterwards, at least to the rank-and-file, did not.

Reading the papers in early 2006, many AIG employees concluded that Greenberg's departure was a good thing. He never stopped complaining about Spitzer and his suing AIG over artwork and personal effects seemed churlish; taking over Starr International Co. and its cache of stock, worth tens of billions of dollars, was a different thing altogether. A man bent on revenge now controlled more than 12 percent of the company and that was scary. (That these sentiments were highly encouraged by the nonstop leaking and spinning of Spitzer and his press aides was less obvious to them; their own public relations and legal machine's efforts did not lag Spitzer's by much.)

All over AIG, the mood brightened. Hank had doubted they could do it, and instead they earned more than $10 billion in net income. Executives used to interrogations and bloodlettings quickly acclimated to Martin Sullivan's open-minded and respectful style. The senior-most leaders joked about the private differences between the two: Greenberg would have a lunch and eat a small plate of steamed fish and vegetables while conducting a half-dozen detailed conversations with his guests at once; Martin knew how to order a good bottle of wine in a dozen languages. He listened and joked easily with his former peers, happy enough to talk about things like English soccer, where AIG was the big sponsor of Manchester United, the perennial contenders for the league crown.

There was much they didn't see: that Sullivan and other AIG executives had made small fortunes when they tendered their C. V. Starr & Co. equity stakes back to that company—Sullivan alone made $14 million—and that Greenberg's role at Starr International had long been permitted in its charter. They saw nothing of the explosion of CDO guarantees at FP or that global securities lending was on its way to be the largest player in mortgage securities on Wall Street.

All AIG employees and investors saw were the ever-growing earnings numbers in the SEC filings and what they read in the media. And that meant one thing: in a post-Greenberg AIG, the kids were alright.

Chapter 8

In the Shipping Business

T he credit-default swaps (CDSs) that would launch a courtroom full of subpoenas, legal filings, and conspiracy theories were themselves hardly a secret. For years, every other Tuesday, FP held a "global marketing call" where its transactions in London, Paris, Tokyo, and Wilton were discussed; pipelines of deals were referenced; and questions were asked and answered. Everything was said and done on the record, and, staff learned quickly, if a marketer left out an inconvenient fact about a deal's risk during the call, there would be hell to pay. If the marketer intentionally left out a detail about risk(s) during trade review, he would be immediately fired.[1]

Al Frost's collateralized debt obligation (CDO) swaps were discussed in detail on these calls, and while veterans raised eyebrows at the headlong foray into the realm of mortgage credit, the revenue was real enough, and no one had heard of any losses coming from insuring tranches of all those CDOs stuffed with European corporate bank loans. Frost told anyone who asked on the calls that dealers liked working with FP on asset-backed security (ABS) CDO swaps because they moved quickly, could handle volume, and knew the product. There were dozens of other marketers and dozens of other risks; no one dwelled too much on Frost, who was seen as an "old reliable" sort who wasn't going to be involved in any violently complex structures.

What no one was told about was the credit support annexes (CSAs). These were standard contracts attached to the swap agreements between AIGFP and the investment-bank trading desks that mandated the swap be marked to the market price nightly. If the swap was for $100 million face value at par and the CDO declined in market price to $95, then FP would be liable for $5 million in collateral. In 2004 and 2005, however, concerning yourself about this was akin to worrying that the sun would rise in the West the next day. CDOs had traded at or around par for years and were, at the least, not known for their volatility.

They were assumed to have no volatility in price largely because of one of Wall Street's best, but least well known, schemes. Known as value at risk, or VaR, it was a complex statistical measure of the likelihood of future adverse events and its effect on a security's price. Because CDOs with heavy concentrations of ABS collateral had been around for only a few years, and that market had exploded in liquidity and popularity, VaR models held that not only was there little probability of CDO losses, but that they also needed little in the way of capital to be held in reserve against losses. This resulted in CDO investors and trading desks being devastated and underreserved when the selloff hit. The entire system was a few degrees shy of a tautology.[2]

Joe Cassano, Alan Frost, and Andrew Forster knew about these CSAs and appear to have told no one at corporate headquarters, according to numerous interviews with former AIG officials.[3] Bob Lewis, AIG's chief risk officer, would later say he had had no idea that the swaps had CSAs attached to them and only learned of them in late July 2007, much to his consternation.

This lack of awareness of a key legal feature of something that the company was using to write billions of dollars' worth of insurance with is in part with a broader senior management mindset throughout 2005: a total obsession with the pending accounting restatement and legal settlement with regulators to the exclusion of all other considerations. Bensinger and Sullivan would testify that they had no idea that FP's six-month-long ABS CDO swap underwriting spree would put them on the hook for a total of $54.3 billion. It was all the more impressive since they had started with a portfolio of $17.9 billion in swaps at the end of December 2004.[4]

In their defense, FP's experience with collateral calls stretched back years but had always been for small amounts on liquid securities. And Gary Gorton's increasingly intricate models reinforced the view that there was an absurdly small probability of ever having material price deterioration in the sector. Cassano, who had ceased his lengthy, wandering weekly phone calls with AIG's CEO when Greenberg was booted, argued that he hid or obscured nothing. Cassano would later tell authorities that all the paperwork was filed and signed off on in Wilton and sent to New York. That no one at headquarters ever asked about anything having to do with the CSAs is what he would repeatedly tell a horde of Securities and Exchange Commission (SEC) and Department of Justice lawyers.

The lines of detailed communication between New York and Wilton were essentially dead. There was no dramatic fallout like Sosin's in 1992, no one event that forced a schism, but rather a simple combination of a lack of curiosity and total managerial distraction. When Spitzer got Greenberg tossed out, he also removed someone willing to spend hours with underlings parsing the risk on transactions that were still on a drawing board. He studied the nuances in Savage's and later Cassano's voices and learned when they had problems or were simply being theoretical. This is a "soft and touchy" data point, inherently unquantifiable, but it appears to have made a material impression on FP's administration.[5]

The FP line on the transparency issue is that they discussed in detail with New York everything they did that that they conceived of as risky before the deal was done. Moreover, since New York had detailed computer and portfolio analysis of FP's book on a real-time basis—in addition to outside audit and legal work—arguments about headquarters not understanding the swaps or the size of the book were absurd.

Equally as important was the sea change in the approach to risk management at FP, as illustrated by a story from the Sosin era. When FP was considering its first deal, an interest rate swap of $1 billion on Italian government debt slated to launch in July 1987, Sosin spent weeks studying and analyzing a litany of risks. He hired a law firm to study legal remedies against sovereign issuers in the event of default and ordered staff to study the financial health of the Republic of Italy and reconstructed its recent dealings with investors. Regardless, the transaction was fully hedged (the hedge was the source of the deal's profits), and multiple steps were taken to protect the unit should Italy sustain a ratings downgrade or default.[6] Sosin privately joked that he had wanted to contact the CIA to see if they had any information that might cast doubts on the seriousness and competence of the major decision makers in the Department of Economics and Finance.[7]

In contrast, to write swaps on hundreds of billions of dollars of debt in 2005, FP plugged a handful of variables into a seven-year-old computer model. Somehow, their model always said "yes."

To Howard Sosin and Tom Savage, the only reason FP existed was to get *away* from this type of business. They both looked at these trades as a total waste of time and resources in a marketplace that was crowded with well-educated sheep, and really didn't cotton to providing liquidity to some sort of investment-bank underwriting scheme.

Joe Cassano saw it differently, though. If you could pick up 10 basis points and the downside was triggered only by Crash of 1929 proportions, he liked the odds. If he was right, he had a multimillion-dollar portfolio of annual cash annuities. If he was wrong, he had authorized Alan Frost to sign a corporate suicide note for more than 90,000 people.

■ ■ ■

The role of Goldman Sachs in AIG's saga had its roots in a little-remarked-upon series of promotions involving a pair of managers known as the "J. Aron guys" taking control of Goldman's Fixed-Income, Commodities, and Currency unit in the late 1990s. Gary Cohn and Lloyd Blankfein, veterans of Goldman's sharp-elbowed commodities trading operation, saw a need to do things differently. As they'd lay it out to the unit's better producers in twos and threes, the firm was on the horns of a dilemma. In the looming post-Glass-Steagall landscape, "mega banks" like Citigroup and Bank of America (which had spent much of the past few years gobbling up Goldman's competitors, big and small) would have the ability to throw around capital that Goldman would never have. Spreads were compressing, with margins immediately following, and whatever their vaunted relationships with clients had once been, they wouldn't hold up in the face of Citi's consistently being able to absorb a loss when it trades $5 billion of five-year Treasuries cheaper than anyone else.

Goldman didn't need to change its business model; the marketplace had changed it for the firm. All that was required was to acknowledge it.

So Cohn and Blankfein said Goldman should discard the way it had traditionally done its bond business, with an extensive focus on the largest 100 accounts according to assets managed and trading-revenue generation. From now on, Goldman's bread-and-butter business plan was to compete to do every trade with everyone who rang up and then, after that, they would beat the bushes for more customers so they could do more trades. The bigger the better, of course, but every order was going to be fought for.

A certain group of longtime Goldman trading and sales staff were disgusted at the idea of becoming a glorified PaineWebber, in wasting time to give narrow bid and offer spreads on $1 million bond trades for a midwestern savings-and-loan or some $20-million-in-assets new hedge fund, many of whom might never call the firm again. Blankfein and Cohn would patiently meet with these people and reexplain themselves and lay out their reasons. A few weeks later, when various trading floor snitches reported back that the grumbling and politicking hadn't stopped, these traders and sales staff found themselves having long midday lunches with Wall Street's executive recruiters, exploring options at other firms, spinning tales of how they were happily leaving an ugly situation before it got much worse.

People like that, Blankfein and Cohn said, were just hard to reeducate.

Another group of traders and salesmen who had joined the firm in the 1990s proved more willing to adapt. With only a passing connection to Goldman's patrician past, they picked up much more quickly on what Blankfein and Cohn were trying to do. This wasn't a bid to compete to get every trade *per se*, but a bid to get what every trade was telling you.

Who was buying what?

What bonds were not moving and why?

Where were people offsides?

Who had conviction and who was sitting on the sidelines?

And above all: why, why, why?

To get that information, you had to pay for it. The way you paid for it was in bidding or offering tons of bonds to customers you ordinarily could care less about. If the customer wouldn't tell you directly, then you could piece it together based on what your desk and perhaps others were doing with them, or other customers like them. Then, armed with that information, they would be able to take the firm's own capital and make some informed bets on a moment's notice and make the real money.

In this formulation, Goldman was not to be the biggest trader, have the smartest people, or dominate any one market. But when it came time to take advantage of market moves, they would be there first and with their own money. Other firms might have bigger years and more dominant franchises, but no one would have a better return on equity. Since this was happening in the late 1990s, when Goldman was still a partnership, this was their own money at stake and return on equity was a key measurement. Blankfein and Cohn (and dozens more newly minted partners from the 1990s) were not terribly inclined to maintain a partnership in an era where even their longtime rivals at Salomon Brothers had sold out to Citibank to secure a more solid balance sheet. No, Blankfein and Cohn would push for a public offering and bring in some additional capital.[8] Because, from where they sat, just about the entire bond world was evolving away from everything Goldman Sachs was, namely relationship- and client-driven and capital-at-risk averse.

Every day, in meetings in offices and on the trading floor, they drilled it home: margins were gone and they were not going to come back. Everything they did would have to become integrated: the growing prime-brokerage unit would open trading accounts for the growing number of hedge funds out there. Because they provided their own capital to these hedge funds, they had an instant customer base. Sales staff would have more clients to call, analysts would have more people to peddle ideas to, and traders could execute trades. What they lost in higher-margin business they would make up by "touching" the customer a dozen different ways. Things they had long hesitated to do—peddle derivatives *en masse*—they would do as markets became more integrated and ways to mitigate risk became more accessible. Above all, everyone was to hustle for that idea that had the big payday attached.

The way Blankfein and Cohn saw it, Goldman's reputation as a repository of old-time investment-banking mores was a helpful asset that existed intellectually, in some vague, public relations type of way. In the world they had to live in, their customers were years removed from the white-shoe image of its past; all they honestly cared about was price and liquidity. To do that, with a competitive landscape that was getting more steep every quarter, was going to require a safecracker's touch if they wanted to remain independent.

■ ■ ■

The compete-for-every-trade mantra forced some profound changes upon the life of Andrew Davilman, a salesman who had joined Goldman in 1994 from Lehman Brothers. An unlikely candidate to become a salesman, he had started out as a mortgage derivatives trader and made the switch a few years later. He was neither inclined to overly socialize with his accounts—the drinking, dining, golfing, and the like that is the traditional lot of the bond salesman—and he was profoundly disinclined to hustle and scrap with every Tom, Dick, and Harry for the small orders that Messrs. Cohn and Blankfein had deemed important.

However, the Dartmouth grad was inclined to eat.

With a wife, young kids, and a house in Larchmont, Davilman began to hustle and scrape for the bits and pieces or revenue generation that made up what is known as *production.* Exactly what was commendable or woeful revenue production for a salesman was a fluid thing. What was good production on one desk was middling on another, and production that was substandard in a manic year like 2005 was heroic in 2008.

Of course, every business has elements of this, but what really kept the traders and salesmen on a desk off-balance was the utterly capricious approach of management. Unless you had a compensation guarantee, whether management was going to increase your bonus or inform that you and the firm were "moving in different directions" in a given year was not something you could ever really plan for. Thus, was Davilman willing to press his trader to give the best price for an order of $10 million Fannie Mae or Freddie Mac pass-through bonds—a trade that might contribute $10 or $15 annually to his bonus—something that was about as intellectually and economically unrewarding as sales-desk life could get.

Except, as Davilman saw it, damned if Blankfein wasn't kind of right.

As Davilman worked the phones in the autumn of 1998 into early 1999, he gradually learned that some really solid real estate companies were having the devil's own time raising enough capital because of a commercial real estate crisis. Specifically, even the better ones, with trophy projects, couldn't get capital for loans higher than 75 percent of the value of the property. There was just too much capacity in the market, and in cities like Atlanta and Phoenix, it seemed like banks had lent in 1996 and 1997 without even thinking about the shape of the marketplace.

Davilman had an idea. Why not have Goldman lend these developers the 15 percent or so difference between 75 percent and 90 percent loan-to-value? They could handpick the best of the market to work with, they would capture a really nice spread to even lower-rated corporates, and have it secured by some readily salable property.[9]

As lenders and its rivals flooded out of the commercial real estate market, Goldman entered. Grateful developers leapt at the chance to work with the firm, and they made a nice return with minimal risk.

Davilman was handsomely rewarded for his efforts, but, management wondered, couldn't he do even better? Wasn't there a way they make additional loans and take returns up into the 13 percent to 15 percent area? There was a hitch, of course. Goldman was not looking to compete with J. P. Morgan and become a bank, so they wouldn't be increasing the dollar volume of loans but their profitability. That was a nice way of saying, "Why don't you come up with a way of using leverage to increase returns without changing the low-risk nature of the deal?" In a warm and understanding tone that left little room for doubt, Davilman was encouraged to make these contradictory goals a priority. He was not without resources, though, since, as he was learning, when Goldman thought something was important, everybody got on board. In short order, he was dealing with people across the entire firm, from investment management to risk management, many of whom he had only the foggiest notion even existed. He hadn't asked for help, he wasn't sure more than a half-dozen people knew about the deal, but a partner thought it was important, and people dropped everything to converge on a salesman on the bond-trading floor. It was, he concluded, the opposite of Lehman Brothers.

Soon enough, he had cobbled together a structure. Goldman and a real estate fund it effectively controlled, Whitehall Advisors, would partner up to analyze properties and to manage the portfolio of loans. Borrowing was a challenge. Drilling down, though, into the type of company willing to do this short-term secured lending, to have the liquidity, to move quickly, and to above all understand what was trying to be accomplished with this did not leave many options.

A phone call to AIG Financial Products was his best chance to get the project going without the months of lead time, hassles, and delays that accompany everything traditional banks do.

As it so happened, Davilman covered FP, and so discussed a proposal with Alan Frost, a marketer there with whom he'd done a couple of CDO swap transactions earlier in the year. After some back-and-forth, FP said they were interested. As Davilman envisioned it, FP would contribute $2 of commercial paper to the fund for every $1 Goldman contributed. Goldman, however, would take the first loss position, as if they were the one contributing the majority of the capital.

It worked out.

They made just under a 15 percent return, there were no credit issues, and thankful real estate developers put Goldman at the top of their Rolodexes, which, one might say, was the point of the whole effort. FP earned a nice return for no real risk. It was, all agreed, a good deal.

Looking back on the handsome deal with colleagues, everyone agreed that the Goldman-coming-together-at-a-moment's-notice aspect was fruitful and moved things along, but in the end, you couldn't beat FP for having the knowledge base and strength to make deals occur. They were pitched the deal, asked for a few changes, and then studied it. After some back-and-forth that involved no shortage of lawyers from both places, a deal was struck. They protected themselves zealously, but coming from Goldman he couldn't really argue with that approach and FP really did move quickly. They got it. No explaining stuff repeatedly; it was like talking to a guy on the other side of the trading floor who saw exactly what you saw.

He was lucky to be at a place like Goldman that allowed salesmen to dream up deals and then execute them, and more than that, he was lucky to cover an account like FP that cared only about getting involved in unique, one-off deals that no one else was thinking of. For Davilman, there was no doubt about it: covering an account like Hartford Investment Management and doing 35 percent of their business was good, but taking that spreadsheet into your bonus meeting was a difficult proposition. Unless the volume of trades was so great that the profits were undeniable, he would need a few Hartford's to make a good year of it. However, as long as FP agreed to get in a deal, it was hard to see an outcome that wasn't going to be positive. They didn't screw around: they understood risk, and as long as it was structured so that they couldn't get hurt, they would make their money and he would get his deal.

Contrary to most stereotypes of bond salesmen, Davilman cared about the accounts he covered and wished to see them do well, if only out of a sense of self-preservation. With FP he would always rest easy, as they were the smartest people on the Street; there was zero probability of their doing something that could backfire. They saw and thought of *everything*. The world could nearly end and FP would likely have been short, or else had gone to cash.

There was never going to be a chance, Davilman thought, that Goldman was ever going to be smarter than FP in any deal or any trade. The process they used to vet risk and to favorably structure a deal was too thorough.

■ ■ ■

By 2001, Ram Sundaram had landed at Goldman Sachs. After Morgan Stanley's mini-implosion in 1998, Sundaram joined Merrill Lynch in 1999. If Morgan *was* saddled with some bad debts, it seemed to Ram that Merrill was a series of bad debts. In the crisis of 1998 Merrill had, apart from UBS, been deepest in the trough: they had exposure to every bad trade, had underwritten bonds and derivatives for every stressed sovereign borrower, and banked and touted every absurd dot-com. They had also hired armies of bankers and traders to whom they had guaranteed lavish contracts. Ram once heard someone refer to Merrill as a conservative place that its employees called "Mother Merrill." Ram would tell his friends that after just a few months there he had no idea what this person was talking about. Layoffs ruled, political factions were everywhere, business plans were made and scrapped at whim, but despite it all, he managed to hang on two years. It was no small feat.

When an old friend suggested him for a job at Goldman, he fairly leapt. There was a job description that included structured credit derivatives, but really, it was all left open-ended with the suggestion that he would develop a portfolio of his own. No one said as much directly, but the feeling he got was that since there wasn't much happening at the moment in that sector, the firm was stockpiling people.

Showing up at 85 Broad Street in early 2001 he was thankful to have the chance to be himself again: hardworking, friendly, and creative. That winter, everything structured credit—that is, bonds and derivatives that could be carved out of other fixed-rate bonds—was in the doldrums. Rates were sharply higher than they had been throughout the 1990s, so the gap between standard credit rates, whether it was mortgages, credit cards, or corporate bonds, was pretty narrow to the risk-free rate of return, around where the banks and brokerages financed themselves. Taking risk or stockpiling inventory wouldn't pay, so few did it.

Business was slow. While it seemed that a lot of people at Goldman appreciated his nonstop idea generation, an equally large amount didn't appreciate that many of his ideas encroached on their turf. So Ram hit the road, literally. Over the course of a few years, starting in Australia, he developed an infrastructure finance business. The Eurotunnel, the Chicago Skyway, the Rome airport—everywhere someone was building something, Ram's unit was seemingly in the mix, selling off old, troubled receivables in securitization, closing gaps in financing, hedging out risks with swaps, everything.

This portfolio, the majority of his business was handy for him in that it put a nice income in his pocket and made him a managing director, but it also allowed him to build out a pair of other portfolios that were most decidedly not helping his profit and loss in mid-2006.[10]

One of these was a systemic risk portfolio and included CDSs on banks, the monolines, and it included some of the negative-basis trades. Some of these were trades that looked good at the time, some might work out if certain conditions occurred, and some simply expressed Ram's view that something very stupid was going on in the bond market.

But he never silenced that desire to do something about the next 1998, about never being dependent on short-term funding again. He had discussed it with various colleagues at Goldman and, starting in 2004, was given approval to start seeking out and buying billions of dollars of longer-term funding from banks and insurance companies. This was Ram's third book.

What Ram was doing was the financial equivalent of the suburban couple who quietly stockpiled loads of freeze-dried and canned foods in their basement during the best of times for the categorical failure of modern society. The couple's risks are one of practicality (storage, spoilage) and decorum (people would think they were alarmist nuts); Goldman's were more basic. There was a fair chance that despite spending millions of dollars financing this stuff, the bank providing this excess balance sheet a few years later might decide that times had changed and the balance sheet was no longer excess. Ram imagined that they might dress it up in the guise of a just recollected duty to its shareholders, but the effect would be the same: Goldman could take its money back and go to hell.

Goldman Sachs was buying disaster insurance for a thousand-year storm. Ram could only hope that enough of the places he got longer-term funding capacity from were around when it got bad. There wasn't exactly a template for this; as far as he knew, he was the only person buying it.

Ten million dollars a year in insurance costs was nothing to Goldman, but it was something to Ram. He was in a perverse position: he was making that funding book into a quite a cost center, one that would pay off only when the bottom fell out. He had the blessings of all the bigwigs, but he had a lot of pressure to manage the various liabilities: he opened protection on banks and monolines at 12 basis points for five-year CDSs, but was long seven-year infrastructure finance loans elsewhere. Ram tried to be amiable on a daily basis, but underneath was a deep paranoia: his entire portfolio was constructed of concentric, fat-tail risks. He didn't need any poking from Goldman's risk managers to hedge and prepare for the worst; he worked 12-hour days trying to offset things like interest rate and volatility risk yet he didn't kid himself that there was a scientific way to hedge all risks and liabilities. The more he looked at the market, the more he was grateful for the revenue thrown off from his infrastructure finance book, since it subsidized his other portfolios. It cost plenty of money to put those trades on, he acknowledged, but there was a good chance they would wind up hedging not only his little group, but the firm. If not, it was just one more thing to worry about.

He liked Goldman plenty, and for a big firm they had a startup's mentality combined with a real teamwork ethos. But he had liked Morgan Stanley plenty, too. For now, having a nice profit-and-loss statement to point to at year-end, Ram knew, was the best hedge of all.

He just needed the right situation to present himself. He didn't sit on a trading desk making markets, so there was going to be no rally in convertibles, Japanese warrants, or U.S. Treasury bonds that he was certain to profit from. So he went back to basics: rates were low, and depending on where a trader could fund himself, the world of structured products was looking cheap. He'd do some work, bust his ass, and something would turn up. It always had.

■ ■ ■

Ram got his wish. As the Fed Funds rate dropped to record postwar lows in 2003–2004, the market for CDSs ballooned. Around since 1994, they were a tradable form of insurance on a corporation's perceived ability to meet its obligations.[11]

On the surface, they were simple enough: The buyer could purchase insurance against default on a $10 million block of corporate debt for a period of between 1 and 10 years. If the company were to default, the counterparty, or payor/insurance writer, would pay the buyer the $1,000 par value of the bond. Obviously, if the CDS buyer owned the paper below par, it would be a home run. Even if they bought the bond above par, and there was some sort of corporate disaster or fraud, they could at least recover par with CDSs.

Ram was not interested in owning corporate bonds and hedging them with CDSs; that market was too efficient. Instead, he saw one of the great arbitrage opportunities of recent times.

With brokers like Goldman funding themselves at just over 1 percent, buying bonds that paid 6.5 percent interest and then buying CDSs as a hedge for, say, 500 basis points (or 5 percent) was an easy trade to make. In this case, the interest rate paid from the corporate bond was more than the cost of the CDS, so traders like Ram locked in a "negative" basis in that he had no credit risk, with a risk-free profit locked in.

The negative-basis trade appears to be one of those arcane and dry ideas some unknown Wall Streeter conceptualized and, when overheard in a bar or train, caused the listener to turn away in boredom, wary of the coming glut of technical moneyspeak. In reality, it was simply a gussied up form of bond arbitrage, the likes of which Wall Street had practiced in one form or another since the early 1900s. Ram, of course, knew this, too. But what he saw was that the low rate environment also made it extremely advantageous to restart CDO issuance, and with the housing boom under way, there was an ample supply of home loans to carve into collateral. What investors didn't love to buy in volume (higher-yielding, riskier assets), CDO desks loved to buy and kept an eternal bid out in the market for this paper.

Ram was thinking that CDOs, which paid an interest rate sharply above his cost of funds, would be a great vehicle for the negative-basis trade if he could find CDSs that would effectively match—or correlate, in trader parlance—to the particular tranches of CDOs he was seeking to buy. But the CDO swap market was many times smaller than the corporate CDS market. To get a CDS on a CDO, you would have to approach a really sophisticated investor who understood risk intuitively and had substantial capital resources.

Ram was beginning to spend time thinking about this because he was starting to think something was really wrong with Wall Street again. He was no short-seller by disposition, but 1998 and the destructive force of leverage and crowded trades was still fresh in his mind.

So who could he buy swaps from? The options were surprisingly limited. Ruled out immediately were the monolines, the insurance companies like Ambac and MBIA that had evolved away from the sleepy business of insuring municpal bond issuers against default and into the growth business of guaranteeing the principal repayment of MBS and CDOs. Goldman's reasoning was simple: it had decided that as an investment bank there was no way they could "face" (be positioned opposite) the monolines directly as a hedge. The officially sanctioned reason was that the monolines never posted collateral as a matter of policy. This meant that if the CDS dropped in value, Goldman, which usually acted as a middleman in CDS trades, would be posting collateral but recieving none. Personally, Ram and a slew of other Goldman executives—including its risk-management staff—had flagged them as overlevered and undercapitalized. There was no way when something bad happened that anyone, let alone Goldman, was going to get paid in full.[12]

Unlike his previous jobs at Merrill and UBS, at Goldman talking about problems in a position, or challenges to maximizing profits, was not considered a sign of weakness or an invitation to steal an idea. Goldman, Ram had learned, pretty much insisted that you never shut up about what you were doing. The reason for this was simple: if you had a good idea that was making money, Goldman's management would want to be doing it as large as possible on as many trading desks as possible until it didn't make money anymore. There were no "lone geniuses" at Goldman.

In a series of conversations with his colleagues in the autumn of 2004, Ram laid out his conundrum. One of his colleagues, it so happened, was Andrew Davilman. He said he thought FP might have an interest and made a call. Getting hold of Alan Frost, the fellow he had been dealing with since his real estate lending proposal, he laid out the trade: *at what price was FP willing to ensure a few hundred million dollars' worth of the top-rated tranche of a Merrill CDO deal?*

Davilman knew there was something different about the issue the minute he got off the phone with Frost, and after chewing it over, he realized what it was: Frost had told him, "Sounds good. I'll get right back to you."

FP never, ever said anything to the effect of "I'll get right back to you." They had a cast of lawyers, marketers, and accountants breaking stones about this minute detail and that one. Davilman had completely braced himself for this process. A few hours later, Frost called Davilman back and told him he would do it for 9 basis points. FP, at least on Goldman's floor, was opened up for the negative basis trade. Ram had his arb, and he happily paid Davilman 11 basis points.[13]

A new avenue to trade was open, yes, but Davilman wasn't
going to get rich doing this, especially since most of the time FP was
involved, Goldman was acting as a middleman—FP was the guarantor
but another customer was the swap (or insurance) buyer. In other
words, if Goldman had a customer who wanted credit protection on
a CDO, Goldman would do it only if it could lay the risk off to
someone else.

This was a customer facilitation business for Goldman, which, as far
back as the 1990s, had seen, according to its risk-management staff, just
how completely and utterly carried away things might get with swaps.[14]
Every swap trade was netted out between a seller and a buyer, with the
only exception being when the firm would bet for its own account. In
the words of a Goldman partner, "Goldman was not getting paid
enough to guarantee any of this shit." In fact, for most of the swap trades
that launched a thousand conspiracies, Goldman earned one or two basis
points on the notional value of the trade.

Credit-default swaps were now that sort of incremental business
Davilman did simply to keep a customer on the phone and engaged. A
team player, he was happy to help Ram out, and he was glad to get
some business going with FP, since they were the type of customer you
always wanted to be in front of.

Still, it was hard work doing every trade, thought Davilman. He was
fortunate, he knew, since at every other firm the creative stuff he
dreamed up and loved would be taken over by investment bankers and
he would get cut out of it, only to watch passively as they screwed it up
into something beyond recognition. But hustling trades where Goldman was a middleman to earn just a basis point or two? That was just
something he did because he had to.

When the swap agreements went out, they had the CSAs attached.
Every swap Goldman did, with everyone from small hedge funds to
AIGFP, had a CSA attached. There was no negotiating on it or the
terms of the CSA, which was industry standard anyway. The bottom
line was that Goldman marked everything to market at least once a day,
so the underlying asset, the so-called reference security, would be
subject to their determination of prices. After all, since Goldman was the
middleman most of the time, they would also be making collateral
postings to their counterparty.

It was all pretty cut and dried. Frost returned the signature sheet a few days after the swap agreement arrived in Wilton with no questions asked and the swap was on.

That trouble was not anticipated is a ridiculous understatement. Everyone from Goldman's then-CEO Hank Paulson to Andrew Davilman viewed AIG and AIGFP the same way: the insurance industry's Goldman Sachs. They did business in a "best of breed" manner and made more money than everyone else because they worked harder and took smarter risks. If you were a Goldman partner, or wanted to be one, it was assumed that you would have a working relationship with your approximate counterpart at AIG. Goldman's trading desks risked capital to win AIG's trading business, and they took losses on trades to keep them happy. It was one of the central, long-standing relationships at the firm, the others being Bank of America, Ford, Fannie Mae, and a handful of others. A generation of Goldman general partners had called on Hank Greenberg and curried his favor; Hank Paulson would call and congratulate Martin Sullivan shortly after he took over.

There wasn't much left of the old Goldman Sachs, but the centrality of its relationship to AIG remained constant.

■ ■ ■

The negative-basis trade would be how institutional Wall Street—the professional money managers and the traders that served them—came to be stuck in the subprime quagmire, in one form or another.

It was to be a mania apart, and there were a few reasons for this. The first is that unlike traditional arbitrage trading strategies, where a trader seeks to take advantage of volatility in the underlying asset, price movement was going to be a big problem for many players. Much of Wall Street's structure, from ratings agencies to the CDO underwriters to the constellations of CDO managers, was heavily motivated to assume that there could almost never be an event or series of events that would lead to widespread declines in the value of real estate, the new collateral of choice for CDOs.

Normal credit research practices and, more profoundly, trader skepticism was thus suspended. Granted, there were reasons for this.

As noted previously, all risk-management models, at least the ones brokers and ratings agencies use, primarily look backward to assess risk that is in the future and were effective to the extent that the problems of the future correlate to the problems of the past; correspondingly, they were useless if problems were new or unprecedented. As was broadly and endlessly discussed—more of a set-up to a Straw Man argument, really, than an intellectual defense—the last event triggering a national home price collapse was the Great Depression. Since there hadn't been depression since the early 1930s, and from where most analysts sat then, a second one looked none too likely either, this was dismissed out of hand.

In 2000, whatever inclination there had been to perform detailed analysis of default probabilities for CDOs largely died. That was when a quantitative analyst at J. P. Morgan Securities named David X. Li released a paper in the *Journal of Fixed Income* that argued price trends from the CDS market could be used in analyzing possible default risks.[15] The thinking went that since prices broadly followed default risk, a mathematical model that tracked price trends could effectively establish a probability of default, as opposed to actually analyzing the loans underlying the securities and formulating individual assesments or, at least, the individual loan pools. Li's theory assigned a correlation number to the default risks inherent in each pool or, more simply, to the probability of defaults in similar loans being correlated.

It is impossible to understate the effect this had on the marketplace. CDO underwriters began to price and structure CDOs based on the belief that a *theory* of price association could be an effective predictor of defaults. Worse—vastly worse—so did the ratings agencies.[16]

The second development was that the system of hedges, and the leverage used to fund the investment in CDOs, permanently changed the landscape of economic relationships on Wall Street. The explosion of CDSs—approximately $920 billion in outstanding contracts in 2001 to $62 trillion in 2007—meant that a massive amount of swap risk was spread thoughout a group of a dozen swaps dealers. The best that could be hoped for was that the amount of contracts they paid out on would be netted evenly against the contracts they received payment from.

Adding to that was the fact that the collateral of the CDOs was entirely similar. If a housing crisis hit, it would matter very little if the originator of the loan was Countrywide or Citigroup or New Century. CDOs, starting in 2002, had absorbed so much real estate paper that the promise of securitization, the diffusion of risk, had been perfectly upended, guaranteeing that most CDO holders were wholly leveraged to the housing market.[17] To that end, with about $1.5 trillion in CDOs outstanding as of late 2005, whatever happened to CDOs was going to move instantaeously across national lines.[18]

Thanks to the the aforementioned dismantling of the Glass-Steagall Act in 1999, a bank like Citigroup became a marriage of the raw daily trading and securities inventory risk of its Salomon Brothers unit with the long-term loan exposures that every bank has to manage. That Salomon Brothers had run for generations on its own capital was lost to memory; it was now part of a massive conglomerate that used customer deposits to fuel trades and business lines, the size of which had never been imagined on Wall Street.

If something happened in the CDO market, it would happen to banks first, fastest, and longest. Banks had, of course, gotten themselves in tight spots under Glass-Steagall, most notably Citibank in 1989 under the weight of bad foreign loans and even worse domestic commercial real estate loans, but those were specific banks in specific markets. Equally, their troubles were contained. The fact that Citibank had made a slew of stupid loans in the 1980s didn't mean that Wells Fargo or a former giant like Securities Pacific necessarily had.

Now, because of the massive tilt toward both mortgage origination and capital markets activities across the banking universe, very few banks were going to be able to escape a housing crisis unscathed. They all had it on their books in one form or another. Real estate risk was everywhere in the modern bank: there were mortgage origination operations, trading and sales inventories, warehouse credit lines to mortgage companies, proprietary trading desks, CDO structuring books, prime brokerage operations and their loans to hedge funds, and, in an audacious new twist to the old conundrum of balance sheet expansion, structured investment vehicles, or SIVs. A form of perpetual arbitrage portolio, SIVs sprang from the loins of banks in the late 1980s and early 1990s and sought to issue short-term debt and buy longer-dated mortgage- and asset-backed securities with the proceeds. At $10 billion and larger, few knew how big they were or even that they were there.

A search of any analyst's report on a brokerage firm from 2002 to 2007 for the words *structured investment vehicles* is certain to be a waste of time. Yet putting these allegedly off-balance-sheet assets back onto balance sheets proved essentially fatal to banks in both London and New York.

If the storm came, the banks were in no position to act like banks. They were levered to the gills and had little unencumbered capital. No one would ask whom banks turn to for capital in a dark moment.

The investment banks, to turn a phrase on its ear, had morphed from their age-old roles in the shipping business to new ones in the storage business. They would learn there was a considerable difference between the two.

■ ■ ■

Ram Sundaram, for all of his running and cunning, was a token player in the largest trade in the history of the world. Talking to the likes of Deutsche Bank, Merrill, UBS, Royal Bank of Scotland, and others over 2004 and 2005, he saw that whole sections of skyscrapers in the financial districts of London and New York were now dedicated to manufacturing and selling variations of a CDO theme. Other sections of other skyscrapers were dedicated to buying the CDOs and seeking someplace to sell an index or get a swap written for hedging purposes. The collateral for these loans was everywhere and everyone that Ram saw: the houses and loans representing the hopes and plans of generations of American people.

About $1 trillion was deployed in this trade, mostly to one side. There was no vibrant debate or coterie of natural short-sellers or even a broader marketplace in which CDOs existed. If it came time to exit the trade, $1 trillion worth of an asset that had no natural buyer would be heading to the exits at the same time. Standing between par and zero were maybe 10 brokers and banks, each one more levered up than the next with similar paper.

Moreover, if anything happened to the health of about $3 trillion in real estate loans, whomever had written the CDSs in this cycle was going to have to write a massive number of checks in a small amount of time for an amount of money that Ram could not concieve of.

Ram was a freethinking man by nature, so he constantly reexamined his thesis, such as it was. Certainly, everyone was making money hand over fist in CDOs—his own firm, Goldman, would issue more than $50 billion of the things when all was said and done—it's just that he could never put behind what happened when he saw funding get pulled.

He would continue doing his negative-basis trades and trying to buy swaps on CDOs. He had bought up a lot of longer-term funding capacity and was confident that he would be able to help the firm ride out what might come.

When that might occur was anyone's guess.

Chapter 9

The Preservation Instinct

They stopped writing the collateralized debt obligation (CDO) swaps at FP because one man spoke up about an imbalance of risk–reward and a general deterioration of the subprime market.

That man was Andrew Forster, FP's London-based head of Asset Finance and a man who had Cassano's ear and his respect. Almost as soon as Frost had gotten moving on writing the swaps, Forster, according to his colleagues, had begun having misgivings. The former J. P. Morgan derivatives trader appears to have taken an orderly approach to voicing his concerns, letting Al Frost—who was a peer of his in the FP food chain, not someone who reported to him—continue to get a torrent of deals through.

In private conversations and in emails, Forster tried to persuade Cassano to see his point: subprime was a big problem that was only going to get much bigger.

Some of this is only natural as it was his profit and loss statement, ultimately, that was going to reflect any losses. But mostly it was because he was worried sick over the stuff.

That Forster could derail something that Cassano had come to view as a gravy train speaks to the love/hate relationship Cassano had with FP's traditions. It was tradition that FP stayed away from mortgages but it was also tradition that the place was run in a decentralized, collegial fashion. Though Cassano was not shy in making his points—making him appear dictatorial—he was in actuality devoted to consulting with his senior managers before making serious decisions. So when Forster started raising red flags early in the summer of 2005, Cassano encouraged him to flesh out his thoughts, even though the unit was booking millions of dollars a month in apparently riskless revenue from writing the swaps on CDOs.

On July 21, 2005, before the London and Paris offices scattered across southern Europe on their multiweek August holidays, Forster put together a conference call with Al Frost, Gary Gorton, and others to hash out these concerns. In an email Forster sent around framing possible subjects of discussion prior to the call, he noted, "We are taking on a huge amount of subprime mortgage exposure here and it is clearly a fast evolving market."

The balance of it reads like a short-seller's inventory of concerns: the inconsistency of ratings agencies views on asset-backed security (ABS) collateral, the fact that CDOs could have a swath of collateral down-graded to triple-C before they touch the CDO, whether they knew anything about the people managing the CDOs. In hindsight, the key takeaway from Forster's email appears to have been the least remarked upon: "Are we happy that the [ratings] agencies have it right and that we should be treating everything the same in our model?"

Forster, according to colleagues, was no less convinced after this call that his colleagues had a handle on the growing number of challenges in the subprime market. So they continued to write CDO swaps.

■ ■ ■

At the same time that Forster was letting it be known that he had concerns, a man named Gene Park, who worked in the corporate and structured transactions group in Wilton, was not shy about telling anyone he knew that he was growing plenty suspicious of mortgage credit.

In the heroic retellings of the tale, most especially in Michael Lewis's *The Big Short*, Park is the paradigmatic voice in the wilderness, warning about looming disaster.[1] Specifically, a ne'er-do-well friend of Park's, perpetually without cash, managed to secure a series of loans to buy a house despite a risible credit rating and no job at the time, something that shocked Park to the core; combined with a natural wariness over manias, Park became convinced that the market's mortgage absurdities were destined to end in collapse.[2] As the story goes, his warnings went ignored until he eventually convinced Cassano under the weight of his carefully groomed argument.

There is certainly some truth to this account: Park did hate subprime and mortgages as a rule, the friend (and his house) did exist and he told a half-dozen of his closer colleagues about his skepticism about mortgage credit. But that's about as far as things went. Cassano would testify under oath to regulators that Park never said a word to him and there does not appear to be a trail of emails or public conversations that would support Park's account.

There is a reason that Park's efforts probably did not go farther: Joe Cassano really didn't much care for Gene Park, according to many of their FP colleagues, and wasn't going to place much faith in stories about old buddies, stupid mortgages, and what it meant for Wall Street. He respected Park as a producer—he gave him the multisector CDO wrap business when Frost assumed a new role in January 2006—but he just didn't see eye to eye with Park on most things. Much of this is because of who Park is: unusually laid back, even for the generally unassuming FP culture, his one "weakness" was an inability to generally suck up to Cassano. Where others "yessed" him and then went about their business, Park would try to engage Cassano in a discussion or reason with him. While greatly amusing his colleagues, he completely failed in getting Cassano to take the wisdom of his points. Despite this, Park was a solid producer and broadly respected for his ability to execute all manner of deals.

So when Andrew Forster began raising questions in the spring of 2005, it was a no-brainer for Cassano to give his full attention to his London office colleague, friend, and key manager.

Forster sought to make a detailed analysis of the issue and to bring in senior colleagues in London and New York to bat the issue around;

Park simply wanted to stop doing the business. To Cassano, FP didn't just get into, or out of, businesses based on the feelings of one man—there was a process and a methodology. So Forster prevailed upon Cassano to give him a few weeks in the autumn of 2005 to really investigate the issue, something Cassano readily granted. Forster interviewed traders, analysts, mortgage originators, and others in the mortgage food chain and gradually refined the thesis he had been fleshing out in the late July 21st email and conference call. He told Cassano that he had been wrong to be skeptical; he should have been afraid. They were writing swaps on CDOs backed by poorly structured mortgages with massive concentration to single geographies like Florida and California. The ratings agencies were entirely mistaken, if not out to lunch. Cassano had sat in on a one or two of these meetings, along with Park, and seen some of what Forster saw. Apparently, it was enough. He agreed to stop the CDO swap business straightaway, over Frost's bitter objections.

On February 28, 2006, Park drafted an email memorandum that would be sent to dealers summarizing their new thinking on the issue: "We feel that the CDO of ABS has increasingly become less diverse over the past year or so and is currently at a state where deals are almost entirely reliant on subprime/nonprime residential mortgage collateral. . . ."

Save for one final deal, a $433 million CDO that had been shepherded through by Park himself that was yet to settle, they were out of the CDO business. Like American General Financial's Fred Geissinger, Cassano didn't make any grand declaration or even inform AIG's New York headquarters. It was just a business that they were in when it seemed right and now they were out of it.

■ ■ ■

When the CDO swap business was essentially shut down in the late autumn of 2005, FP had become the terminus of the CDO trade. They had just shy of $73 billion worth of exposure to CDOs that were comprised of residential mortgages that were issued to the economically marginal borrower in front of a looming macroeconomic slowdown. FP, via the credit support annexes (CSAs), were now dependent on the valuations from the massively overlevered broker trading desks that were responsible for perpetuating the absurd and abusive cycle of mortgage origination.

Seen from a few years remove, the question wasn't if FP would get hurt doing this business, but just how badly could things deteriorate? We know now the answer was, "a lot."

Cassano, Frost, and Gary Gorton appear to have believed, for varying reasons, that risk only came from having to pay out on the swaps should credit impairment occur; the CSAs locked them into mark-to-market risk. There appears to be no record of this even being considered or discussed. Indeed, FP appears to have had no real-time CDO pricing information, on the belief that CDOs issued at par stayed at par. Similarly, hedging, via an index or a custom-structured derivative, would have probably cost as much as the portfolio brought in annually. To FP, this was free money and was going to stay that way.

Gene Park was of course right: FP should never have entered the business. But that doesn't imply Cassano and Frost were necessarily equally wrong. Al Frost's job was to drum up deals and revenue from the major investment banks and he did. Cassano's job was to ensure that all decisions made at FP were logical and were made with all available information.

He failed.

Cassano, who had personally overseen the intake of hundreds of millions in dollars in premiums from writing CDO swaps, made the mistake that many unsophisticated investors make when he assumed the past safety of CDOs were a guarantee of future performance. Swaps on CDOs were treated as if they were insurance policies, amenable to a standard analysis—in this case Gary Gorton's models—and not a dynamic instrument created in a marketplace in flux. Because they refused to consider this, the issue of being at the mercy of CSAs became foreordained.

But Cassano did not fail in a vacuum. Hours of testimony given to various congressional and regulatory panels did not turn up a single instance of a New York–based AIG senior manager sending so much as an inquisitive email about a swaps portfolio that amounted to 75 percent of AIG's equity base. That Martin Sullivan and Steve Bensinger said nothing is now well established. But neither did Financial Services chief Bill Dooley, his CFO Elias Habayeb, Risk management chief Bob

Lewis and his head of credit-risk Kevin McGinn. Anastasia Kelly's legal department was similarly silent. These people saw everything FP did in real time and had plenty of authority to force at least a reevaluation. It was, in fact, their job to do this.

But they did nothing.

Cassano justly deserves blame for failing to at least consider the swaps in CDOs in a critical light; save for Anastasia Kelly (who retired) every other person in the line of oversight of the FP swaps book is now gainfully employed as an officer at a publicly traded company with as much or more responsibility than they had previously.[3]

That is less explicable.

■ ■ ■

It didn't help matters that the ratings agencies had put in place a series of policies that provided every incentive for FP or other monoline guarantors to get into the CDO business.[4]

Starting in 2002 the ratings agencies made it less capital efficient to guarantee the traditionally low-risk municipal business that had long been the monoline's bread and butter. Via lower capital reserve charges—that is, the amount that an FP or its competitors, Ambac and MBIA, had to hold in cash reserves against the swaps they wrote—on supposedly diversified and noncorrelated CDO pools, it made more sense for monolines to ease up on municipal guarantees and to move into the CDO business. Since the market provides what its regulators will demand of it, the word got out quickly that a dollar of monoline capital went farther in the CDO guarantee business.

It worked like this: if a monoline or FP guaranteed a $500 million slice of a CDO they would have a 10-basis point reserve requirement, obligating them to hold $500,000 of capital in reserve against the possibility of default. In turn, they would get nine basis points in annual premium, or $450,000, annually over the expected 10-year life of the deal. According to this formula, the premiums could generate the 12 percent annual return that the ratings agencies were looking to see generated from these portfolios.

This represents an inversion of the practices a ratings agency is supposed to reward. Because one sort of insurance writing generated marginally higher profits it was rewarded while the other insurance writing—for a line of business where default is exceedingly rare because of the power of taxation municipalities have—was penalized.

When ratings agencies connected maintaining the monolines' triple-A status to the meeting of their internally generated profit models, as opposed to consistent patterns of superior cash-flow generation and balance sheet management, it can be safely said that Wall Street has slipped its moorings.

Unsurprisingly, with a mandate to get CDO deals done, more deals got insured and trillions of dollars of triple-A paper was created. As if that wasn't enough, it heightened the competition to guarantee CDOs, keeping premiums lower. When FP left this market, Ambac and MBIA happily picked up the slack.

To FP, this was hardly some ivory tower diversion. In guaranteeing nearly $54 billion worth of CDOs in the second half of 2005 the fact that they had to reserve $54 million in total was thought to be the height of smart capital deployment.

■ ■ ■

When Bertil Lundqvist got the call from Eliot Spitzer he was contemplating getting out a little early. It was a Friday in December 2005, not much was going on and his boss Hank Greenberg was out of the office. Lundqvist, the general counsel of C. V. Starr & Co. had a ton of work to be done but a chance to get out at a civil hour didn't come around all that often when you worked for Hank Greenberg.

Getting out early soon became the last thing on his mind.

The attorney general cut to the chase.

"Bertil, I want you to tell Hank that unless he settles the accounting charges for $750 million, I will expand my investigation into the Starr Foundation."

"I'm sorry, can you repeat that?" said Lundqvist. It was an old lawyer's trick, of course—the connection was fine—to buy five seconds for processing what he was hearing but it served its purpose. Spitzer, audibly annoyed, spoke slower and louder and repeated his demand for three quarters of a billion dollar settlement or he would launch an investigation into a *charity*.

Good to have that cleared up, Lundqvist thought.

Lundqvist assured the AG that he would drop everything and relay everything to his boss.

"Oh, and Bertil? I want it by Monday. Thank you."

He picked up the phone to call Hank Greenberg and when he found him, he and Greenberg were happily going to ruin David Boies's weekend, along with more than a few of his partners.

■ ■ ■

"Eliot wants $750 million or he'll do—*what!?*

Boies got the phone call during the firm's annual retreat weekend in Jamaica. Over the past year, the incredibly high-profile Boies had devoted nearly two-thirds of his time to Greenberg's wars—with Spitzer, with the Securities and Exchange Commission (SEC), with the hovering federal prosecutors and with AIG above all—and had become his confidante and strategist.

It was surreal. This case had officially become unlike anything he had ever been involved with.

A summer intern in Spitzer's office had come across documents relating to the 1968 sale of the just deceased C. V. Starr's shares to back to Starr's companies the previous summer—per his estate's instructions—and had misconstrued some of the conversion features of the transaction to mean that Greenberg and others had been engaged in some massive self-dealing.

That the intern had made a serious, if honest, mistake was beyond doubt. A week earlier they had sat down with him and his chief lieutenant, Michelle Hirschman, and showed them Starr's will and testament, fairness reports from a law-firm, Morgan Stanley's 1970 analysis of the transaction, years worth of audits and disbursements and, apparently, it wasn't somehow enough.

A few weeks later Spitzer released a letter to the Starr Foundation's board—simultaneously leaked to the media—arguing that the sale of Starr's shares at what he claimed were low prices ripped off his estate and foundation to the tune of what now amounted to billions of dollars. He effectively ordered the Starr Foundation to conduct a full investigation or he would. Incredibly, in what would have been a career-threatening breach of ethics in any law firm or prosecutor's office any Boies, Schiller partner had ever heard of, in filing the letter electronically, Spitzer copied the judge presiding in the New York Supreme Court matter, as well as the judge presiding in a Starr International Co. case.[5]

Later that night, over drinks with his partners Lee Wolosky and Nick Gravante, they pondered what the hell was *really* going on here. On the one hand, this was as ugly an approach as any of them had ever seen. Spitzer was using his popularity and media caché to destroy Hank Greenberg. There was really no other purpose to pursuing this approach. Executives who are accused of jiggering numbers often can rebuild a life, if not a career; people who loot charities generally leave public life for good. A whole lot of Manhattan had a plaque on it somewhere that said it was funded in whole or in part from a Starr Foundation grant. Much of that goodwill might be forgotten in a few years.

Looking beyond that, though, Spitzer was getting sloppy and perhaps even desperate. The attorney general's office had millions of pages of discovery and with all the powers they had, *this* was their strongest approach? This was the way they forced Hank to the table? If Eliot had something—and he couldn't since the Starr Foundation's construction was beyond kosher—he wouldn't play these games. Short-term it would naturally be a win for him since everything was a short-term win for him with his media access. Longer term, however, it might be the opposite.

Here and there cracks were beginning to show in the financial reform juggernaut that was Eliot Spitzer. A Bank of America mutual fund small-fry named Ted Sihpol who steadfastly refused to fold when Spitzer's office squeezed him to bolster its case in the fund-timing scandal mortgaged his house and beat the attorney general's best trial lawyers in open court. Ken Langone and Dick Grasso, the centerpieces of the attorney general's battle to reform the New York Stock Exchange, were positively tying Spitzer up in knots. Then there were courthouse rumors that some of the easy victories in the insurance bid-rigging cases were not so solid. And in Greenberg, well, Spitzer had met a foe who would happily spend $10 million to delay a deposition until he had gotten the documents he requested. Whatever Langone and Grasso spent on defense, Greenberg was going to double.

Everyone could see Spitzer was going to be the next governor. Someone was going to take notice of the inconvenient fact that the battles that had garnered him so much favor and publicity were now getting harder and harder for him to win. Threads would eventually be connected and uncomfortable questions asked.

From where Boies and his partners sat, he had nothing on their client. Boies called the attorney general early the next day and told him "no."

■ ■ ■

The AIG short was not working out as planned for Jim Chanos. He had shorted it in the mid- to upper $50 range more than a year prior and the stock was now bouncing around the upper $60 level in the spring of 2006. The stock opened the year at $70.11 and would spend most of the year in the upper $60 range. Just when it looked promising and drifted down into the upper $50s it would spike up past $70 again. It was rare, in Chanos's experience, to have sustained the level of drama that AIG had: auditors refusing to sign off, the AG suing the CEO and CFO, $1.6 billion charge to square a half-dozen things away, and not have an appreciable share price collapse.

But investors wouldn't budge.

He and his analysts picked apart every 10-Q AIG released. Nothing, not a single thing contradicted their thesis. AIG, as they saw it, wasn't even pretending to be anything other than a heavily levered money-management machine. Sure, the insurance subsidiaries did well, but the footnotes of every quarterly release showed they were getting deeper and deeper into everything that was highly levered like real estate and portfolio management. He had no idea what on earth was going on with that guarantee thing AIG appeared to be doing but he doubted it had gone away.

The one new thing on AIG Kynikos had picked up was from his partner Alan Best (who ran his securities borrowing program), who was hearing from his old friends in the stock borrow/stock loan community that AIG was somehow massively expanding their securities lending program. As the story went, they were printing money. Best had told Chanos that if this was true, they were probably making some sort of interest rate bet and that it could well end in a bloodbath. If even half of this was true, Chanos would tell his analysts, this was a total freak show.

None of which explained why most every day a position that should have been paying him would up taking money out of his cash position.

Most every short-seller is patient by nature since they identify troubles that might take years to manifest. Chanos was different. He had a strict discipline: if a short went more than 10 percent against them, they pulled out their thesis and reexamined it. If they still had conviction, they might wait and short more. Another 10 percent to 20 percent and they would usually begin to cover.

Chanos respected his friends and colleagues at other short-selling funds who would ride a short out and take $25 per share or more of pain, ironclad in their conviction that they had uncovered a troubled stock or even fraud. He liked to guarantee that he would always live to fight another day, something he accomplished by not subjecting his investors to massive losses. It did not escape him that in the middle of 2006, there were no more than a handful of dedicated short-sellers left; there once had been many. Heroic stands against market insanity and corporate corruption usually made for nice newspaper copy, but they also tended to kill the short-seller.

Tough positions were Chanos's lot in life and bullish markets the norm. But the legal and regulatory backdrop to daily life was not very pretty for Kynikos. The chairman of the SEC, former congressman Christopher Cox, egged on by senators like Robert Bennett and Orrin Hatch of Utah, now actively sought to investigate short-sellers for fomenting alleged conspiracies to drive share prices down.[6]

He kept the AIG position on though. Everything he was seeing told him that the real estate bubble was going to bust very soon. When it did, banks, brokers, mortgage companies, and a dozen other interconnected spokes of the financial wheel were going to skid to a halt. AIG would probably take a black eye or two in that mess and he would get paid for his almost yearlong headache.

He had no idea what would act as a catalyst, though. In a bull market, betting against the icons of the business establishment when the regulators were on your back was an exercise in just trying to keep your head above water.[7]

■ ■ ■

The ratings agency imposition of ridiculous capital reserve requirements were the only real guardrails for FP.

For most of the first 13 years of its existence FP didn't have a formal regulator, so beyond what Greenberg imposed on the unit, there was no one outside of its auditor to independently analyze and assess its operations.[8] Things changed in 1999 when AIG set up AIG Federal Savings.[9] The thought behind it was simple, according to Ed Matthews. AIG would, in owning a savings-and-loan, have an alternate funding source for the Financial Services unit, which to their way of thinking, could always use another option for strategy or to access the markets if things ever got tight. A secondary consideration was a sense that a well-run thrift could be a nice business in the longer term (but would remain something to be considered in the future).

So Greenberg and Matthews got their thrift. AIG, in turn also got a regulator, since anyone owning a thrift was automatically under the supervision of something called the Office of Thrift Supervision (OTS). Coming into existence in 1989 in the wake of the savings-and-loan collapse, the OTS had a simple mandate: ensure that savings-and-loans never again risk their equity in ill-considered schemes.[10]

The job of an OTS examiner is straightforward because savings-and-loans are straightforward: they collect deposits, maintain checking accounts and issue very plain mortgage loans of the 30-year, fixed interest rate variety. Their investigators were honest and thorough, but given the lack of complexity of 90 percent of the thrifts, they were not likely to have developed skill sets for analyzing complex liabilities and capital markets operations. Less well-funded and prestigious than the SEC or Department of Justice (DoJ), aggressive, and already-trained analysts were hard to come by and harder to retain.

That was a shame since AIG was nothing but complex liabilities and capital markets operations that required skill and experience to wade through. Examining it for safety and soundness was a multimonth job that could take several hundred people. OTS had maybe a dozen, sometimes more, and maybe a month to get it done.[11]

Some very hard decisions were forced upon OTS in terms of investigative efforts. The 2006 audit of FP is evidence the first of this. A detailed summary of the nearly completed first quarter's business activity, it lists revenue figures for each of the major business groups and the percent it changed from the year prior. With a more seasoned team, the 396 percent increase in credit revenues should have been a major conversation starter.

In a not quite two-page summary of FP, this is what was noted about the credit-default swap (CDS) portfolio:

> The Credit revenue segment, which primarily represents revenue on credit derivative and asset transactions, showed a significant dollar increase due primarily to an increase in the aggregate notional amount of super senior credit derivative transactions.

There is no further analysis or breakdown of this, nor an attempt to quantify the risk it posed. Despite having access to the unit, its officers and its books, the analysis shows that OTS appeared to not have enough a basic level of curiosity about massive revenue and balance sheet growth.

However, it does give the sense that they had left their car running downstairs.

■ ■ ■

Toward the end of November 2006, a man who gave every appearance of being on top of the world would have been happy to stop the merry-go-round and get off. Goldman Sachs employees anticipated a record-breaking bonus season, as the firm had set aside $16.5 billion for its bonus pool, or more than $620,000 per employee.[12] Dan Sparks, Goldman's mortgage chief, was due for some handsome tribute. Having taken over the position as the sole partner in charge of the 500-person mortgage and real estate finance group just four months earlier from his friend and fellow partner Jon Sobel, the 39-year-old Sparks was due a career-high payout because of his group's huge production.[13]

But none of this made Sparks feel terribly enthusiastic. That's because in the third and fourth weeks of November 2006, in an event happily ignored by the balance of humanity save for the few thousand souls then trading or analyzing securities made from home loans of varying stripes, the series of separate-yet-linked economic events that would become known as "the credit crisis" began.

All said, for something that would in relatively short order pose a grave threat to the economic safety of the free market, the credit crisis had a dull beginning. It started in Excel spreadsheets, row after row of sterile numbers on a seemingly benign report titled "Early Pay Default" that usually was scanned and then saved in some sure-to-be-forgotten electronic cache on a trading desk assistant's computer. This time, sharp eyes at every firm looked at the numbers and came to the same ines- capable conclusion: a record-breaking number of mortgage borrowers were defaulting within six months of taking a loan out. There had always been a tiny sliver of borrowers who fell victim to some horrific life circumstance, or were plain old scammers, but this was more than that. Loan pool analysis at respected mortgage companies like Ownit Mortgages and H&R Block's Option One Mortgage were showing north of 5 percent of their recent origination were not even making it to six months.

That was a sign, as a trading desk chief at Credit Suisse put it, "of the looming apocalypse." But the final default number wasn't what made grown men pale. It was the trajectory of the number; it was growing by half again every month. Where were all the mortgage originators going to be in three months? Nine percent? *Eleven*? If an important client of Wall Street like Ownit[14] was at 5 percent, where were the really aggressive places like Novastar Financial going to come in?[15]

Valid questions, all.

What these numbers said to an experienced analyst was more than just horrific underwriting standards and the mounting specter of widespread fraud. They saw that a large segment of borrowers had been buying homes on the expectation that they could either rapidly refinance into a lower rate, sell it for a profit, or borrow against the property's (presumably increasing) value to get the cash they needed.

But that was very 2004. The Fed had been raising rates for over two years and there were widespread slowdowns in home sales, with prices beginning to slip in many of the hotter markets in the Southwest, Florida, and most of all California.

In Wall Street's impersonal and clinical fashion, this burgeoning destruction of personal wealth begat a series of questions that were parsed with Talmudic seriousness:

- If you (plausibly) assume that nearly 10 percent of the borrowers would default within six months of the loan, how many of the more serious and law-abiding borrowers were likely to fall behind as rates rose and, perhaps, the economy slowed?
- More importantly, how long until the problems of "the marginal borrower" dribbled into the new home sales market?[16]

Regardless, one thing was very clear in the autumn of 2006: many mortgage originators were going to collapse.

Sparks had seen an inkling of some of the problems in early summer over the issue of "put backs," or loans they had the right to return to mortgage originators because they had defaulted. As Goldman was forced to put back an increasing amount of crummy loans to the likes of Fremont General and Mortgage Lenders Network (MLN), they simply refused to pay. Goldman's lawyers thought they had a trump card in these negotiations when they would point out that the borrower didn't even make the first payment, but the originators still refused. It became easy after a few rounds of this to conclude they were playing these games because they didn't have any money.

So Goldman cut warehouse lines and bought credit protection on many of these lenders in the event of bankruptcy, because it had hundreds of millions of dollars' worth of exposure. Still, Sparks's suggestion that the sector itself—including Countrywide Financial—was showing every warning sign of beginning to contract, if not collapse, was met with scorn in many sections of Goldman. Especially dubious of Sparks's suggestion were the investment bankers and the bond salesmen, who relied on the transactions they generated from their capital-hungry clients.

Always thinly capitalized, in their fat years the independent mortgage companies had not seen fit to grow their capital base and were unprepared for the deluge of loan put-backs that Wall Street brokers were forcing them to repurchase at par value. It was, as traders at J. P. Morgan would joke among themselves, merely a question as to who then would be "the host monkey," the first independent mortgage company to fall. On December 5, they (and their competitors throughout Manhattan and Connecticut) had their answer when Ownit Mortgage Solutions announced it was ceasing operations the following day.

That many others were infected with the combination of low capital levels and troubled loans was something no one doubted. Jokes about disease and viruses were apropos as it gradually dawned on the trading desk rank-and-file that most firms had so-called warehouse lines of credit outstanding to these originators that allowed them to fund their loans. (The big brokers had lent the independent mortgage companies [IMCs] billions of dollars so they could have product for their massively profitable mortgage-backed securities desks. The IMCs would use this capital to make and fund loans and then sell those loans back to the brokers. Obviously, this set in motion a disastrous cycle: If they didn't use the capital to make loans, they would lose it. So they made loans to increasingly marginal borrowers to maintain their credit lines.)

Gradually at first, and then picking up some steam, hedge fund investors and other money managers started cutting back on their exposure to the type of person who could take a loan out in January and default by Memorial Day. The brokers followed suit. At J. P. Morgan, their trading desks joked about "host monkeys," but their management ordered the warehouse lines pulled at Ownit and reduced sharply everywhere.

■ ■ ■

By the last week of November, Dan Sparks was spending most of his time trying to figure out whether the selling in subprime loans was a correction or a capitulation.

It felt like neither.

There was a lack of immediacy to this, a lack of, for want of a better word, violence. Weak hands were not being identified and forced into the open and then out of the market. Prices were not careening. The selling across the sector was constant, but it was not panicked. It could be considered orderly, save for one factor: there really weren't any buyers. That was what shocked him—a sales force as good as Goldman's couldn't surface any buyers. All the archetypes that seemed to exist in every market—the savvy bottom feeder, the overseas account hungry for yield, the inveterate optimist—were sitting on their hands.

He understood why many of his colleagues and customers hoped this was a correction. Corrections are generally good for a market, forcing weaker and less experienced investors to capitulate and sell. But this *drip, drip, drip* was different. There was no coalescing event. Rates didn't spike, and no massive player collapsed. Outside of the Early Pay Default reports, nothing forced anyone to change the way they thought about the business.

When he traded emerging market debt in 1998, he saw a correction become a capitulation. When Russia defaulted on its debt, it forced *everyone* to value assets differently. Wall Street's then-massive proprietary trading units (who all had variations of the same trade on) had to simultaneously sell most everything they could because one of their biggest trades, Russia's debt, was for the time being nearly worthless.

This was not that, at least yet.

Sparks did not fear a correction. If you could take the pain and had managed your risk well, corrections could be a blessing over the long haul, since whoever was left alive after the smoke cleared had an ample supply of cheap, good paper to trade and most customers were happy to find someone to do business with. Finally, every correction had that one key customer that threw up his hands and took the losses when he sold a portfolio to the highest bidder, setting prices lower and forcing rational decisions to be made from lower valuations. That didn't happen. It was like people *couldn't* sell for fear of something.

As November faded into December, it became clear to Sparks that no one was really willing to buy this paper at anything like current prices. There were bids here and there but no real stabilization— somebody nibbling at this price or a fund covering a short at another. Certainly, none of the brokers of Wall Street had any real appetite for the paper they had underwritten.

His own trading desk, which was long something called the ABX. HE index to the tune of about $1 billion, was having trouble reducing its exposure. A series of credit-default swaps based on an index of 20 separate subprime mortgage bonds, they were a popular way for traders to speculate on or hedge against payment defaults in the underlying subprime mortgage bonds. If the index dropped in value, that was taken as a signal that investors were getting bearish; a rise was bullish.

He talked to clients who talked to his competitors at UBS, Merrill, and Citigroup and found himself even more confused. At Goldman, subprime was something they owned because their customers traded it. At those other shops, it was a key to their business model, yet they appeared to be cruising along as if nothing was changing. Everybody knew UBS ran a huge book, into the many tens of billions of dollars worth of subprime bonds, loans that they were in the process of carving into bonds and CDOs made from subprime bonds. But the valuations they were showing their customers, who were also Goldman's customers (and Lehman's customers and Credit Suisses's customers) indicated (at least on the CDO front) that everything was hunky-dory.

Sparks could care less where UBS or the others marked their own books. But in an era where all investment banks had such close connections to hedge funds via their prime-brokerage operations, decisions made on UBS's mammoth trading floor in Stamford definitely affected him. If UBS was marking bonds and CDOs higher than Goldman, a hedge-fund that used both firms as a prime-broker (and there were dozens that did this) would have its portfolio's value assessed using valuations from both brokers. If there were sharp disparities, the fund's management would have pointed and justifiable questions for the firm with lower marks. The concern was hardly academic. A hedge fund's management is paid a percentage of the profits they generate, and if a major investment bank said the value of a CDO or subprime bond was sharply lower than another's that was a big barrier to higher returns for their investor and higher pay. The fund manager could use the higher valuation, but if an investor were to ever litigate there could be big liability if the manager went with the higher number and the position lost value.

Finally, this was a problem for Sparks because Goldman was lowering its marks on everything to do with subprime bonds. He had personally overseen a wide-ranging process of lowering valuations across the subprime mortgage universe. As part of that, the prices of hundreds of CDOs were lowered, many below par, which in turn triggered margin calls. There were few buyers for anything to do with this universe, plenty of sellers and what trades did occur, were occurring at lower and lower prices. Four years later, he stands by his thinking: an honest trader marked his book up when his positions appreciated in value and took the pain when they dropped.

Wall Street hates the outlier, the analyst with the recommendation to sell a stock short or to buy a much beaten down laggard and because of Dan Sparks and his traders, Goldman was now the outlier. As the firm with lower marks many "questions" were directed to them—and specifically Dan Sparks.

Sparks had been certain that most of the marketplace held this view. As such, he was wholly unprepared for the firestorm that came his way.

The complaints took many different forms. Some merely called their Goldman sales coverage and, well, complained. Some called a bit further up the food chain to Tom Montag, the newly appointed head of the Securities Division, and announced they would pull back their trading through Goldman. Some didn't call at all; they just ended the relationship.

Some picked up the phone and called Lloyd Blankfein directly. His staff handled the overwhelming majority of these, which often ended up back on Sparks's desk. A few got through to Blankfein, who stood behind Sparks in the face of what were some serious allegations of stupidity, perfidy, and sloth.

Anger, threats, lost business—all of it was understandable to him. This was careers and livelihoods and for his customers, a matter of moral importance since they were trusted with investing the hard-won capital of pensions, families, and foundations across the globe.

The issue of leverage made matters worse. If an investor owned subprime paper or CDOs at par (or a price of $1000—the last zero is dropped in trading shorthand) and it dropped to $90, they were down 10 points, and that was bad, but at least they had title free and clear to a $90 asset. It was a little more complex when borrowed money was involved.

If they used leverage from Goldman's prime brokerage of four-to-one to buy that CDO at $100, that meant that they had borrowed $4 for every dollar of investor capital they put in. To maintain their equity of 25 percent (or $25), they had to inject $2.50 into the account.

Multiplying this $2.50 times the millions of dollars worth of bonds a hedge fund typically held shows just how rapidly losses can eat through a fund's capital. In the example above, a $50 million tranche of CDOs that dropped $10 in price would require $1.25 million in cash to be deposited with the prime broker before the close of the next business day. To add some immediacy to it, consider that to varying degrees across the fund's portfolio there were other margin calls on subprime bonds and CDOs based on Goldman's valuation.

Then multiply that fund by a factor of 100.

Usually, when markets are in the process of revaluing assets and a section of the investment world—and the trading desks that serve them—are caught off-guard and saddled with losses, they function fairly decently. Customers are willing to trade and receive "price discovery" on both the securities they want to buy and to sell, with brokers competing for orders as prices, like water, generally find a new level. Time after time, whether in the wake of the October 1987 crash, the week after September 11, and during the bond-market tribulations of 1994 and 1998, the investors who didn't lose their shirts picked up the phone to brokers and got back to business.

This time, however, it felt to Sparks like people who managed CDOs were just stalling. They were too afraid to sell, but furious over every last penny Goldman marked them lower.

■ ■ ■

Sparks understood what his clients were going through—as a trader he had lost his fair share of money over the years—but there was nothing he could or would do about it. The value of these securities was what the marks said they were.

A true believer in Goldman's culture of "long-term greediness," Sparks, like many of his colleagues, was alternately bemused and baffled at the so-called mystique that had emerged over how Goldman conducted its business so much more profitably than its competitors. It sure as hell wasn't because people were that much smarter or harder working in his building, nor (as Sparks now knew first hand) because its customers were overly fond of the firm. If there was a reason, Sparks and many of his colleagues insist, it was because the firm's traders and sales staff bought into the marking regime. It was interesting, bordering on unique, how the highly educated trading corps at Goldman accepted the value of precise valuation, similar to how a young recruit eventually surrenders himself to the Marine Corps ethos at some point in boot camp. It wasn't questioned or much talked about, it was just done. If there were questions or disagreements, the trader could leave.

Much had changed at Goldman Sachs over the years. It employed over 25,000 people, it was publicly held, and there was an incessant spotlight on the firm culturally and politically that no one could have envisioned. But if you could argue there was one constant from the early days as cotton merchants, it was its slavish devotion to the idea of market pricing. The philosophy behind a trade, or why a trader got into it in the first place is one thing, but at Goldman a trade is only what its price said it was at that moment in time.

If it sounds complex, it really wasn't.

Broadly, when a security's price changed in a material fashion— 5 percent moves up or down and then again for dollar volumes made or lost—other people at Goldman got involved. Every firm on Wall Street employs some variation of this system. Goldman's was different simply because they uniformly acted on it.

Much of the diffusion of the credit crisis, or the parts that directly bear on the investment banks, can be traced to traders, risk-management and unit-chiefs ignoring exceptionally clear warning signals from their own risk-management staffs and systems. Merrill Lynch, UBS, Citi, Bear, and Lehman all had numerous occasions where senior management overrode their risk-control staff to maintain or expand their holdings. The difference at Goldman? The risk-management chief, Craig Broderick and the small army of analysts who worked for him, had unlimited authority to question, dispute, or analyze anything the firm did with capital. He worked down the hall from chief financial officer David Viniar and was able to raise any issue with him or Blankfein and Gary Cohn, Goldman's president and chief operating officer, at a moment's notice.

Goldman's experience was by no means perfect, especially in remaining heavily engaged with underwriting and trading the loans that helped the explosion of leveraged buyouts get done, but it ensured that from the third week of November 2006 onward, a wide diversity of experienced eyes were focused on a series of portfolios that most of the firm wasn't aware even existed.

Goldman was a trading shop, but unlike Salomon or Kidder or First Boston (now known as Credit Suisse) and dozens of other Wall Street firms going back through time, there weren't many "star" traders. There were no shortage of very rich traders, but none with accounts that no one saw or understood. It was a common occurrence for a risk-control staffer to have a trader pulled off a desk to discuss his valuation or risk parameters on a portfolio.[17]

By the last week of November there were risk managers in Sparks's office, and he was constantly on the phone with CFO David Viniar. The subprime paper hadn't tripped the 5 percent price-decline limit, but it did hit the dollar-loss targets. It was for the good of all involved, but being in that kind of spotlight wasn't what he wanted and many traders felt it actually limited their thinking and forced them to act hastily.[18] Then again, limiting traders' options is exactly what the system is designed to do. Often, the trader is emotionally connected to his positions, so people with no agenda and no economic connection asking tough questions leads to better answers.

Put another way, the Goldman system flags a purely quantitative data point (losses in dollar amount or percentage declines) and suggests a host of qualitative considerations. If a trader with a PhD can't enunciate the reason for staying with a losing trade to a junior risk analyst, that's a problem. If that trader can elaborate a host of reward scenarios comfortably to anyone up through senior management, then that would give management a sense that the trader is engaged with the problem.

Goldman's management also had a keen understanding that it was only an investment bank, as opposed to a commercial bank, and could not assume that it would have unlimited access to funding or capital. Supposing that a position of $100 million that dropped 10 percent would "come back" in full in two weeks was a very different proposition for Goldman than it was Merrill or J. P. Morgan. If Goldman got any part of a large trade wrong, there would be no customer deposits or massive retail network to replenish the capital and smooth over the earnings blemish.

That hedges failed and earnings projections were missed and "asymmetric events" occurred was understood by Sparks and his colleagues. In fact, all of Goldman's downside projections—the worst-case scenario—included a total loss of capital. Over the years, the firm had found that if traders understood what it looked like to model for losing their capital, it encouraged more effective hedging strategies.

What Goldman's management was really good at, if everything else was stripped away, was ensuring that through wars, depressions, and everything in between, the firm was run with an eye toward the next looming crisis. If you have the ability to drop everything and run out of a building the fastest when it catches fire, you are fortunate. If you can do it for nearly 140 years consecutively, then it's fair to say that it's a talent you have worked hard at developing.

■ ■ ■

Sparks's first meetings with the CFO Viniar and Gary Cohn came about one week after he started marking the subprime world down.

One of the benefits of the pricing regimen was the relatively efficient information flow that allowed Viniar and Cohn to know most everything Sparks did, so meetings tended to be thankfully brief.

Cohn and Sparks had known each other for years, so Sparks felt he had credibility when he said that he had no idea what to expect from the position. Credibility was important since they didn't have a ton of warmth for each other.[19] In response to questions of what the future might bring, Sparks could only reply that they were hedging it as best as possible with credit default swaps and the newly launched ABX index but without buyers, who knew?

Sparks wasn't going to have his traders stand in the gap and support the market, being the only bidder in an effort to stabilize a fallen market even if Goldman had underwritten quite a few of these deals. Since 1989 he had seen plenty of investment banks become either parts of commercial banks or become former investment banks. Much of that was because their trading desks got in the way of a market seeking its natural level.

So though backing his decision was never in doubt, neither was their message: get the losses back.

One of the things Sparks and other senior Goldman officials found people misunderstood about their firm was the widespread

misperception that its culture was one of deep and abounding collegi-
ality. Nothing could be farther from the truth.

While Goldman Sachs for many years was a partnership, and it
avoided the brutal internecine strife that had destroyed or weakened
rivals, that did not mean a unanimity of opinion or deep reservoirs of
goodwill existed in their building. "Partner" was merely a legal designation that meant risks and rewards were borne among those whose
capital was at work in the firm; it did not mean they were a band of
brothers locked arm in arm facing what challenges may come.[20]

Cohn, and later Blankfein, made certain Sparks understood that
they did not accept his assessment of brutal market conditions as good
enough. It mattered little that he was accurately valuing his portfolio in
the face of client pressure. He would come up with a way to earn back
every penny he lost and it would be done straightaway. The firm was
publicly traded and its stock was then bouncing off the $200 per-share
level. Investors had profitability expectations and Lloyd Blankfein and
Gary Cohn were going to meet them.

Though it need hardly be said, Cohn made sure Sparks knew it was
a good year, actually a remarkable year, and so they could afford to eat
the losses. Next year, though . . .

Sparks said he took the point.

A few days later Sparks ran into his colleague Ram Sundaram.
Without bothering to catch up on the market, Sundaram told Sparks
that his department's marks for subprime were the only honest marks on
Wall Street.

"Everybody is full of shit, totally full of shit," he said. "I see
everyone's marks."

■ ■ ■

In December 2006, Viniar convened a meeting of traders, controllers, and
accountants to discuss the rising risk profile he perceived in the mortgage
market. Anyone who didn't get the seriousness with which management
was taking matters now did. They were to free up capital by selling as
much subprime as possible and be ready for what may come.

In the hour-long early morning drive in from New Canaan,
Connecticut, to Goldman's 85 Broad Street headquarters, Sparks tried

to look past his conviction that something truly ugly was going to happen into where opportunity might lie afterward. It wasn't really clear to him that the people who couldn't stomach subprime at a price of 95 were going to want it all over again at 65. But maybe he was wrong. Perhaps with enough yield and some liquidity, buyers came back. If they did, well, Sparks would have proof that this was all just a correction and the market would take care of everything else.

If it didn't, then Sparks had some decisions to make. In that case, everything he did was going to have a real price tag attached to it.

■ ■ ■

A short-seller could be forgiven for thinking that in the year 2006 AIG had a printing press on loan from the U.S. Mint in the basement of its headquarters. Their results were simply breathtaking. The $113 billion in revenues led to profit margins that were astounding: 19.1 percent pretax and 12.4 percent net. If Chanos was foolhardy to short a company that could generate so much profit, his analysis was at least correct. Life insurance profits and revenues grew nicely but the engine was capital markets in all its glorious forms.

Win Neuger continued apace with his efforts at streamlining the stray moons and out-planets of the Asset Management constellation while turning in a $2.3 billion operating income performance for the year (virtually identical to 2005.) Unnoticed, save for those obsessive enough to swim though various subsidiary filings, was the $892 million differential between assets and liabilities in the then $70.2 billion securities lending portfolio.

The gap should have been cause for an immediate halt to the program. There is no indication, however, that anyone from AIG's risk-management or accounting units said a thing. One explanation for this is that with massive cash inflows to the program—from $60.4 billion to $70.2 billion—no securities needed to be sold to meet any redemptions. Regardless, since none of the life insurance companies had the remotest idea this was going on, and with the bond market humming along, any redemptions were minor. Thus, the program continued to show an expanding profit, although Neuger took care to remind his charges that they were still far short of his goal.

A less charitable explanation of the above is that this had become a giant Ponzi scheme. There were benefits to this, like all schemes requiring new cash to meet its existing obligations. If the *annus horribilis* had come at the beginning of 2007, for example, they may have been able to get out of the cauldron for under $1 billion.

As it was, Neuger's corporate star remained ascendant and he earned $8.78 million for his work.

Two veteran portfolio managers presented Neuger with evidence of the illogic of what was going on in the program and said that they had an opportunity to stop things before they got any worse. One of the men stayed and the other soon left. The man who left was Michael Rieger, the blunt portfolio manager of $54 billion AIG Global Investment Corporation (AIGGIC) ABS portfolio.

Initial attempts at civility having failed, he had a brief and meaningful conversation with Neuger in which he explained that if the market corrected the entire securities lending portfolio become entirely mismatched. A less technical way of saying this is the portfolio, supposedly calibrated to have bonds with maturities that matched when they would have to give bonds or cash back, would become wildly out of balance, with much less assets than liabilities.

Even though the investors in the global securities lending (GSL) program were all AIG family members, this wasn't like when you borrow a few hundred dollars from an older sister in a tight spot; no awkward smiles and IOUs would suffice. When the investors in GSL needed their bonds back, it was because they had policyholder needs to meet.

Theoretically, given the size of the portfolio, the loss in value could outstrip the supply of corporate cash were AIG forced to step in and meet the obligations. This risk was disclosed nowhere in corporate filings.

Neuger, ever the veteran Wall Street manager, thanked Rieger for his concerns and wished him well. Shaking hands with some of his colleagues as he left for a hedge fund in New Jersey, the deeply religious Rieger seemed to them to be profoundly grateful not to have killed Neuger.

■ ■ ■

The number from 2006 and going into 2007 were so good that it shut down a conversation that Frank Zarb, Bob Willumstad, and a few other board members had been having on whether Martin Sullivan was a long-term CEO.

The original transition plan from 2005 was a thing of beauty: the legendary CEO's handpicked and personally guided replacement. No civil wars or fratricide, no adrift on a lifeboat trying to learn stuff, nothing. He would keep a lifelong friendship and AIG would get a CEO hand-taught by the best. Whatever they had hoped, however, died in March 2005 when Greenberg was deposed.

From the day that Willumstad joined they had pondered whether Sullivan was going to be a transitional CEO or someone that would stay longer term. Zarb and Willumstad were in the transitional camp, though they had never put their foot down and said as much. The company was always striving to meet some regulatory goal or put something else behind them so there was never the time for indulging in long-term succession planning. They needed a CEO, Martin Sullivan was the candidate, and that was that. In the early days after he assumed the CEO role, Zarb would laugh to himself sometimes: one of the world's most powerful companies had a shotgun marriage CEO that no one was certain was up for the job.

It couldn't be denied, however, that while everything went to hell Martin hadn't. He placated regulators and kept defections to a minimum, and as a finale he presided over a year where AIG posted record earnings for an insurance company.

People would walk into fire for Greenberg because the alternative of not walking into fire was believed to be worse; people would walk into a fire for Sullivan because they liked him.[21] A story that made its way to the board illustrates this.

While working on the third-quarter earnings release in 2006, a working group of Sullivan, CFO Bensinger and an associate general counsel were going over the last draft of the press release and in strolled Brian Schreiber, the head of corporate strategy and, many believed, a likely candidate to replace Sullivan should he depart within the decade.

The details of the release were settled and only some of the wording of the release was being squared away. Schreiber picked up a copy of the release and began suggesting some substantial changes on the fly. Everyone looked at Schreiber with bafflement, wondering why they had had to do all the detail work only to have him launch into a last-second analysis of how everything could be changed. Told several times with differing degrees of politeness that they were only looking at the release to make sure it didn't have any profanity in it and things like that, Schreiber huffed and eventually threw the release into the middle of the table.

Sullivan, who had ignored the problem, looked over his glasses and asked if Schreiber was "going to take all his toys and head home?" Said in a way that drove home the point without humiliating Schreiber, everyone—Schreiber included—was soon laughing at the silliness of late-night meetings to go over press releases no one really read, save for the earnings numbers.

People were happy, and investors were happier. Zarb and Willumstad were forced to shelve their concern over Sullivan. Numbers didn't lie. AIG appeared to have its second legendary CEO in a row.

■ ■ ■

The problem started with leverage.

In the early spring of 2007, a pair of hedge funds housed within Bear Stearns Asset Management (BSAM), the High-Grade Structured Credit Strategies funds, began to teeter as the selloff in subprime and the absence of any bids for CDOs took its toll. There was a fearful symmetry to it: prices dropped and with the fund's running at astronomical 20-to-1 leverage ratios it took precious little to wipe out what little equity cushion existed in the funds. The fund's managers, Ralph Cioffi and Matthew Tannin, ordinarily would have injected some cash to meet the wave of margin calls that brokers were sending them. But there was none.

To juice returns, Cioffi and Tannin had invested all of their investors' $1.6 billion in capital; every mortgage-bond and CDO desk on the Street happily—and greedily—provided leverage to the funds, grateful for the last client willing to buy their CDOs stuffed with increasingly preposterous collateral. It worked wonderfully for several years: they earned tens of millions of dollars and regularly provided double-digit returns to investors who couldn't have imagined that bond hedge funds would provide such brilliant returns. A big part of doing this was getting remarkably advantageous repurchase agreements from brokers that gave them 99 cents on the dollar for the subprime collateral they posted. That meant that on the trading desks—known as repo desks—at a Merrill and Citi (the Bear fund's two biggest counterparties) they had this paper marked at 99 cents.

This implied that the CDO-squareds (CDOs made up of other CDOs) and late 2006 subprime collateral—bonds whose real value existed in a computer model and pretty much nowhere else—could readily be sold in the market for 99 cents on the dollar.[22] In addition to being a work of professional fiction, this assessment put everybody at a place like Citi and Merrill at cross-purposes. The repo desk had their mark, but the mortgage desk had to have known that this sort of paper was worth much less than 99 cents on the dollar. But if the mortgage desk marked the bonds where they would likely trade, had there been any trading occurring in these securities, then not only would they immediately sustain billions of dollars' worth of losses but much of their customer base would have been devastated.

So the risk-management, accounting, and valuation units of Citigroup and Merrill were in the dark; their repo desks were praying to God that there was nothing that would lead to them to have to take this collateral onto their books and their mortgage desks had billions of dollars of reasons to hope a miracle happened and prices held up. Multiply this state of affairs by seven other trading desks and that was the mortgage market on Wall Street in the spring of 2007: hope and willful ignorance fused into one big ball of misery.

At Goldman, it was different. The misery was there aplenty, especially for Andrew Davilman, who covered the BSAM funds, but as of early May they were attempting to be honest about where they and the market stood. As it turned out, the firm and the values in the market were far enough apart that they were prepping a big write-down. An email between chief risk manager Craig Broderick and some mortgage department staffers illustrated this point.

We're in the process of making some significant downward revisions to the marks on the mortgage portfolio esp. CDO and CDO squared. . . . This will potentially have a big P&L impact on us, but also to our clients due to the marks and associated margin calls on repos, derivatives and other products.

Broderick added that the firm sales staff should "take a shot at surveying" their client base to figure out who was most vulnerable. This was not being done for sales management goals, naturally, but rather a combination of legal and strategic reasons. Customers were going to go out of business because of these marks and others would be in some hot water. There were big players in both categories and it was probably smart to try to identify who was who.

Hedge funds die fast, but they can inflict a ton of pain on the firms that gives them repo lines and act as a prime broker. And the litigation can drag on for years. It was time to prepare for what was coming.

■ ■ ■

Goldman would not be one of the sick or the dead at least that quarter: Sparks, per Viniar's instructions, had figured out that keeping the firm's power dry—or capital on the sidelines—was pointless. Everything that was purchased, no matter how good the price, soon dropped again and was sold for a loss.

So they shorted the mortgage market.

Starting in late 2006, Sparks and his traders—led by Michael Swenson and Josh Birnbaum—bet against the MBS market in a variety of ways, including shorting stock and buying options on a host of different mortgage lenders. Where it really paid off, however, was buying CDSs on the ABX index that had been launched in only the prior January—the same index that cost them a pretty penny to reduce their long position in.

Over the course of the first and second quarters, the hedges contributed between $3 billion and $4 billion in operating income to the mortgage unit, which was blessing enough. A much more important thing for Goldman's health, perhaps even its survival, in the coming months was that the income from the short allowed them to seamlessly mark their $10 billion CDO book down about $1.5 billion. If the market rallied, they would make more than anyone else; if it dropped more, they would lose less.

They were marking them down not because of these reasons, however—it was very much in their economic interest not to use more than a billion dollars of income against some notional losses—but because that's where the market was telling Sparks and his trades they should be valued. Every CDO Goldman traded was a loss and getting customers interested at *any* price seemed like a joke. There was another, uglier reason though: no one could really figure out how to value these things independently. The blend of busted mortgage issuers and their delinquent underlying collateral made a fundamental valuation of many CDOs impossible.

(What no one talked about at Goldman was that they had sold billions of dollars of this paper over the previous year and spent a good amount of time in the first quarter extricating themeselves from varying commitments to structure more deals. Customers that had been angry now began to hate the firm. Sparks, for his part, felt he was in some kind of horrific Catch-22: he was having to hurt a franchise he had helped build in order to save it.)

Using the price levels from their few customers still willing to trade CDOs, as well as spreads from the ABX, they cobbled together a series of prices where different classes of CDOs could be said to be fairly valued. They then used one additional criteria: Knowing all this, what price would they be comfortable owning CDOs in a market like the current one?

With the lowest marks on the Street and record profits in mortgages, toward the end of that May, Goldman sent out marks to BSAM's funds showing their tens of billions of dollars worth of CDOs were worth maybe 50 cents on the dollar. It would take a few weeks yet but at that moment, the BSAM funds were dead. They didn't have any cash reserves to satisfy the tens of millions of dollars they borrowed from Goldman, nor would anyone buy the non-CDO paper at even fire-sale prices.[23]

Davilman considered himself lucky since the repo desk had always been wary of extending much leverage against sub-prime collateral, a long-running headache for the firm's mortgage salesmen. Now, it seemed prudent. After the fund's began to totter in mid-June, Merrill Lynch—which had not been shy in encouraging customer criticism of Goldman's marks—seized $850 million of collateral from the funds because they couldn't repay their repo lines.[24]

Merrill would have been better off if they had just let the repo loans fail.

Convinced the market was better than it was, the plan to auction off the seized collateral failed miserably, with only $100 million trading at distressed levels. The few bonds they sold set clear prices within the market; the $750 million balance that Merrill was stuck with, like BSAM before them, told everyone all they needed to know about how the bond market valued CDOs at that time.

That was the easy part though. Goldman now had to face its customers, who were, as Goldman's Broderick had foretold, getting angrier and poorer every minute.

Chapter 10

The Down Staircase

O n July 11, 2007, Andrew Forster called Alan Frost in Wilton and told him that he was spending all his time focusing on credit-default swaps (CDSs) and subprime. Nearly two years to the day that he had hosted a conference call "to get juices flowing" about the risk in FP's mounting subprime exposure, the deliberate and reasoned approach that had made him both rich and respected at FP hadn't served him well in this one instance. He should have taken the tack that Gene Park advocated and simply stopped all CDS writing earlier that summer and tried to get out of their existing swap obligations.[1]

Forster had every reason to be panicked. On July 10, ratings agencies Standard & Poor's and Moody's began to downgrade dozens of residental mortgage–backed securities (MBSs) worth nearly $10 billion dollars. Forster knew borrower delinquencies had been mounting from the early autumn of 2006, and he could surmise that there was more to come since the downgrades represented a new ratings methodology.

Poorly telegraphed and a year late though it was, both ratings agencies (Fitch would follow later) were now seeing what had cost Dan

Sparks headaches and no small number of customers: the mortgage market was a nightmare of bad loans, fraud, and strapped borrowers.[2]

"The problem we are going to face is that we are going to just have enormous downgrades on the stuff we [have on]," said Forster.

"We are fucked, basically," concluded the man who had been worrying over the swaps book, though official channels and behind closed doors in Cassano's office, since the summer of 2005.

■ ■ ■

On July 26, Goldman's Andrew Davilman, though on vacation, sent Alan Frost an email giving him a heads-up that the next day Goldman would be sending in a collateral call for more than $1 billion. From Davilman's perspective, he was just being courteous. He had been moved to a different department within Goldman's Fixed Income Clearing Corporation (FICC) division to try and develop sales in corporate bonds and swaps, and his sales relationship with FP was one of the few remaining mortgage relationships he retained.

In actuality, the collateral call was for $1.8 billion, and the instructions were to wire the amount in after the close of business. For Goldman, the margin call was the cumulation of weeks worth of work, carefully coming up with valuations based on trades in CDOs that had similar characteristics. In two cases, Goldman's traders checked the marks at Merrill and Citi, who were publicly insisting that the market— even after Bear's hedge fund's collapsed—for most CDO paper was near par (or $100). In both cases, both firms refused to buy even small blocks of similar CDOs at anywhere near par. Where people were willing to buy and sell these types of CDOs was at $85. This made a margin call a foregone conclusion since 19 of the 23 CDO swaps FP wrote were written with provisions that had the credit support annex (CSA) go into effect when the market value dropped 4 percent.[3]

The margin calls were driven as much by Goldman's massive trade support, pricing and risk-analysis infrastructure as they were by its own traders. One of the senior members of this unit said that in late March 2007, when Merrill clearly was trying to flush its bloated inventory out by pricing 20 CDOs on a single day, they had been laser-focused on CDO prices.

"We couldn't find many, if any, examples of these deals trading up or even having [price] support. They didn't trade or they simply had no buyers. We saw there was going to be a big problem because there didn't appear to be any bids."

For AIGFP, which had prospered during every financial debacle from the crash of 1987 to the debt crisis of 1998 to the dot-com bubble, the credit crisis now had both their name on it and a dollar figure attached to it.[4]

The margin call came out of the blue. If the management of FP was stunned they kept it to themselves, but in New York there was total shock. Stasia Kelly, the general counsel, had never even heard of a credit support annex, nor had the CFO Bensinger or Martin Sullivan. It is unlikely that Kelly or Sullivan had any knowledge of a CDO beyond what was found in *Bloomberg* or the *Wall Street Journal*; Bensinger's awareness appears to have been little better.

Cassano's approach to handling corporate headquarters was to insist that Goldman was wrong and that it would back down. He had no other choice, which would become a recurring theme for FP.

He deputized Jon Liebergall, the head of North American Marketing, to begin to build cash balances and keep a running tab of cash movements within the unit. It was a good choice: Liebergall was what one of his colleagues called "an athlete. He simply excelled at whatever slot he was dropped into." A nearly 20-year veteran, the garrulous Liebergall had worked his way up to running the municipal securities unit and had spent time as a big producer in other departments as well. Respected by the rank-and-file at FP, he also had something of an encyclopedic knowledge of FP and its processes.

In choosing Liebergall to be the point man for the margin calls, Cassano would be the "Mr. Inside," dealing with what was sure to be a growing roster of internal questioners and analysts.

A July 30 phone call between Jon Liebergall, who was thrust into the role of overseeing the collateral dispute, and Forster is illustrative of the pickle they were in.

To both men, who were friends—Liebergall began the call recounting the stomach flu that had run through his house and its predictable side effects—as well as unit chiefs at FP, Goldman's marks were "ridiculous." Sadly, however, there was no way they could readily disprove them since, according to Forster, the bonds could be valued anywhere "from 80 to 95." As an over-the-counter security with no available market other than what CDO-bloated dealers quoted them directly, they had no ability to counterargue with Goldman. Actually, the horns of the dilemma were worse. Even trying to establish their own price discovery could be dangerous, Forster told his colleague, "If we start buying the physical bonds back . . . then any accountant is going to turn around and say, well, Jon, you know, you traded at 90, you must be able to mark your bonds then."

On the phone call, Liebergall worked out with Forster that they had about $2.7 billion in cash on hand for the next few months. They were confident that it was enough.

All they had was the power of the purse. If they had a strategy, it was this: avoid paying and play a wait-and-hope game for a few weeks, and just maybe the market would rebound a little.

It didn't.

■ ■ ■

The Office of Thrift Supervision (OTS) was trying to grow up. In 2007, in what appears to be penance for its prior year's effort, OTS staff came back to FP and conducted a professional and serious examination. Examiners formulated questions about the CDO swap portfolio—it even got some of the future market risks (such as collateral substitution) correct.[5]

According to a *ProPublica* article, the improved analytical thrust of the OTS was because of the effort put in by a small group headed up by Clarence K. Lee and his team from the Office of Complex and International Organizations unit. The good news is that Lee's group appears to have asked the proper questions and organized the data in a way that replicated the way that the people in the industry looked at it and thought about it.[6] The bad news is that, again, they took everything that FP's management—almost certainly Cassano—as the final word on the matter. It wasn't that FP was lying; it's that the examinations were so one-sided. There is the "second loss" chestnut, designed to assure auditors and management that losses would certainly stop at the lower-rated tranches. There is the "99.85 percent certainty" meme, referring to FP's view that the loss estimates on its models will have that level of accuracy. There is the liberal use of the phrase *worst case* to emphasize that the FP stress tests have measured every last input.

Since the swaps were housed in a portfolio, and on a server, in Andrew Forster's asset-finance unit at FP in London, none of the OTS's U.S.-based team was going to pull the swap contracts and discover the CSAs.

This suggests a point about financial regulation in the United States: an emphasis on practices and protocol rather than results. While checking paperwork is a start, no one at OTS (or the Securities and Exchange Commission [SEC] or Pricewaterhouse, or, obviously, AIG headquarters) sought to impose the sheer volume of insurance FP had written against so much as a model of what subprime losses had been like in recent corrections. Because FP is by design overwhelming and regulators by nature don't have the experience and resources that the companies they regulate do, they have to stick to what is verifiable (processes and paperwork) and what is true (corporate computer models that told of minimal risk) as opposed to what is buried and prospective.

What is buried and prospective takes dozens of hours, raises more questions than can be answered, and is expensive to the point of bordering on prohibitive. To pick off the looming nightmare of the CSAs is basic stuff for people who have looked at them before. Getting there would require Lee to keep the entirety of a staff of a few dozen people working 60 hours or more a week for a little over $100,000 a year when an equivalent private-sector job would pay three to five times more. So companies and their regulators go for what is true and make sure that paperwork is in order.

All told, OTS found the issue and made an effort, a stark contrast to the year prior. There was some boilerplate language about AIG's engagement with FP in oversight over the swaps portfolio and the concession that while the prospect of CDO losses were "remote," the subprime market's brewing troubles might pose a challenge. With little evidence to the contrary, all was officially well with AIGFP for another year.

■ ■ ■

For Ram Sundaram, this whole period was intensely frustrating. Anyone who cared to do the real work knew that the market was offsides tremendously in its prices. To his way of thinking, dealers—and most of their clients—were either using model prices, which were only as good as whatever the inputs were, or were using stale ones, a sure sign that desks were choosing not to update their prices in a serious fashion.

As the swap holder against numerous CDOs, this was bad for his Principal Funding and Investment group, the little proprietary unit he ran with its noncorrelated grab bag of businesses, including some negative-basis trades. Ram and a few colleagues had spent several miserable days trying to get accurate marks so they could value their own trades, and it was clear that they would have to simply develop values themselves.

On July 26, 2007, in a late night email to colleagues across several departments, Ram let them know he was frustrated with Goldman's process for coming up with valuations in CDOs. Some of this was skin in the game, to be sure: he had a lot of money to make or losem depending on which way things cut, and as a managing director, he was only one good year away from being made partner. Primarily, though, Ram laid out that the way this was being handled was "embarassing" for the firm. The fact that the marks quoted for many CDOs on Goldman's own desks were as bad as its rivals was one thing, but when they were suddenly issuing margin calls into the billions of dollars, they had better have their marks immaculate and current.

An example Ram quoted in the email stands out: one CDO was quoted on July 25 at 99, but when he demanded a current bid the next morning, the trader bid $77.5.[7]

To his mind, the market was giving them a pretty clear proxy for all this, and he happily spelled it out for his colleagues. Markit, the company that launched the ABX index of credit default swaps based on subprime mortgage bonds, had launched the TABX five months prior, an index that dealt with the triple-B and triple-B-rated tranches of the ubiquitous ABX. To Ram, it was a pretty clear window into how the most volatile and risky subprime collateral pools were being viewed in the market. The way he read it, both the ABX and the TABX provided unambiguous, multimonth confirmation that sub-prime collateral—the engine-oil of the CDO machine—was dropping in value. If it was the case that the collateral of this paper was distressed, then there was no reason for any CDO made of the stuff to trade near par.[8]

Ram's advice would gradually be adopted at Goldman, but the more immediate issue was trying to get the margin call squared away. The full-court stall was on, but Goldman treated it, according to FP emails, like it was the last stand at the Alamo. There were a few reasons for this. The first and most important was that Goldman, as previously noted, had used many of the FP swaps as a way to write protection itself for customers on the same CDO. In 2004–2005, this was a way of keeping its customers happy and confident enough to keep buying the arcane stuff its CDO desk was spitting out.

More immediately, Goldman was now having to pay out counterparties on the swaps where they were middlemen. So in the case of the collateral call it made to FP on July 27, Goldman would sooner or later presumably have to post the same amount of collateral to someone else.

In his email to the mortgage department in May warning about the pending write-downs, Goldman risk management chief Craig Broderick had noted that the issue of valuations in CDOs was "getting a lot of 30th floor attention right now." In Goldman's old headquarters at 85 Broad Street, the 30th floor was where the president and chief executive's offices were. Naturally, any loss is a concern and something they should be fully engaged with, but vastly more important was determining the effect a write-down of CDO values would have on the swaps market, where Goldman was an active counterparty.

Unlike other Goldman managements in earlier crises, the credit derivative swaps market would give them no benefit of the doubt. It was an actively traded window into what investors thought of their ability to repay debt. If the CDO and subprime freeze turned into something worse, and investors percieved that Goldman had billions of dollars of exposure to troubled counterparties, then the cost of funding itself would skyrocket overnight. Ram had worked mightily to line up the longer-term funding to forestall such a nightmare, but neither he nor anyone else kidded themselves. Like all investment banks, if word got out that a major counterparty like Fidelity or (bond management giant) PIMCO was wary about extending short-term credit, its future would be measured in days, if not hours. One way to forestall that was to avoid the large imbalances in cash inflows and outflows resulting from margin calls in CDSs.

No edict from the corner office was required; the books would be marked immaculately and often. Cash was at stake, and as the future grew darker, cash would be the way that Goldman avoided becoming the prey. It was why, on the day that the margin call went out, Goldman bought $100 million in default protection on AIG. AIG was eternal, the thinking at Goldman went, large enough and strong enough to live forever. Goldman, however, was just another investment bank in lower Manhattan.

Tom Athan, an executive VP who ran FP's credit derivative trading, emailed Forster on August 1 describing a conversation he had just completed with Goldman as "a tough call with Goldman . . . they are not budging and are acting irrational." All of Athan's arguments fell on deaf ears, which was hardly surprising. He had spoken to Ram, who was sure to have done much more work on pricing out CDOs than Athan had and was becoming religious within Goldman on the pricing failures within the CDO market.

The email minimized the salient fact, however. Ram told Athan that this was a "test case" because "the CSA has to work or they cannot do [these] trades" across the firm. Goldman wasn't going to budge because it really couldn't. If it allowed cash to flow out, as its management was prediciting was likely, then it could be signing its own death certificate.

FP's Al Frost, who made a lot of money for FP and himself by having good realtionships with Wall Street's investment banks, saw a pretty dark future looming. He made this point in an email to Athan and Forster two days later when he described Davilman, with whom he'd just gotten off the phone, as "more discouraged and despondent about amicably resolving the dispute between our firms as long as I've known him."

Certainly, Davilman could see down the road a bit and realize that he was dealing with an account that had been lucrative for him but was now just shy of legal action, which for a good salesman is always a sad state of affairs. More substantively, Davilman saw what Frost and his colleagues couldn't see: FP was grasping at straws.

Athan's phone call with Goldman was a case in point. He and his colleagues disagreed with Goldman's assertions but offered no marks of their own. Athan, a man who had run a $75 billion portfolio of CDOs and other structured products for more than a decade prior to joining FP, certainly had a keen understanding of the CDO market and of valuation disputes. Yet when he and other FP executives went to the market to get quotes, they got "numbers for valuation purposes." All of the big investment banks that had fought so bitterly to win FPs business for years were now unwilling to commit to trade anywhere near the numbers they provided; for legal purposes, they wouldn't even discuss the prices where they would trade. Instead, FP argued procedure and the spirit behind the CSA.

On August 10th, Cassano authorized $450 million to be wired into Goldman's J. P. Morgan account and both sides agreed to a "side-letter" that stated that the dispute was not officially resolved nor that Goldman accepted the wire as fulfillment of the margin call. The day before, Goldman had agreed to recalculate its margin calls using the midpoint between bid and ask, which reduced the amount demanded to $1.2 billion, a drop of $600 million.

At Goldman, the heat from the 30th floor to get *something* in was growing. No one at Goldman had expected FP—smart, independent, and deliberate—to simply accept their word. Or be happy about it. But this was like nothing they had anticipated. Two weeks of ceaseless struggle for 25 percent of the original amount? On Goldman's trading floor, an ugly feeling set in: this is going to be near to hell to get these guys to play this straight. That was the reason between August 2 and August 10, the firm bought an additional $475 million in credit default protection on AIG.

In an email to Forster on the 16th, Frost wrote that "this is not the last margin call we are going to debate." To the point he told him that, per Davilman, Goldman's desk was seeing Merrill begining to drop its marks to its customers. There was the possibility, said Davilman, of "some significant margin calls."

Forster, who was on vacation, replied that he had heard rumors that Goldman was marking down "asset types" it did not own "so as to cause maximum pain to its competitors." Allowing that the rumor "may be rubbish," he said it was "just the sort of thing Goldman would do."

It is doubtful that Forster's opinion of Goldman improved after the firm issued a $1.5 billion margin call on September 11, 2007. Two days later, Goldman purchased $700 million in swaps as insurance against

AIG's financial health. No one at Goldman had any big-picture concern about AIG, but everyone who was dealing with AIG thought there was something really wrong. Anybody else would have been "closed out" and the collateral seized, but AIG was different than everybody else, so Goldman had to bite their tongues for now.

■ ■ ■

Jim Chanos decided to move on. His bet against AIG didn't work out and he wound up ordering that most of it be bought back, or "covered," in the late spring 2007 in the low $70s. His conviction hadn't wavered, but Kynikos's clients didn't pay for moral victories, only performance.

He would redeploy the capital he had tied up in AIG into opening a short on Fannie Mae and Freddie Mac. Redefining his thesis, Kynikos was becoming a pure play on the collapse of the securitization industry: he was short Moody's, he was short New Century and other mortgage originators, he was short Bear Stearns, and now he could be short Fannie and Freddie, the mortgage guarantors who, like FP in the CDO market, were (the much bigger) terminus of all activity in the residential real estate market.

Like all short-sellers exiting a trade that didn't work, Chanos wondered if he was just flat-out wrong, or if Kynikos was onto something big but no one saw it yet.

■ ■ ■

Robert Willumstad, who had become chairman of the AIG board in November 2006, and the rest of the board were made aware of the swaps in mid-August. Briefings from Cassano himself were, to his mind, proving pointless, as he told them repeatedly that everything was in control and they were not only *not* worried about substantial credit losses, but he was expecting that the collateral requests would soon abate. Per Cassano, it was a case of Goldman being Goldman.

Most of the board accepted this explanation because Cassano's track record and Sullivan's unswerving support were weighty, plus the numbers—through the first half at least—threatened to blow 2006's record-setting performance away. Through June 30, 2007, AIG had posted $8.4 billion in net income, up a remarkable 25 percent from last year. It was very hard for a board to start issuing demands when the CEO has the company on pace to smash a record-breaking performance.

The consensus emerged that this was all troubling, but if management could oversee this kind of performance, then they could handle what was looking like a unit-specific dispute with a broker.

Willumstad, Frank Zarb, and a few other board members saw it differently.

Willumstad was no expert in this stuff, but he did manage to get a few straight answers out of Cassano about the size of his portfolio and he did some math. If, as of mid-August, they were being asked to post $1.8 billion, and things remained as ugly as they were for another few months, they could easily get asked to post $5 billion, maybe more. Maybe Goldman would take another 75 percent haircut, but maybe they wouldn't. This could get really rough if the entire $72.8 billion portolio got marked down 10 percent; at 20 percent it would be a material event. Willumstad didn't need to be told that if you could lose 20 percent, then you could lose 30 percent.

Not in the mood to mince words, he called Sullivan to ask him about Cassano and his grasp of the situation. Sullivan was even more supportive of Cassano in private than he had been in public.

That was great, Willumstad told him, but can we believe him when he says that the problem is in hand? After all, even if no one at headquarters had known about these CSAs before—and he had no idea what to think about that, either—their effect was clear enough: AIG, despite being on track to earn over $16 billion in net income, could be brought to its knees by an esoteric derivative contract no one knew existed until just days ago. He made sure Sullivan heard him spell this scenario out.

Sullivan pledged to Willumstad that the financial services staff was on top of this on a weekly, if not daily, basis, and he would keep the board appraised. Loyalty was something he could appreciate in a manager, but it didn't seem like Sullivan had any real insight or feelings into the situation beyond what Cassano had said. To Willumstad, this all suggested to him the systems issue again. No one on the board had been told of this much swap protection having been written. Shouldn't it have triggered something, somewhere in risk management?

In the course of a few days in the summer, AIG went from shooting for the record books to once again trying to head off management's self-imposed damage to the franchise.

■ ■ ■

The swap portfolio continued to be a headache for AIGFP because the market continued to fall apart.

In October 2007, Goldman's rivals started to fold their bets in the multiyear quest to garner riches through the CDO market.

UBS, perenially caught up in the tail-end of every financial mania, had made a wager with its balance sheet that it could dominate in the MBS and CDO markets via capturing huge market share. They have had at least $100 billion, and often times much more, of this paper on their books. Like all previous attempts by its management for Wall Street success, it ended terribly, and on October 1st it announced a $3.4 billion write-down of these assets. This would be only the start of their losses.

On the same day, Citibank took a $5.9 billion write-down, and Merrill Lynch weighed in on the 24th with $7.9 billion in write-downs. Merrill, which had $26 billion plus of CDOs and subprime collateral on its books at the beginning of the month, had said earlier in the month that its charge was likely to be about $5.5 billion. They were the first firm that the cratering mortgage market would make swallow their own carefully scripted words; they would hardly be the last.

At FP, there was no more arguing that this was something Goldman was capable of ginning up to squeeze a rival.

For AIG, the shadow began to fall shortly after the Merrill write-down. A Reuters story, citing a just released RBS Securities report, noted that $64 billion of its CDO book was backed by subprime, which was causing havoc across the Street, with Reuters predicting the stock would "take a pasting."[9] AIG told Reuters (among others) that any credit losses would be absorbed by lower-rated tranches and at any rate, they didn't mark that portfolio to market. The Reuters reporter didn't play up a telling piece of data, however: The bulk of Merrill's write-down, $5.8 billion, came from losses on so-called super senior tranches, precisely the sort of paper that AIG's models had told it was unlikely to sustain any blows.

Rumors mounted of a large write-down and gained steam when a Citi analyst wrote that he expected a $1.6 billion write-down on October 25.

CNBC's David Faber, a morning fixture on trading floor TVs around the globe, reported that to the contrary, "people in a position to know" were expecting no such write-down. The firm denial and the high-profile reporter announcing it helped send the stock back over $60 from its year low of $59.06.

■ ■ ■

In the securities lending portfolio at AIG Global Investment Corp., what had been a challenge or concern had now emerged through inactivity and the program's dubious nature into a full-bore calamity. The experience of TransAtlantic Holdings, a majority-owned, AIG life insurance subsidiary whose assets were managed in part by global securities lending program, is telling.

In the second quarter of 2006, when TransAtlantic managers noticed that they had doubled their securities lending activity to $1.5 billion, they sent an email to the program's management asking for an explanation of the increase. The reply was immediate (if rather dense) and helpfully pointed out that there was heavy demand for the bonds in their portfolio and that every transaction was negotiated carefully, with the maximum amount of collateral posted. TransAtlantic's managers backed off, but remained suspicious.

The suspicion was not unfounded. Toward the end of 2006, Peter Adamczyk, one of the managers of the securities lending program, replied to an email query from TransAtlantic about the safety of the lending program's investments by noting that as of December 31, 2004, AIG was exceptionally disciplined and rigorous in its approach to security selection. The date was a huge red flag. Adamczyk did not reply when pressed as to why something from two years prior was applicable. Furthering this incredible vein, Adamczyk made a presentation to TransAtlantic's board on December 6, 2006, where he insisted that the program's investment criteria was "rigorous and risk-controlled." Regardless of some erratic behavior—that is, the two-year-old marketing piece as evidence of safety and soundness—TransAtlantic remained invested with the program because returns were still coming in.

That would soon end.

In the summer of 2007, as trading ground to a halt in the sections of the MBS and ABS markets that the securities lending program had been busy in, its managers began to frantically sell longer-dated paper and seek more borrowers so new cash could come in and shortfalls could be met. At that point, there was an alarming similarity between Bernard Madoff's fund management operation and Win Neuger's securities lending apparatus—without new cash coming in, both would not be able to continue.

On July 12, as the Bear Stearns hedge funds collapse roiled the mortgage markets, TransAtlantic's finance officials sent an email to Craig Mitchell of the securities lending program asking about subprime exposure. He replied, "TransAtlantic has no exposure to MBS/ABS/CDO securities." One month later, however, during a more in-depth inquiry, they learned that "no exposure" really meant that 80 percent of their almost $540 million investment was in securities that could be considered subprime.

To satisfy a furious TransAtlantic management, the securities lending staff promised to carve out a seperate lending pool that would have nothing to do with subprime. What they didn't know was that the securities that they chose to do this with—Alt-A, home-equity loans and home-equity lines of credit—had seen also seen sharp deterioration of underwriting standards. These markets would, one after the other, begin to seize over the autumn.[10]

By the end of December, the gap between asset and liabilities in the global securities lending program would amount to $6.3 billion, every last penny of which conceivably posed a threat to the safety of the policyholders.

■■■

On November 1, 2007, Goldman Sachs delivered a $1 billion margin call to FP and increased it by another $1.8 billion a day later. Société Générale also issued an $82.5 million margin call, something Cassano would claim in an email to financial services unit CFO Elias Habayeb

Goldman had "spurred on" because they provided SG with the marks on the CDO.

Under a week later, AIG released its third-quarter earnings, which included a $1.95 billion charge for what was broadly categorized as mortgage-related writedowns. Between October 25, when CNBC's Faber spoke to "people in a position to know,"[11] and the release date of November 7, nearly $2 billion in material losses had been uncovered. In instances like that, where a reporter was given such demonstrably false information, it would be assumed that the public relations staff was either incompetent, deceitful, or both. AIG's was none of those—quite the opposite, in fact.

Once again, it was the issue of internal controls. Most companies looking to take a charge have a clear indication of the amount that will be written down well before the end of the reporting period. Nearly four weeks after the quarter's books closed, however, AIG's management was still telling its PR staff that the company was in the clear. This is because they had appeared to have had no real picture of their portfolio and the marketplace. The human element—Greenberg's encyclopedic knowledge of finance and all things risk and volatility— was now gone, and in its stead was a man who trusted other people to get those things done.

Into this breach was stepping PricewaterhouseCoopers. The write-down was forced by auditors who were unwilling to accept the values placed on mortgage securities and loans held on its balance sheet. On October 31, Pricewaterhouse had called Habayeb and posed a host of increasingly specific questions to him about AIGs valuations and their methodology for arriving at them; Habayeb turned right around and posed the questions to Cassano, who replied straightaway and answered all that was asked of him. But the devolution of the CDO market into a collapse gave the auditors the ammunition they needed to put their foot down. PwC let AIG management know that they were going to study the issue for a while longer but would be back to them shortly with some concrete proposals.

This was no ordinary conversation.

An auditor's job is to audit and in the United States at least, accounting firms expend much effort to accomodate their clients wishes—arguably too much—and much deferrence is given to management. When an auditor has to tell a client the size of AIG that they have "concrete proposals" about the best ways of valuing themselves, it is a sign that PwC is very concerned about its liability if the status quo is maintained.

On the 14th came a $1.7 billion call from Société Générale and a $610 million call from Merrill Lynch. Andrew Forster, along with FP's head of risk managament, Pierre Micottis, had spent many days analyzing the margin calls this way and that. Goldman was in every instance sharply lower than any other investment bank.

About one month later, an FP computer programmer working next to Financial Services president Bill Dooley—who was visiting FP at the time—overheard him discussing with AIG management the size of "the hole," meaning the possible liability the CDO swaps book had. One estimate had it at about $11 billion, Dooley allowed, and another had it—the absolute worst case, he said—at $32 billion.

Naturally, this made its way around the office in London and Wilton. All anyone could ask was, "Where do you get that much cash?" and the answer was, darkly, "Thats's the $32 billion question!"

Much more damning, however, was the sentiment of Kelly Kirkland. One of the original members of FP who had run their European operations and a member of its operating committee, whom Cassano had brought back as a consultant to develop tradable derivatives off of an index of fund-of-funds investments in well-known hedge funds.[12] In early October 2007, Kirkland overlaid the CDO swaps portfolio against a series of calculations he had run of bond volatilities and the ABX indexes.

When asked what his assessment was of the result, he replied, "That's easy. This stuff is fucked. We are fucked."

Chapter 11

Midnight in September

T he last two weeks of November 2007 were spent at FP in a routine that involved Andrew Forster sending around emails comparing the marks of Goldman Sachs and Merrill Lynch. Invariably, Goldman's were between 15 and 30 points lower than Merrill's. Forster, who in every sense of the word distinguished himself in the crisis, seems to have been one of the last market players who saw Merrill Lynch as a credible source of market information and liquidity at this point. With its CEO forced out at the end of the October, even the most yield-addicted collateralized debt obligation (CDO) investor had grown tired of the firm's marks being "conversation starters."

This doesn't imply customers expanded their admiration for Goldman—the precise opposite as its clients and rivals eyed sharply lower valuations, after the astounding third-quarter performance of 2007, as proof of some gaming-of-the-system gambit—but the firm actually traded where they quoted CDOs. Citi's engagement with the market had dropped off the charts after the first week of November when its CEO Chuck Price resigned.[1]

251

It was an unenviable spot to be caught in. Forster and his colleague, FP risk-management head Pierre Micottis had to analyze Goldman's methodology while developing their own even as, in fits and starts, many of FP's other credit-default swap (CDS) counterparties began to drift down to Goldman's pricing levels. In turn, Jon Liebergall had to manage real and potential cash reserve balances for FP based in large part on Goldman's marks, even as his peers and boss decried them as mistaken and unreasonable.

Absent a system of their own, and with the CDO market on another leg down—October had been surprisingly stable—FP posted $1.55 billion of collateral on November 23 with another side letter attesting to the continued dispute between the two. Goldman, especially David Viniar, was grateful for the collateral as Goldman was itself posting collateral daily on the swaps it had written, several of which were with the soon to be famous short-seller John Paulson.[2]

The consensus at Goldman was that Paulson and other clients would be sharply less forgiving in a valuation dispute than they had been with FP.[3] In this vein, the swap position insuring against AIG's default was taken to $1.74 billion.

■ ■ ■

On November 28, PricewaterhouseCoopers let AIG know that it was time to talk.[4] They scheduled a call with Steve Bensinger and Martin Sullivan at 8:30 the following morning and they wanted most of the senior corporate management on the call as well. Later that day, audit chief Mike Roemer got an email off to Cassano suggesting he should listen in; Cassano agreed readily and suggested that Forster and Micottis join him.

As a fact-gathering exercise, it bordered on pointless. PwC's Robert Sullivan emphasized the need to factor in margin calls and declining CDO valuations to the valuation of the FP as a whole. In case no one got it the first time, he then repeated the point. Moreover, Sullivan said every effort should be made to get as much market information as possible about how their counterparties were valuing their books. This was similar to telling an NFL quarterback his job is to throw touchdowns and win games.

But the 10-minute call wasn't really about "facts"—though a few did surface. It was to serve official notice to AIG that however imperfect a market-price methodology might be, it was preferable to whatever FP had at that point. In case they missed it, and no one on AIG's finance staff did, the line about learning more about how "their counterparties" valued their books was surely an unambiguous reference to Goldman Sachs.

PwC was planting a flag. AIG's management, as was becoming its wont, would only partially comprehend that they would from now on be the ones taking the orders.

The PwC subtext obscured Cassano's otherwise solid performance. He explained to an apparently baffled Sullivan and his colleagues that collateral calls are a fact of life, but what was complicating the situation, massively so, was the illiquidity in the market. As an example, Cassano said the head of CDO trading at J. P. Morgan, Brian Zeitlin, had told FP his desk hadn't done a trade in a month. They were scrambling to develop a system that was more effective, in their eyes, than Goldman's was. The problem was getting good pricing inputs.

Allowing for all that, Cassano said, if they agreed to Goldman's marks and methodology, they were looking at a $5 billion write-down. According to the notes, upon hearing this, AIG's Sullivan said it would wipe out the quarter's profits and that he would "have a heart attack."[5]

This struck Cassano as odd. He had emailed Martin's secretary the morning before, copying Bensinger, a detailed and explicit chart walking through every conceivable valuation scenario and mark-to-market loss possibility he and FP were looking at. Even if you didn't understand the nature of what was being presented, if you only looked at the document a loss scenario of $5 billion was directly pointed to. It dawned on Cassano that no one—or at least the CFO and the CEO—was paying any real attention to what he was saying.

After everyone got off the call, a second call took place between the PricewaterhouseCoopers group and Sullivan, Bensinger, and Roemer. This time PwC was much less mealy-mouthed. PwC's Sullivan let Martin Sullivan know that there were major risks going unaddressed, and PwC was beginning to analyze this in the context of whether it constituted a "control deficiency."

It was possibly the worst news imaginable at that moment. A violation of section 404 of the Sarbanes-Oxley Act, dealing with the adequacy of its internal controls, at a point when the market was beginning to aggressively discount those with mortgage and CDO exposure, could be very, very painful indeed.

PwC's list was broad and deep. Worse, it was entirely correct.

- There was FP's last-minute revision downward of its swap book mark's last quarter and the fact that FP, in their view, was "managing the process" of valuation and keeping them in the dark.
- The filthy little secret of the global securities lending program had been uncovered. If PwC had known about it before the issuing of the second quarter's 10-Q, they would have forced a change in disclosures.
- How FP and American General Finance had independently arrived at the conclusion that subprime was problematic and stopped doing new business while its mortgage guarantor unit, United Guaranty, and AIG Global Investment Corporation (AIGGIC) kept on doubling down.[6]

The list went on. At the end, Bensinger managed to interject that he wasn't certain that any of the above amounted to a risk-control problem or material weakness. (The notes appear to indicate that PwC's Sullivan didn't really respond to this.)

Martin Sullivan, a savvy salesman and a veteran handler of the difficult situation, noted strongly that he appreciated the early warning and that he deeply wished for a close working relationship with PwC as they sought to address every issue raised. It would not be the last talk PwC had with Sullivan.

Regardless, AIG was again on notice. Its auditors were clearly going to start asserting more control, and there was a very real possibility that investors would be appalled at what they saw. Shareholders and stock prices was the distinctly "precredit crisis" way of thinking about the world, however. In a bond crisis, all that mattered was liquidity and credit rating. Traditionally, what happened to the stock price was of little concern to bondholders, who simply cared about cash flow and where they stood in the capital structure. With CDSs traded actively among hundreds of hedge funds, and a globally interconnected media using swap spread changes as a proxy for financial health, a cacophonous echo chamber had been born in which rumor, hope, and fear would play out in seconds and be reflected in a company's swap prices.[7]

It used to be that a company was what its stock price said it was. Now, it was what its swap spread reflected about it *at that precise moment.* For AIG, this was a deadly development because the swaps market heavily influenced stock prices and eventually bank lending decisions the more the crisis progressed.[8]

The next day, Roemer, after talking with a few attendees from the call, sent Cassano an email thanking him for his "great job of walking through an incredibly complex situation. PwC made special mention of this."

Discussing the PwC part of the email, Cassano told his colleagues in London that the pressure seemed to be turning everything at AIG on its head. His own management didn't read his summaries while PwC thanked him just before pressuring him to adopt someone else's valuation methodology.

■ ■ ■

At a point that December it began to dawn on Andrew Davilman and his colleagues at Goldman that for all the brilliance of FP's executives, they completely misunderstood fundamental aspects of the 2007 CDO market.

The first is that at some level FP was giving the impression that they viewed Goldman as simply making it all up. This was the most disappointing of all since as far as they could tell from what Davilman and his colleagues were hearing from their accounts, no one gave a crap about price discovery anymore except for them. It's all Goldman seemed to do that summer and into that autumn: dozens of controllers, risk managers, accountants tried to establish accurate bid and offer levels for a market in which all anyone cared about was selling.

They had their work cut out for them. Creating substantive trading values for CDOs—defined as the price where a buyer and seller could agree to a trade—involved a fair amount of deductive leg work based on similarity of structure and collateral. Everyone, and Goldman was no exception as Ram had plainly illustrated, had gotten very used to models. They were easy, fast, and, in a rising market, an acceptable way of defining price.[9] In a market where liquidity dried up, it was incumbent upon you to use as many real and observable "proxies" as possible when you are valuing swaps and posting collateral. The ABX indexes weren't perfect at all, but they were a really clear signal as to where people would pay for CDOs at the moment.

The second is that cash wasn't just king; it was more precious than that. Whoever survived in this market would do so because they had a combination of less leverage and more cash than their competitors. As such, with a massive deleveraging occurring, the price that brokers and other natural CDO buyers could pay was now very different from what they could pay when access to capital was easier. When it's your cash, you do tend to pay a different price than when it's someone else's. The upshot was that much less traded, or when it did, it was fully hedged, after lengthy negotiation and at a price the trader could (theoretically) own the paper for an extended amount of time.

Rather than build their model around this, it seemed to Davilman, Sparks, and their colleagues (like structured product trading chief David Lehman) that FP emphasized details that in the end had no real reflection on market fundamentals, like whether the values assigned in collateral calls were at the midpoint of the bid-ask spreads. Of course it *did* have an effect—one value was higher and required less collateral be posted after all—but it was a classic case of "majoring in the minor" details while missing the crucial and obvious issue.

The CDO market was collapsing, and Goldman seemed like it was alone in providing documented levels for valuation and trading purposes. CDOs weren't Treasuries; no two were alike. When a customer brought out bonds for sale at 95 and there was an 80 bid and the bid was hit, well, that information was very, very valuable and told you a lot if you studied it as hard as they did. AIG, on the other hand, seemed like it was doing nothing but inventing straw men and playing for time.

Getting FP's model off the ground was proving to be a Sisyphean task. Going back to early November they had discovered some deeply embedded flaws that had outsized effects in skewing valuations for CDOs. In emails and calls at the time, Cassano told, at various times, Dooley, Habayeb, and even PriceWaterhouse that, "This model is not ready for prime time. Don't make me rely on this." According to Cassano's later testimony to the SEC and Department of Justice (DoJ), he was overruled by Habayeb and PwC and ordered to use it on the view "that something was better than nothing." For a guy who was accused of hiding everything, the document trail, it must be noted, is pretty decisively tilted toward two-way communication.

When the model—called the Binomial Expansion Technique, or BET—finally became serviceable around November 9, it reliably kicked out values that were sharply higher than even Merrill or other troubled CDO dealers. From an observer's point of view, it proved useless in the markets of 2007 and 2008.

■ ■ ■

Willumstad was facing some difficulty managing the board's rising blood pressure. Like investors, the board had grown accustomed to the algebraic increases in profit from the second half of 2005, through the miracle year of 2006, and into the first six months of 2007. Like the AIG boards of 2004 and 2005, who were appalled to learn of the Brightpoint and PNC deals, they got religion really quickly, though.

Fred Langhammer, a former CEO of the Estee Lauder cosmetic empire whom Willumstad described as "one tough German," had a really simple way of handling the issues PwC's team had raised.

Fire Martin Sullivan.

He told Willumstad he was open to all manner of wording on the issue: "Early retirement," "pursuing other opportunities," or whatever phrase the PR department dreamed up. He wanted him out. Pay him or threaten him, but he had to go. Recruited to the board by Zarb in early 2006, he had come on when the company was just emerging from a set of problems that could be traced to, as he put it, "No one having an idea about what was going on."

This looked like a clear repeat of all that.

Willumstad told Langhammer he took his points but getting rid of Martin was going to be no real long-term solution. Willumstad's case would have been easier to make had Sullivan, in a second series of conversations with various board members, been more expansive in describing his plans for handling the issues PwC raised. Instead, he simply replayed his comments about seriously working with PwC to craft solutions, that it was good to get early notice of their concerns and the like. His support for Cassano remained unflagging.

The quarter and the year ended in less than a month and as usual there was no shortage of questions what the final numbers would be. Again, they would have to wait and see.

■■■

Thoroughly entwined now in the money business, AIG management had called a December 5 investors meeting in response to skyrocketing investor anxiety over its portfolios of securitized bonds.

For decades, AIG stood the world on its ear with its reach, adaptability and its raw prowess. Even when it did wrong, it didn't seem to stick. Currently, the opposite dynamic was in effect: everything they did was star-crossed and snake-bit.

AIG hustled anyone who could be said to have direct managerial control or knowledge of anything to do with subprime or CDOs into New York and ordered to prepare a detailed briefing. It happened so rapidly that, as Sullivan was to joke, Edmund Tse, the foreign life executive who had originally been slated to prepare a presentation on those markets, "didn't get the memo" and showed up, speech in hand.

Held at the posh Metropolitan Club on Fifth Avenue, Cassano told Wall Street's analysts and investors that despite dropping $1.1 billion in value for over the previous two months, the super-senior portfolio would come back and, crucially, "It is very difficult to see how there can be losses in these portfolios."[10]

Cassano, whose discussion was thorough and broad-ranging, appears to have talked everyone's ears off. Anything he couldn't answer, Andrew Forster or Gary Gorton did. He made one crucial mistake, however, in not dwelling on what to him was probably obvious: there was a distinction between economic loss (having to pay out on the swap policies as the CDO's underlying collateral defaulted) and mark-to-market losses. Focused intently on cash leaving FP to pay off CDO holders in busted CDOs, he assumed that the world shared his indifference to accounting "adjustments."

He was epically wrong. The valuation "adjustments" that FP was dismissing out of hand looked to the outside world like a nightmarish investment that it could not exit. No one, least of all at PwC or Goldman Sachs, was wondering in December 2007 whether in six years a measurable percentage of the loan pools underlying the CDOs would be irrevocably defaulted.

He also didn't mention the collateral call disputes with Goldman. What little he did discuss of this issue seemed to imply that those issuing the calls would "go away" after AIG signaled disagreement with their marks. Others were amenable, he said, to finding "a middle ground."

There was much confusion he could have avoided had he also drilled into the reality of a collateral call. Much of the outside world, it would later emerge, interpreted the FP collateral postings as zero-sum payments to Goldman Sachs. That Goldman would return every cent of the collateral when the market came back wasn't mentioned either.

In their quest to provide disclosure that trumped what other big companies in the crosshairs were doing, AIG's legal and media relations staff saw defeat snatched from the jaws of victory. With his whole heart, documents and interviews show, Cassano believed everything Gary Gorton's models told him. But FP was no longer about Joe Cassano, much the way it had stopped being about Howard Sosin when he ran afoul of Greenberg over long-dated swaps.

The investing public was now used to reading and seeing 24/7 news coverage of loans so surpassingly abusive that they seemed alternately comic and tragic. Defaults, delinquencies, and foreclosure were very real to the average investor now, and to hear Cassano say there weren't going to be losses severe enough in those bonds to hurt the CDO seemed a stretch. They needed patient explanation of the difference between frightening write-downs and actual economic losses, or the difference between Citi, Merrill, and AIG on this front, not Martin Sullivan's lines about "that's why I sleep well at night."

For a few days at least, though, the old AIG magic worked and what they said was embraced as the stock climbed $3.20 on December 6 to close at $61.35.

When more adjustments loomed in a few weeks though, it became difficult for many to dismiss the sense that Cassano was wildly off-base; that Sullivan had spent countless hours reassuring investors, accountants, and employees that things were OK based entirely on the assurances of Cassano now cast his own credibility into question. When the DoJ and the SEC got involved to piece together who did what in the collapse, this meeting became their starting point.[11]

On January 16, Cassano sent a lengthy email and large spreadsheet attachment to Michael "Woody" Sherwood, Goldman's co-head of Europe, that served as the basis for demanding $1.1 billion in collateral be returned. The claim was that FP's improved model provided broadly higher prices for the CDOs.

Most disputes over collateral calls are resolved, line by line, with a reference to market pricing or something approaching it. This had none of that, relying instead on the model generated numbers to refute Goldman's valuations. It could have been a social-science argument or the like, for all Goldman could figure out. What FP appears to have not considered was that Goldman was executing trades, sooner or later, at the marks they provided. Astoundingly, several of the marks FP's model provided Goldman were at par. With economic history in the balance, and AIG's liquidity stretched, FP appeared to be flirting with the delusional. There was *nothing* backed by that collateral trading near par at the time.

Goldman's efforts at professional and peer-to-peer engagement were failing and concerns were setting in. The CDS position insuring against default was now $2.1 billion.

■ ■ ■

On February 6, 2008, Willumstad met with PwC's Bob Sullivan and Tim Ryan to listen to their concerns over internal controls. They had another laundry list. Ryan delivered the news, barely pausing as each new data point was made. PwC had:

• A lack of confidence that chief risk officer Bob Lewis was up to the job or even had the necessary skill set.
• An uncertainty whether Martin Sullivan was up to the job of changing the culture. More directly, Sullivan had: "a difficulty in holding people accountable for internal control–related matters, making difficult decisions, experience with large scale change, and lacking in execution skills." He was, less politely, a terrible chief executive for anything other than a perfect operating environment in PwC's eyes. Considering that AIG paid their accountants $380 million in fees between 2004 and 2007, this was strong stuff.

- CFO Bensinger was no help. They cited his "lack of leadership, unwillingness to make difficult decisions regarding FP in the past and inexperience in dealing with these complex matters." Like his boss, the auditors perceived him to be the worst CFO imaginable for the moment.
- Granting the board's right to make its own decisions, PwC said Cassano had to go "for the culture of AIG to change."

There was at least a dozen other suggestions, some longstanding concerns, some not, but all spoke to the fact that AIG and its subsidiaries had all the wrong managers and the wrong risk systems in place at the most dangerous moment in financial history.

Starting with Cassano, change was going to come all right, though he kept some of this to himself. Willumstad thanked Ryan and Sullivan for their time and set about figuring out how to implement change where, it was now obvious, it was not welcome.

■■■

In what would become the first indication that AIG was entwined in a Gordian knot of its own making came February 11 when the company filed an 8-K that remains legendary for its opacity and jargon-laden descriptions. The one part all investors could read though was where it said PwC asserted that "a material weakness" existed relating to the "fair-value valuation of the AIGFP super-senior credit-default swap portfolio."

FP could now yell, scream, or cajole, but according to its own auditor, it didn't really have a leg to stand on when it disagreed with the marks from Goldman or other brokers. The only threat they had to play against Goldman—possible legal action—was now completely removed. Even in a litigious age, it made little sense to go to court when your own auditor said you had no idea what you were doing.

The stock dropped 11 percent to $44.74—it was down more than 25 percent since the December 5 presentation—and, lost in the clamor, was the news that Fitch had put the company's ratings on alert for a possible downgrade. If Willumstad had needed any cover, the earnings release on February 28 gave it to him.

Sullivan, who had joked about having a heart attack when a $5 billion loss was discussed in late November, now had to deal with an $11.47 billion write-down that reduced annual earnings to just over $6 billion down from over $14 billion.

Sullivan didn't have a heart attack and survived the ugly investor reaction. Joe Cassano, however, did not. On March 1, it was announced that he was departing AIGFP after 21 years. Sullivan, who hadn't found it easy to stop calling his former friend and boss "Mr. Greenberg," was given an easy out when Cassano volunteered to "retire."[12]

In what might have been his greatest trade, Cassano struck a $1 million per month contract after a brief negotiation directly with Sullivan. Incredibly, someone in AIG's legal department didn't deem the consulting contract material and so it was not disclosed in an SEC filing, a mistake that would become a cornerstone of the argument that AIG was hiding things from the public eye.

The night of the 29th, in the Capital Grille in Stamford, Connecticut, Bill Dooley and Cassano hosted a dinner for 15 of the top executives at FP. Halfway through the meal, Cassano asked for silence and told everyone that he was leaving the next day and that he would do his best to ensure that "everyone would be looked after and taken care of."

The notion of compensating his staff, especially his unit chiefs, was exceptionally important to Cassano, who though he was renowned for his brusque manner, was also a corporate tribal partisan of the highest order. Tremendously proud of what he had built—or continued is perhaps a better way of putting it—he understood fully that 2008 was a wash and wanted to give his key staffers some reward for what had been, for many of them, a hellish ordeal of public and internal scrutiny and 80-hour weeks to fix something none of them had a hand in creating. It went even deeper than that though. Childless and a workaholic, FP, as he saw it, was his family so having taken care of himself—he was, after all, not holding himself out as Gary Cooper—he would try to take care of *everyone*.

Known for his refusal to delegate, Cassano had had to parcel out even some of his most basic administrative duties over the past year since, as some of the senior staff knew, his wife was fighting breast cancer. Refusing to use it as an excuse, he would spend time with her and then stay up and work the night around. Exhausted but unwilling to leave his unit to its fate, the consulting deal seemed like it would allow him to stay with his wife during the recovery period and help FP get back on its feet.

Sullivan, for his part, acceded to the soon-to-be-infamous retention payments because he was deathly afraid of a mass exit of FP leadership and senior producers. The idea of having people in those seats who at least understood what was occurring in the portfolio, who could wind it down and perhaps make some money back was worth an extra $60 million or so. Moreover, an FP exodus at that moment might cause some sort of panic in swaps or might spook a ratings analyst. From where Sullivan sat, this was money well spent.

Over the next three weeks, Dooley and a handful of senior FP managers hammered out the deal. For 2008 and 2009, all employees would get their 2007 compensation level; executive directors would get 75 percent of their 2007 compensation. Though it set a certain proper leadership tone of sacrifice, the reasons for the payment differential were more mundane: the top 15 executive directors often earned between $2 million and $4 million a year, so getting a "haircut" was less painful than it appeared.

With contracts drawn up and signed quickly, and staggered dates for partial payment set, the matter was quickly shelved. To those at FP, this was the basic stuff of Wall Street life: to keep valuable people in their seats, you would give some guarantees.

For a company that prided itself on being the antithesis of all that was Wall Street, FP's most distinctive feature was in some ways its compensation plan. The deferred amount was calculated on a graduated basis such that a $500,000 bonus had no deferred amount, then 10 percent on the next $100,000, then 10 percent on the next $100,000, and so on, up to 50 percent on amounts over $1 million. So, on a bonus of $1,500,000, the amount of deferred was $10,000 + $20,000 + $30,000 + $40,000 + $250,000 = $350,000. The deferred amounts were paid out pro rata over the average life of FP's portfolio, which averaged between four and six years. The employee had no say on when the deferral was to be paid out—it was paid out according to the plan, and consequently the deferral was taxable only when paid.

A nice kicker was that employees with deferral were paid interest at the London Interbank Offered Rate (LIBOR) plus "a spread," or bonus interest payment, that Cassano determined. In some years, the spread got to be as high as 20 percent. That spread came out of the general FP bonus pool, calculated as 30 percent of FP's earnings less expenses.

The compensation scheme was hatched by Greenberg and Matthews, who wanted FP to have not only some of their own cash on the line, but to think longer term about risk and liquidity. There may be better plans to encourage long-term employee commitment and the alignment of risk and rewards in the financial sector, but if so, they aren't readily apparent. By the summer of 2008, there was about $650 million of employee capital in FP; nearly $100 million of this was Cassano's.

It was the textbook definition of irony that the CDS imbroglio happened at FP. There may have been no other workplace in finance whose employees were more incentivized to avoid short-term risk and to stay at the firm building long-term equity.

■ ■ ■

Donn Vickrey was impressed when he saw the press release come across his newsfeed on February 11, 2008. It was, after all, not every day you saw a double-A-rated company that was an icon of the business landscape file a "material weakness" disclosure while simultaneously taking a $5.2 billion charge to earnings.

So he grabbed a few minutes and began to try to make heads-or-tails of the documents. Two days later, he had written his first report on AIG.

Vickrey occupies a rare niche in the investing firmament, one that it all too rarely practiced anymore. Half detective and half accountant, he uses his perch as the founder and president of Gradient Analytics to warn his customers—money managers who pay upwards of $30,000 annually—about the probability of looming financial troubles based on Gradient's detailed scrutiny of corporate financial statements.

Proud of his track record in spotting troubled situations or even outright frauds, since 2002 he had been early—or was the first—to raise the red flag on looming investor pain at Krispy Kreme, Cardinal Health, Arthrocare, and UT/Starcom among others. Recently, however, two companies that alleged Gradient was skewing research to benefit its short-selling customers, had sued him and the company. He strongly protested his innocence and probity but the costs and stress of the suit took a hard toll.[13]

So what he found in AIG not only shocked him but posed a dilemma: he was certain that there were deep accounting issues that had not been explained in full to his clients or the public but he was hesitant in weighing in too strongly on a company that paid more in legal bills than his courtroom opponents made in revenues. Eventually, however, the numbers spoke too loudly. He'd be careful, but he would release it, reasoning that a company with that many CDOs on its balance sheet has more to worry about than an accountant north of San Diego.

The first report was released on February 13 and bore a grade of D, implying that there was the likelihood of an accounting restatement in the future. He had three points: (1) management credibility was at issue since they had had this problem for some time and had assured investors the matter was under control and then, suddenly, a material weakness appears; (2) they wrote swaps they had modeled without "analytical rigor"; and (3) whatever was precisely wrong with the company was not going away with one charge.

On March 3, he released another report, this time with a grade of F attached. In it, Vickrey wrote that, "One of the more disturbing aspects of the AIG situation is management's steadfast claims that non-cash losses indicate the amount of losses the firm is likely to incur. Clearly [PwC] has a different opinion and so do counter-parties."

The issue of counterparties and the auditor intrigued him. He knew that the flip side of the "credit crisis" was a grab to hold on to cash (or to raise it) at all costs. If counterparties were involved—and Vickrey knew nothing about the mechanics of swap settlement—he understood they had every incentive to do anything possible to take in collateral. That, coupled with the auditor's seriousness—Vickrey correctly surmised that PwC's new analytical rigor was a function of its concerns over audit integrity—led Vickrey to conclude AIG was in for an absolute blood-bath. He went on to add that debt downgrades were likely. Naively, he assumed that lower operating margins and higher costs would result, not imagining that counterparties on the swap contracts would require the instant posting of billions in collateral and drive the company out of business in a day.

The response from his client base was surprisingly muted. He got a detailed and angry email from one client and a few follow-up questions from some other clients that were either polite or lost interest in AIG mid email. The reports did get out there, however, and he was able to get some mileage out of them as the media used him as a source to discuss AIG.

The accounting sleuth game was impossible to figure out, Vickrey thought. You raise a few points about a high-flying donut company or a scammy pharma company, and you're in the middle of a war between the company and its critics that lands you on *60 Minutes*.[14] You use blunt language to describe a host of concerns over many aspects of the accounting of a legendary company, predict legal troubles and downgrades, and a day later a single hedge fund client long the stock emails you in disagreement.

■ ■ ■

On March 3, Goldman submitted another $1.7 billion collateral demand to FP, bringing the total demanded since July to $4.2 billion. Like plagues of old that slipped into the New World on rats stowed away on ships, whatever the market malaise was had evolved out of securitized products—bonds backed by pools of loans—and was affecting anything that bore an interest rate.

Bear Stearns, an investment bank that had boasted of an unbroken string of quarterly profits until December 2007, was the first to go. With between 20 percent and 25 percent of its bottom line attributable to its massive mortgage-bond trading franchise, and another 20 percent coming from its prime-brokerage unit, it was fairly easy to see a death foretold, to be literary about it. Once its prime-brokerage customers got worried about Bear's 33 times leverage—and did the math on the declines sustained in its multibillion-dollar mortgage portfolio—equity investors had little ownership claim on the company. At least that's what swaps traders thought and pushed Bear well past danger territory into the realm of the walking dead. Hedge-fund clients who kept their cash and securities on account at the firm pulled out en masse and away went its easiest source of leverage and borrowing.

A firm that had profitably stood since before the Great Depression was gone in less than one week. Had the government not stepped in and brokered a favorable transaction for J. P. Morgan, it would have filed for bankruptcy on Monday, March 16.

A day later, Goldman sent another collateral request for an additional $600 million, bringing the total amount on demand to $4.8 billion. Later that day, FP posted $1 billion in collateral.

On May 8, AIG announced a $7.81 billion loss—and a $9.1 billion charge on the swaps book—for its first quarter. The cumulative mark-to-market loss to date on the swaps now stood at $20 billion. The premium they took in was perhaps $40 million. The stock price was down 25 percent year-to-date and was trading at 1.4 times book value, sharply under the 2.5 times in the Greenberg era.

Swap spreads moved out 15 basis points to 115 basis points for a five-year CDS.

With the grim news came a combination stock and bond offering, which sought to put $12.5 billion back in the equity account. In a rare unabashed piece of good news, they raised $20 billion, a clear vote of confidence in the enterprise. As part of that process, a group of J. P. Morgan Securities officers, including Tim Main, the head of financial institutions and governments group, and a senior executive from the firm's mortgage operations, visited Martin Sullivan to provide an independent valuation for the swaps portfolio. FP's models had a loss of between $1.2 billion and $2.4 billion but as the mortgage veteran began to make his case he cited his firm's fundamental bearishness about housing and the many, many inputs he was basing his evaluation on, including the ABX, the TABX, what secondary market trading there was and so on. The executive said that he had to be frank about the portfolio, so the real charge would be $9 to $11 billion.

Sullivan turned whiter than a ghost and shot Bensinger a furious look. There were some other topics to be covered and the topic drifted away from CDOs. Later, on the drive back to J. P. Morgan's headquarters on Park Avenue, they didn't talk much about Sullivan, because, as the mortgage executive put it, they were stunned. After all, what can you say when the CEO of a trillion-dollar-in-assets company is off his mark on his most important portfolio by at least a factor of four?

When had such a disconnect from the market ended in anything but resignations?

A few days later, Bensinger was removed at the board's insistence.

■ ■ ■

It was announced on April 25, 2008, that Dan Sparks quit. Citing "personal reasons," he was exhausted, stressed out and fed up from being the focal point of customer fury and internal worry. Working 16-hour days, he had done what he could do for the firm. The billions of dollars he had helped make and the losses he had helped avoid weren't enough internally nor externally; at that point Goldman had taken about $4 billion in mortgage write-downs, vastly better than his competitors. It didn't matter. The share price was dropping and everything he had done on the AIG front seemed destined to fail—no one thought they were going to get the collateral posted to them.

Goldman offered him other positions, but he wanted to go home to New Canaan and spend a fair amount of time back in Texas. Sparks was richer than he had thought possible and was looking forward to having something approaching a personal life.

Sparks was completely mistaken. His biggest challenges were still ahead of him.

■ ■ ■

In the midst of raising $20 billion, there was a moment of surpassing strangeness. One day after the sale was complete, the AIG board increased its dividend 10 percent. Companies forced to raise cash under hasty circumstances conserve it, they don't "kick it back" as a dividend to those who just gave it to them. Furthering the unreality, Sullivan gave a speech in London in which he said the dividend helps them position for future growth. This was nonsensical in the extreme: cold hard cash in a bank account helps them weather a volatile market, not cash shipped back to investor pockets.

Judging by the volume and tenor of calls coming into AIG's headquarters, calls were running five to one against it. Institutional investors decried the unserious message or lack of discipline this showed.

If it was an attempt to put a floor under the stock price, it failed. The stock closed under $38 for the first time since 1998.

To Hank Greenberg, it was very easy to see what was wrong: everything. Most especially the way Sullivan had let headcount increase by almost 20,000 between 2005 and 2007, and total expenses increased 10 percent from 2006 to 2007. Against this, revenues dropped slightly. He had filed an SEC 8-K complaining about management failure and his Starr International had been reducing its equity stake for months.

Greenberg, in late night calls to David Boies and to old friends and AIG alumni, railed about the violent lunacy that had taken hold of his once glorious company. They weren't running a business; they were not even pretending to be engaged with issues.

Greenberg was not without some allies. Eli Broad, the billionaire former board member, shared Greenberg's disgust with Sullivan's team. Broad had written Willumstad a letter on May 12 seeking unspecified management improvements, specifically the removal of Sullivan. Broad still owned tens of millions of shares but when he got Legg Mason investor Bill Miller, one of its biggest current owners on board with him, the board chief was forced to take notice.

June was a different story. On top of regulatory inquiries into FP's swap valuation, the board revolted and demanded Sullivan's departure. On June 16, they got it and Sullivan resigned. The board approached Willumstad directly and asked him to take the job; with hesitation, he accepted.

Stepping and pledging an immediate analysis of all businesses, Willumstad began just that: he put everything on the table. More importantly, however, he recognized that AIG had just true constituent at that moment: the ratings agencies. Via telephone and face-to-face meetings, he sold the agencies on the idea of holding off until he could release his 90-day assessment of its strategy for the immediate future. At each of the three agencies, he promised them that there would be no boilerplate in his assessment; it would be an action plan. Units would be on the auction block, investment bankers would be hired, and deals would be sought.

He also met with Larry Fink, the chief executive of BlackRock, the money-management powerhouse that specialized in mortgage bonds and hired a team of his CDO specialists to analyze the FP swaps portfolio. He saw it as not only fresh, expert eyes, but as a tool to add credibility to their side of a collateral dispute.

The plans didn't stop there. Willumstad was going to try to find buyers for FP, American General, and International Lease Finance Company (ILFC), too. AIG was an insurance company and was going to go back to those roots.

The earnings for the second quarter, released on August 6, were terrible again. There was a $5.4 billion net loss and a $5.6 billion charge. The spread between assets and liabilities on the global securities lending program was almost $15.5 billion. If there were redemptions on this portfolio, the company's cash position would be wiped out.

Working like an animal, Willumstad sensed he could maybe pull something together. He thought he could get a decent price over the next year for most of those units, even FP, with its track record and staff, could attract someone.

■■■

In early 2006, one of his staff had brought Doug Slape, the chief analyst with the Texas Department of Insurance (TDI), an interesting point he had picked up in skimming a regulatory filing of AIG's American General unit. It looked to the analyst like AIG had made some shifts in its securities lending program.[15]

Slape told him to look into it but nothing appeared urgent. The TDI's 2005 audits of AIG indicated no problems, and he thought little of it. Thus, began a nearly two-year effort for the TDI to get their hands around what was going on in New York and AIG's magically expanding global securities lending program.

Eventually, as Slape tells it, his analyst came back to him a few months later with some more state insurance regulatory filings and having made a few calls he confirmed to his boss that AIG had indeed changed the language regarding its lending program's parameters—what they could invest in—and had gone about exploding the size of the program. In insurance regulation land, where paper is king, this was a big no-no.

Slape made sure that the team of analysts that would conduct the AIG audit later that year focused on this. Not filing a form announcing that a substantial change in its risk-profile for a key program was really strange. As it happened, the analysts were examining the global securities lending program in the late autumn of 2006 when the first troubles emerged in the subprime market. One of the analysts, with AIG assurances of triple-A-rated security and liquidity ringing in his ears, did a little test. He assumed that most of these ABS bonds would be all right, but that a minority could get downgraded. To model what that looked like, he simply looked at where AA-rated ABSs were trading. The differential in dollar price, even in November 2006, was massive. The loss of hundreds of millions of dollars from a minor series of downgrades was very real.

TDI "saw the pressure on this portfolio" and began to closely monitor it. Since there weren't yet clear indications that the portfolio was stressed, they couldn't really do much. It's true: TDI's mandate was to monitor insurance companies doing business in Texas for possible risk to Texas consumers, not guard against every jackass idea some company proposes.

The disaster of the summer of 2007 took risks that had long been held to be theoretical and made them real. The securities lending program was looking like it was going to hurt a lot of people, and not just in Texas. That August, in response to increasingly pointed queries from TDI, AIG officials flew down to Austin and assured them that every single dollar that any investor wanted, at any time they wanted it, would be returned to them.

That wasn't good enough. TDI ordered the portfolio shrunk and AIG said that under orders from both Win Neuger and Richard Scott— the head of taxable fixed income—they had been doing just that. It was pretty hard not to notice the major tone shift from AIG but for Slape and TDI, tracking the program was difficult since it was so opaque. It could be approximated via hours of sifting through state insurance filings, but it was disclosed nowhere in SEC filings.

Slape said they worked closely with the securities lending program to monitor its goals throughout 2008. In late June, AIG disclosed that year-to-date, the securities lending portfolio had dropped $13 billion in value.

This set in motion a frantic series of events. Led by Eric Dinallo, the superintendent of the New York State Insurance Department, the 11 states where AIG had regulated insurance subsidiaries pressed the company to step in and support the program. If AIG balked, they had the right to seize the companies to protect policyholders. Should that have happened, AIG would have collapsed within a matter of days, something federal regulators were very anxious to avoid, according to Dinallo.

AIG did step in and guarantee the securities lending portfolio, and it injected $5 billion in capital into the subsidiary pool to ensure that capital would be available at a moment's notice. In what would became the recurring theme of the credit crisis, precious and life-giving capital, raised from investors at once loyal and opportunistic, was deployed, in the view that it would send a message to customers and counterparties.

It would not be enough.

In the bitterly cruel logic of markets, AIG was perceived of being the weak member of the herd. If the primary financial feature of this credit crisis was the market's major players demanding collateral and scaling back on business with each other, the other one was a manic bid to pull in one's horns and conserve cash. As the trading business slowed, Goldman and Merrill Lynch, J. P. Morgan, and Morgan Stanley began a manic cycle of returning the securities they borrowed from each other and the big commercial banks to get their precious cash collateral back. In a nutshell, Goldman and others decided that having billions of dollars stored up in a company that had consistently failed to predict or even comprehend its spiraling liabilities and losses was a bad idea in that market. To meet these demands from the companies that had sought so bitterly just months before to do business with it, AIG had to dip into the corporate cash drawer. The back of that drawer was getting closer and closer.

At AIG's public relations office at headquarters, a *Bloomberg News* article served as an all-new catalyst for frenzied calls and worry. *Bloomberg's* Miles Weiss, a regulatory affairs reporter who ordinarily did not cover AIG, penned a piece on June 27 that used the state insurance filings to suss out AIG's support to the collapsing securities lending portfolio.[16] In meetings with PR and investor relations staff, Chris Winans, the former analyst and reporter, patiently explained to his younger or less experienced colleagues that the whole mark-to-market issue didn't apply here. Shortfalls in the portfolio and investor redemptions equaled pure cash losses. It didn't take long for his colleagues to understand that AIG's choice was between watching life insurance subsidiaries scramble to get its assets back so they could meet what they could of their obligations to policy holders or AIG futilely using its remaining cash—its life's blood—to stabilize a portfolio grown so large it far outstripped all of its available cash and credit lines.

For the first time, investors began to imagine what was unimaginable: AIG might not make it. There was no mathematical formula that could sum things any differently: FP and the securities lending portfolio were wiping out the firm on an hourly basis.

Win Neuger had conceived of "Ten Cubed" as a path to increased riches and prominence. It was now threatening to become one of the most dangerous ideas in the history of the free market.

■ ■ ■

A Goldman analyst, Tom Cholnoky, had released a "sell" report on August 18, 2008, in which he made a series of critical statements that over the next two weeks would lead the investment world to capitulate on AIG. Outside of the fact it is a "Sell," which in itself was always news, the report isn't all that earth shattering in terms of laying new analytical groundwork. It simply cogently outlined everything that had been happening with AIG and logically footed the numbers, concluding that AIG was in a *lot* of trouble. Coming from an analyst of Cholnoky's stature and with a compelling pulpit at Goldman, his arguments were the proverbial tipping point that forced institutional investors to take heed. Swap spreads soon went above 250 basis points and the stock was creamed again.

For Willumstad, in the ordinary course of events, this would have been a major fire alarm. As it was, the only thing he cared about the report was the effect it had on the ratings agencies. He argued, cajoled, and nearly begged for them to hold off. He had secured oral commitments, he reminded them, for a 90-day window and he was making headway. They agreed to hold off, or so he thought.

The plain fact of the matter was that selling any part of AIG was proving to be impossibly complex. Many subsidiaries had cross-ownership of each other's equity and with insurance subsidiaries, pulling out the equity also entailed a possible removal of its policy surplus (or the amount that its assets exceeded liabilities.) So the sale or spinoff of

ILFC, an obvious choice to raise capital, actually threatened to harm National Union, another key AIG subsidiary, which owned a substantial chunk of ILFC's stock.[17] Ripping that out without a carefully detailed plan to immediately replace it with something of equal value would be a disaster to an otherwise profitable unit.

It went on and on, subsidiary after subsidiary. Transactions were indeed possible, it's just that it would take months, if not a year, of maneuvering to construct a deal that took a unit off the books without hurting other units.

Everywhere Willumstad went, doors that should be opened, were closing or were already shut.

■ ■ ■

Over the course of that summer, Willumstad began to confront another unthinkable: squaring things with Greenberg. He saw both sides of the story. If he was on the board in March 2005 he would likely have pushed for Greenberg to go, but this war with Greenberg was stupidity itself. Thousands of man-hours had been taken away from running AIG's business as executives were deposed and testified, documents produced, factions developed internally—it was a management nightmare.

Greenberg saw it the same way. A deal man to his core, he had worked out a laundry list of possible scenarios: tap his Rolodex for major investments from abroad—not from some mutual fund holder somewhere, but a big-ticket infusion from the sovereign wealth funds— begin the process of asset sales, and above all, speak to the *right people* in government. A temporary loan to AIG, if it came to it, was in the national interest and could be paid back readily, no matter what the interest rate. Policymakers needed to understand AIG wasn't some stupid investment bank; it was the company that greased the skids of the free world.

His strategy for handling collateral calls was easy. Given the opacity of the market and the reliance on computer models to generate requests for AIG's precious cash, Goldman Sachs and the other investment banks could go screw. If they didn't like it, this was New York and there was a courthouse on every corner. He liked his chances against a firm that was a long way from the men like John Whitehead and John Weinberg, whom he had considered friends and advisers.[18]

He had Willumstad up to his apartment for dinner, and he laid this out and more; he found Bob to be a good listener and clearheaded about many things. Getting down to it, he had three demands: there would be some sort of payment for this nightmare AIG decided to put him through, an indemnification for any looming headaches from either the New York attorney general's office or the feds, and most importantly, an apology. He had built this company from a series of niche insurance companies to something that the U.S. government used to get information about what was happening abroad; it was an indispensable company. When things got ugly, AIG tossed him to the Street like a used napkin, sued him, mocked him, and tarnished his legacy. Hank Greenberg wanted the public to know that AIG had a big change of mind about him.

In turn, he was going to go work 24 hours a day calling all the people on Planet Earth who could get to the word "yes" on large investments. The idiot investment bankers they hired were probably putting together slide presentations for some midlevel committee in Singapore. He wouldn't have that problem.

Willumstad had no problem with the money and could probably get some sort of statement out there to Hank's liking, but as he heard it, Hank wanted him to call off the dogs on the legal process, somehow protect him from what had happened on the Gen Re deal, and he couldn't do that. If Hank had to go to court, he had to go to court, and AIG shouldn't have a contractual obligation to backstop his legal fees or any damages he was assessed. He wanted a settlement—AIG had spent $1.2 billion on legal and consulting fees since he left and they needed his help—but there were things he couldn't deliver.

They agreed to explore it further over the next couple of weeks. They didn't know they wouldn't have that long.

■ ■ ■

In Greensboro, North Carolina, one of the many minor tragedies of the AIG saga was playing out. United Guaranty Corporation (UGC) was a mortgage insurer that AIG had bought for $200 million in 1981 and had gradually built into a leading provider of mortgage insurance. The company played an important link in the mortgage food chain, insuring pieces of loans that exceeded 80 percent of the value of the property.[19] Long run by a former senior Wachovia banker named Charles Reid, who made it into an industry leader, he had cut a deal with Greenberg and Matthews in the 1980s when he agreed to leave banking to take over the CEO slot: he would grow, but only at his pace, to which Greenberg replied, "You can take some risk, but only at our levels."

Reid was given full reign to approve or deny any business he wanted, and UGC grew. By the early parts of the decade, Billy Nutt took over and ran the company in much the same fashion. After Greenberg left, as the mortgage market heated up, Nutt faced pressure to grow, to meet forecasts to keep up with competition and hit contract incentives. AIG's headquarters, which had just seen American General Finance and FP exit business lines because of concerns over the sub-prime market, said or did nothing.

As the quality of the borrower diminished, as mortgage lenders willingly embraced more risk to feed the Wall Street machine, United Guaranty had to engage in incrementally riskier levels of underwriting to get business done. The results were predictable: they found the marginal borrowers and lent to them in the middle of a market bubble.

An AIG unit chiefs meeting from mid-2007 is a good example. As UGC posted its first losses, about $100 million, Nutt was explaining to Martin Sullivan and other senior management that while they hit a rough patch, they were writing excellent new business and, at any rate, the competition was getting killed. Sullivan smilingly told Nutt that even if he didn't write another dollar in business for a few months, "We would still love him." AIG staffers had a phrase for this sort of response: "classic Martin." It was the decent word or gesture, directed at a manager who was clearly fumbling, both publicly and on the job. But it also carried a serious message: better to be safe than sorry. The trouble is that the time for this was two to three years earlier.

There was perhaps much to be desired in how Greenberg approached management but the man's entire worldview centered on risk. There was a price at which risk could be tolerated, and there were prices in which it was plain old bad business. His every interaction with Charlie Reid had been to focus on the economic trade-off between the profits that came from growth and the risk it took to get there. Sullivan, and to a smaller extent Nutt, chose the easy road of growth.

At the end of 2009, UGC—a throwback company that sought to take a leadership role in the Greensboro business community and civic life—had booked about $3.9 billion in losses and was laying off 20 percent of its local workforce.

■■■

Starting in late August 2008, Willumstad had begun keeping the Federal Reserve in the loop about AIG's liquidity needs and especially about what would happen if they were downgraded. It was fairly useless, he thought, since it was unclear that anyone was paying the slightest bit of attention. People treated him politely enough, but no one gave the sense that they understood AIG was a risk to the entire system. He wasn't waving his arms and announcing that they were collapsing, but he made clear that things were looking terrible.

As Labor Day passed, it became clearer that the ratings agencies weren't going to hold off. Like everyone else, their reputations were in tatters from years of benign neglect or even incompetence. Like some sort of cosmic leveling wind, they sought to act most boldly at the mathematical moment when it was most dangerous for them to do so.

On September 7, Fannie and Freddie were bailed out and placed into receivership. In the course of the bailout, the government wiped out the billions of dollars' worth of preferred stock the company had raised just months prior. It gave Willumstad a chill since AIG had itself just raised billions of dollars' worth of preferred stock. On the 9th, he met with Tim Geithner, the New York Fed's president, and told him that losses were mounting at his financial services units and that AIG would continue to post losses. Geithner thanked him but was distracted; Willumstad understood this. He could piece together what was happening in the swaps markets; Wall Street was dying.

Still, he hadn't expected Geithner to take the detailed list of collateral requirements that Willumstad provided him—designed to catch his attention, frankly—and place it on a pile on the corner of his desk. On that document was the number $2.5 trillion, the amount of exposure AIG was calculating that its counterparties had to it, in one form or another, in global derivatives markets. Before he could bring it up, he was politely hustled out. What that really big number meant was that one side of a contract in an energy, commodity or financial contract somewhere on earth, in an amount equal to one-eighth the U.S. gross domestic product (GDP), was going to get severed over the next few weeks if he couldn't get some cash in the door. That would get *somebody's* attention, he thought.

Over the next few days, Willumstad saw that hope was something he was going to have to do away with. Investors began to balk at "rolling," or reinvesting in AIG's ultra-short-term loans known as commercial paper (CP). Over the decades, CP emerged as the preferred way that financial companies kept their balance sheets liquid. Without this, FP and ILFC would have to become fully funded by the parent or stage a fire sale of assets to meet their short-term obligations and shrink the balance sheet. That was not going to happen: they didn't have the cash, and those units didn't have the type of assets they could sell to raise in time.

Going into the second weekend of September, it was obvious to him that this was it. The funding markets collapsed, and both Merrill and Lehman weren't going to be able to make it into the next week as independent companies. Of the pair, Lehman was most vulnerable, since it lacked the diversity of assets Merrill had.

An attempt to peddle some of the insurance units to Berkshire Hathaway's Warren Buffett, the only man alive who knew as much as Greenberg about insurance, and who coincidentally happened to have a triple-A rating and tens of billions in cash, failed comically. Buffett, whom Willumstad reached at his Omaha home, didn't have a fax at his house and never used a computer, so he couldn't get a term sheet sent to him. "Tell you what, Bob," Willumstad recalls him saying, "I'll get in my car and go to the office. Fax it there."

A few hours later came the reply: "No thanks." At $25 billion the price was just too steep and looking at the horizon, and Buffett didn't want to drain that much of his cash. Hanging up, Willumstad thought to himself that at least the stories were true: Buffett really *does* move quickly and does all of his own analysis.

On that Friday night, Standard & Poor's told him that a downgrade was pending, possibly of as much as three notches. When that happened, AIG would have until the opening of business Tuesday in New York to come up with at least $18.6 billion (more if it was more than one notch). That was only the beginning of the cash conversation though. The securities lending portfolio alone was going to need that much again since starting on September 7, the program was hit with what would become more than $25 billion in redemptions.

Teams from the New York governor's office and the New York State Department of Insurance were working to allow AIG to access up to $20 billion of cash held at state-regulated insurance subsidiaries. The problem was that it could happen only if AIG received an assurance—in the form of a guarantee—that AIG would live long enough to replenish the assets it was borrowing.

That was the sticking point all weekend as Willumstad saw it: the private-equity shops swarming over AIG all wanted to have some sort of pledge that AIG would survive. The problem was that Secretary of the Treasury Hank Paulson emphasized in a meeting that Saturday that absolutely no rescue was forthcoming, and that only a private-sector solution was going to work. In several conversations with Willumstad that weekend, Geithner or his subordinates emphasized that point.

So no assurance equaled no buyer.

Waiting in a pleasant waiting room off of Geithner's office at the Fed to brief him on the latest failure, Willumstad just sat there and went over the small details of every phone call and every action that brought him there. He had no idea what he could have done differently.

He then would get ushered into Geithner's office, proverbial tin cup in hand, and try to get him to focus for more than a few minutes at a time. They were both at a substantial disadvantage: there was no time, and given the compressed time horizon, there was an inability to communicate the gravity of the situation. How, for example, could he communicate the fact that the securities lending program alone would probably imperil six insurance companies, other than to note that policyholders were at risk? There was no institutional history of modern insurance companies like AIG simply not having the promised cash on hand to meet its obligation when there was a fire or someone died.[20]

The problem wasn't that the Fed wasn't paying attention to AIG since it had limited jurisdiction over an insurance company; it was that the wide-ranging connections from AIG to the entire global financial apparatus wasn't either understood or appreciated. When, on September 12, Fed vice president Hailey Boesky sent her boss Bill Dudley an email saying that she was hearing that there was "$2.5 trillion exposure" to AIG among hedge funds and brokers globally, she was correct. The problem was that this was something she was hearing, not something they were actively studying. How odd: AIG grew to become as powerful as it did, and yet the New York Fed, located a block away, understood none of it.[21]

■ ■ ■

The weekend of September 2008, known as "Lehman weekend" in New York's financial community, was going to be "AIG weekend" if Doug Slape, of the Texas Department of Insurance, had anything to do with it. He had their legal counsel draw up papers to seize up to four different AIG subsidiaries. Mindful of the broader picture, as well as federal prerogatives, Slape and TDI had watched silently for weeks, waiting for some big investor to come and inject capital into AIG. When it didn't happen, they got busy. "We saw the possibility of deterioration and when [insurance] companies totter, they can go quickly."

They can also go quickly when regulators seize their operating units. There is no gainsaying that Slape and TDI were well within their purview to seize the units, but it wasn't without its risks. Seizing troubled units in a situation like that means that they have to run the units with the assets on hand; many of these units had a large dollar volume of assets still stuck in the securities lending program. There was a possibility that seizing them might lead to temporary, or even permanent, benefit reductions—so-called haircuts—in the assets available for policyholders. The choice was a brutal one for the TDI: act now and preserve a percentage of policyholder assets, or wait a few more days and hope that something fully stabilized AIG.

They decided to hold off for a few more days. In doing so, they were taking the advice of the politically connected Eric Dinallo, the chief of the New York State Insurance Department, who was counseling patience in the face of the massive private-public sector meetings that weekend, September 13–14.

■ ■ ■

Eventually, the stark realities of what an AIG collapse would amount to in a practical sense began to hit home at the New York Fed. In a series of quiet conversations, in ones and twos, a consensus began to emerge that AIG's collapse would be like nothing the United States had ever seen.

The Fed's thinking can be referred to along these lines. Given that almost a dozen insurance subs were compromised, millions of policy-holders were in danger of literally being at risk with no economic backing to support their claims. Internationally, there would be an immediate slowdown to shipping and aviation, as AIG was a key player in insuring both market segments. Other insurance companies would have stepped in to offer coverage sooner than later, but not before disruptions occurred and losses were sustained.

Financially, it would have been true chaos. What cash or liquid assets there was at AIG would have been sent, eventually, to the insurance subsidiaries to meet those obligations. Left remaining would have been a $1.2 trillion balance sheet that would have dwarfed the collapse from the looming Lehman bankruptcy. Short-term debt funds the world over, the repositories of trillions of dollars in corporate and personal cash, had made AIG a core holding and would have sustained severe losses. This would have occurred alongside a parallel deleveraging that would have made the already brutal events of that year seem child's play. As hedge funds and the surviving brokers sold what they could to meet margin calls and redemptions, the Fed—in conversations among themselves—began to imagine a protracted dislocation in equity markets and many, if not most, bond markets.

As the world went to cash, much real economic activity would slow. The next stop might be political unrest and, at the margins, perhaps lasting damage to U.S. interests among nations that were productive trading partners.

A simpler way of phrasing the above is that AIG's collapse would have had direct and immediate adverse effect on the producers of goods and the traders of goods, by making prices higher and products, at least temporarily, less available. It would also have had a devastating effect on the retiree accounts and insurance policies of tens of millions of people worldwide as insurance companies were seized and annuities devastated. The careful economic planning of generations of families and small businesses would have been ruined. No one owned a crystal ball, so perhaps only a fraction of this would have come to pass, or if it did, perhaps it wouldn't have happened all at once.

It is not clear if any of this was ever committed to paper or was formally discussed. Two of the people who spoke to Fed president Geithner about the matter at the time say—in comparison to Willumstad's view—he was fully engaged and aware of the broad risks of an AIG collapse. It doesn't matter really. The point is that there isn't much evidence that the Fed's analysts began to prospectively frame this out until September 14. When they did, however, they went a mile deep. The conclusion presented itself.

As Geithner was getting that analysis is about when Willumstad called and said that all private-sector solutions were failing. To start with, over the course of about five days, AIG went from trying to borrow or raise $30 billion to, at a point on Sunday the 14th, trying to raise nearly $80 billion. Any chance of possibly raising anything like the amounts needed was doomed because of their moving cash needs. The world wanted their cash back from AIG, they wanted collateral returned, and, most of all, they didn't want to do any more business with AIG. And they wanted it all within the next few days. Who would lend an acquaintance a large amount of money, say a percentage of their annual salary, if the person kept increasing the amount needed and then finally admitted that no matter how big the amount lent, it might not be enough? That's what AIG's banks were looking at.

Meanwhile, the next day, Lehman collapsed, with its $600 billion balance sheet freezing markets and devastating money-market funds. The heads of banks the world over—who had stopped doing mean-ingful business with AIG days or a few weeks ago—were now stopping doing business with each other.

There was little appetite to lend into that, and without assurances from the government, any deal was dead. He informed Geithner that he was going to have AIG file for bankruptcy that afternoon, but before that he was going to draw down about $14 billion on its credit facilities.

■ ■ ■

AIG had been written off on Goldman's trading floor for a long time when mid-September rolled around. Ram Sundaram's Principal Funding and Investment and a regular mortgage-trading desk had about $22.4 billion of CDSs on with AIGFP as a counter-party. They had about $7.6 billion of FP's collateral and $4 billion in swaps on AIG to hedge what they argued was the difference owed to them.

Goldman Sachs CEO Lloyd Blankfein, at meetings at the New York Fed that weekend, made a very big deal about AIG's refusal to post the collateral differential. He indicated that he wouldn't ease off collateral calls or stop pulling money out of the securities lending program—Goldman was a big customer—until he got his collateral.

To the traders and sales staff, they thought it was a nice try but futile. Blankfein couldn't disclose that he needed the money because, unlike his competitors, he didn't run a bank. If he ever mentioned or tipped that he was needing cash, there was the belief that the firm would be gone within 48 hours.

That Monday, Lehman collapsed, and Bank of America rescued Merrill from its guaranteed collapse (likely within 48 hours) by buying it. The more shrewd Goldman staffers had long concluded that Bear and Lehman would go, followed closely by Merrill. It was their turn now, followed, they supposed, by Morgan Stanley.

On paper, they were "flat," or had no material exposure to AIG. In such a case, from an accounting standpoint, AIG could live or die and it wouldn't matter to Goldman. This is the line that their public relations staff has adhered to. In practicality, the collapse of AIG would have created a panic that would have likely sucked more excess capital out of the capital markets than any event in history. Goldman would have been the primary victim in such a scenario as hedge funds redeemed their assets or collapsed (leaving Goldman with worthless collateral), eventually forcing the firm to virtually fund itself.

Ram's bid for buying longer-term funding capacity may have forestalled it's reckoning, but it would have come. Whether it would have led to collapse like at Bear and Lehman (and nearly Merrill) is less certain, but it would have been a body blow, a truly grievous wound unlike any in its history.

Goldman's situation was akin to those old war movies, where the crafty submarine captain, finding himself in a tight spot, is being depth-charged. There is always the scene where the anxious crew stare at the ceiling as the explosions get closer and leaks sprout. In the movies, the crew's ability to endure the terror always leads to their escape as the ships on the surface motor away. In real life, the sub crews that found themselves in those situations usually never saw the surface again.

No one thought there was anything about what was happening that was like a movie. Andrew Davilman would note with dark irony to his closest friends that he supposed his next big business venture with FP was now on ice. It was to be a derivative products company known as White Oak. Goldman had spent millions of dollars developing it and he and Goldman's bankers were planning on doing a road show that autumn prior to its launch. What White Oak would be was a smarter MBIA, charging fees to "wrap," or guarantee, the credit on structured credit products such as the top-rated tranche of an investment-grade bond index. Goldman would provide the products and the clients and FP would do the guarantee. For a while there, it didn't seem like an idea that could lose.

■ ■ ■

Geithner told Willumstad to stay put and at about 4 PM he'd receive something. He advised strongly against accessing the bank credit facilities, or "revolvers," since it would, he said, send the wrong message.

Simpson Thatcher's Dick Beattie, still the adviser to the independent directors on AIG's board, got the document first and analyzed it. Turning to Willumstad, he said, "Well, you finally get your chance to work for the federal government."

"What do you mean?" Willumstad replied.

"They own you now," said Beattie. A few minutes later Treasury Secretary Paulson called Willumstad. After listening for a few moments and nodding, he hung up with a curt "I understand" and told Beattie he was wrong.

"What do you mean?"

"They just fired me."

And indeed the federal government, acting on behalf of the American people, did essentially own AIG and, to make a fresh start, was installing former Allstate chief executive Ed Liddy as CEO.[22]

The Fed's term sheet, full of misspellings, provided an $85 billion credit facility that effectively wiped out the existing shareholders in the creation of a warrant that gave the government a 79.9 percent equity stake. It was structured in such a way that it was more practical to draw it down than not. It was obvious that even with a "normal" economy returning, most of AIG's crown jewels would have to be sold to pay it back.

Whatever AIG had been, it would be no longer.

■■■

Nick Ashooh, the head of corporate communications at AIG, had sent everyone who worked for him (and as many as he could who didn't) home late on the 16th and told them to take the day off. Having spent the night in a hotel room downtown, Ashooh was walking around the normally busy and crowded hallways and offices of AIG, marveling at the surreal silence that corporate trauma wrought. A bit down the hall, he bumped into a ruddy and slightly disheveled man wearing a suit with a loose tie, carrying an overnight bag and a puzzled expression.

Asking if he could help the man, he was surprised to find his offer readily accepted. Grasping Ashooh's hand and forming it into a handshake, the stranger smiled as he shook his hand.

"Hello, hello. My name is Ed Liddy, and I'm the new CEO. Who are you? And who"—circling his finger in the air—"who works here?"

Nick introduced himself and spent several pleasant minutes with the puzzled stranger.

After a few minutes, Liddy smiled and asked Nick where he should go next, allowing that he had no real idea what was going on. Ashooh said he had no idea either as he guided him to the elevator. As they rode down through the Art Deco carcass of AIG, Ashooh thought that it would be a very good thing indeed if this time someone in the CEO's office did have an idea what was going on.

■ ■ ■

At AIGFP, a feeling of exhaustion was in the air. Equity trading chief Jake DeSantis was walking around one of the kitchens, trying to think about what it all meant and how it came to this point. They had set the company up so that they had no real connection to Wall Street, isolated in a woody development in Wilton, Connecticut, and yet there they were, at the center of the most lopsided one-way trade in history.

He was grabbing a cup of coffee when a pair of assistants, just as haggard and depressed as anyone else, came running through, cleaning out the drawers and cabinets hastily by throwing things into plastic bags.

"What's going on?"

One of them replied, "The Fed is coming here. Corporate called and told us to get rid of the . . . things."

"Things?"

"Well, the nice teas and coffee, the sodas, the Perrier . . . we canceled the lunch service." As she went back to throwing out the candy and brown sugar, it hit DeSantis at that moment.

The government owns us, and now we have to look like it.

DeSantis had grown up in modest circumstances in the hills of western Pennsylvania and went to MIT on a full scholarship, so he had an intimate knowledge of what humble was and looked like. This was just dramatic play acting, pretending that they hadn't had catered lunches just days before. He shook his head at the absurdity and began to laugh.

DeSantis thought of the gym, with its hundreds of thousands of dollars of weights, machines, and the latest exercise equipment. You couldn't miss it when you walked in the door.

He wondered how they were going to make *that* disappear in the next hour.

■ ■ ■

As the AIG he had known and loved began to sink beneath the waves, Greenberg sat in his Park Avenue office and made phone calls.

Lots and lots of phone calls.

He had made calls all of his career, and he always seemed to get what he wanted: the information. Because he valued information so highly—and discounted opinions so readily—he had developed a system of getting it that only the few understood. The good information, the raw intelligence about business conditions on the ground or political developments in a far-off locale, was rarely had from talking to the division chiefs or the head of such-and-such region, but from the men and women three or more ranks below him.

So Greenberg always found the guy whose responsibility it was to do what he wanted—what he needed—to know about. That man was still hungry; he understood what could kill him, and he knew what he didn't have or what he needed to win. That man, out of equal measures of both fear and the desire to please, would tell Greenberg everything he needed to know. Political problems on the ground, regulatory headaches, organizational sluggishness, strong rivals or his own weak team—it was always the same. With good information, you could act; with bad information, you could react. The difference was what had once set AIG apart.

People feared him, he knew, but so be it. He needed what he needed to make the decisions that had to be made, and if people couldn't handle it, they could go work on a leafy and pleasant suburban campus for Chubb or for some other company. Those people would stay comfortable and never be rich, and they most assuredly would never be great. The head of the CIA didn't call Chubb executives, nor did the State Department, when it had to understand the minutiae of business life in some far-flung locale, consult with Travelers.

And it showed, he would tell those close to him when he read of some inevitable corporate screw-up, it always showed. Corporate America built models and hatched plans, they hired gilt-edged advisers who knew everything (and repeatedly told you that) and they spent reams of shareholder cash. The best-looking and smartest people they could hire fanned out across the globe and sold and promised and wrote contracts and, he thought, as often as not, they failed.

Which was all Greenberg's way of saying that all the other corporations never sought to understand what could go wrong; they never understood the risk.

That was not a weakness of Greenberg's. He hunted risk and stripped it out of every problem and considered it separately. Everyone who reported to him was trained to do the same thing. He taught them that the men who had built AIG into something that had been worth nearly $190 billion looked at each challenge as having three components. There was the operational problem, a financial component, and then separate from everything, there was the risk. Operational and financial problems could almost always be solved or understood, but the risk, well, that was your challenge right there.

Managing risk, in Greenberg's eyes, was not using your balance sheet to make something more attractive to a customer by loaning them money like some brain-dead appliance retailer, it was trying to understand if their customers would even want what they were selling four years from now and pricing their insurance accordingly.

Buildings fell, houses burned, airlines changed the sorts of planes they used, and energy use shifted as emerging powers grew into global economic forces. If you could reasonably approximate the cost of doing business when plans failed or markets reversed and the balance of power shifted, then you could begin to understand the cost of risk.

He kidded himself not. Understanding risk was not something many, perhaps most, could readily grasp. So, with a healthy sense of paranoia, he had a staff that kept watch against the most obvious sorts of threats. One of the core ones was that Wall Street worked for you. At the end of the day, for 35 years at the helm of AIG, Wall Street brought his people ideas, came to them for favors, looked to his company for capital, and it was never the other way around. Everything AIG did was, in a sense, to become and remain self-supporting. He had never seen, not once, a company that was reliant on the capital markets not run into some epic trouble.

And the first thing that happened after he left AIG—pushed, as he saw it, by ungrateful traitors on a board afraid of a power-mad attorney general—was that the company went to work for Wall Street. They hung up a shingle and happily solicited business insuring the most diabolical instruments Wall Street had ever cooked up, for pennies per billion dollars of risk.

Pure, unrefined risk.

It got worse—much, much worse. They had taken the AIG subsidiaries, the most powerful property and casualty underwriters in the world, and stuffed them full of these instruments. The men who followed him, whom he had nurtured along, trained, cajoled, and corrected—these men had treated capital like it was the divine right of kings; that the markets that were closing for other legendary names across the island of Manhattan were eternally open for them.

Now, teams of bankers and lawyers and company executives sat around tables at the company he had built and prayed for some bailout from Washington. In three and one-half years, it had gone from AIG's telling Washington what was really going on in the world to AIG's praying to political hacks for deliverance.

Above all else, this is what hurt: the yelling, the blaming, the false shock. Had they learned nothing in 35 years? There was plenty to scream about in business—a plan failed because someone didn't do something, contracts weren't honored, fraud, ignorance, and more. But you never, ever screamed about risk. You merely lived with it or got rid of it.

Risk just was. You couldn't change risk because it existed apart from everything else. You could only set the terms on which you owned it or sold it.

AIG as he knew and loved it was dead—its $1 trillion dollar balance sheet—and there was nothing he could do. Everyone he had known or made rich or promoted, the men and women who respected but feared him, they were going to be wiped out. There would be nothing left of his life's work except footnotes and lawsuits.

This was Hank Greenberg's world in the middle of that September. He thought all of these things as the futility of calling his lieutenants struck him. There were no more lieutenants, just the people who had come with him when he left AIG and his lawyers. They all knew less than he did, but they made calls, too.

Like a field marshal desperately staring at a campaign map, but with divisions that had long since fallen on the field of battle, Hank Greenberg studied the situation, thought some more, and picked up the phone again.

Epilogue

The bailout of September 16 was not the end of AIG's collapse.

Despite the Fed's $85 billion loan, no trading desk wanted to have anything to do with the company; collateral calls and demands for the return of the securities lending collateral continued. This was less a rejection of the United States' full faith and credit as it was something much more primal: a modern-day financial equivalent of the way medieval castles pulled up the drawbridge and barricaded windows and doors. This was unprecedented, as other U.S. interventions in the capital markets had always stabilized a panicked market.

The reasoning for doubting the adequacy of the Fed's bailout was investor belief that the entire Western world was one big, highly levered real estate trade. Anecdotally, they had a hell of a case. From the consumer level, where just months before, home equity lines of credit and real estate speculation were acceptable subjects of conversation at soccer games and parties to Wall Street, where *guaranteeing* a midlevel trader on a mortgage desk $2 million or more for several years had become a standard protocol, the effects of the real estate boom (and securitization) seemingly defined the American economy.[1] For almost two years, traders and investors had listened—and believed—as the leaders of the American corporate and regulatory landscape insisted that matters were well in hand.

They weren't, of course, and traders and investors who had been devastated by a fearful combination of executive deceit and incompetence no longer had a margin of trust. AIG's $85 billion loan from the feds was for their working capital—debt maturities, collateral calls, and the like—and was hardly seen as enough to give it a sound footing.[2]

So AIG began to slip beneath the surface again. By October, it was en route to what would become a $25 billion quarterly loss. An inconceivably large number of itself, it was guaranteed to trigger more downgrades, which would inevitably bring up to $35 billion in additional collateral calls.

Like a bad game of chess, the Fed's every move seemed to be checked. An $85 billion loan was soaked up in weeks; the benefits from Maiden Lane II, a $19.5 billion so-called special-purpose vehicle set up to hold the riskiest mortgage bonds from the securities lending portfolio, were neutered when the looming downgrades began to threaten the credit-default swap (CDS) portfolio.[3]

So the Fed went with what was *perceived* to have worked (even though every move—each more unprecedented than the next—had failed to stabilize the situation) and Maiden Lane III was set up to staunch the potentially fatal hemorrhaging of cash from FP's epic misadventure with CDSs.

This time, the plan worked. AIG, while it would go on to lose billions of dollars additionally, would never again come close to collapsing. The Fed, however, unleashed a firestorm of criticism and resentment with this plan, which it had never imagined possible. In popular imagination, the Fed became a sort of diabolical trinity: the unambiguous symbol of New York financial cronyism, the inept regulator, and the clearinghouse for a rigged market all in one. Though no small amount of criticism is due the Fed, much of the rage directed at it was unfair or misplaced, but then precious little was fair in the wake of the credit collapse.

Here's what happened.

On October 3, Standard & Poor's (S&P) placed AIG's credit rating outlook on "negative" and Moody's went a step farther and cut it, citing the loss of cash flow and profits from looming business unit sales. Even as AIG sought to negotiate a lump-sum payment to its CDS counterparties that would remove collateral posting obligations, the collateralized debt obligations (CDOs) that FP had written swaps on dropped another $19 billion in value. A deal perhaps could have been struck, but not before another round of collateral posting was due.[4]

For the Fed's part, every possible solution to FP's increasingly dire situation was a major conflict of interest or was a remedy that would only get them into the next month, at best.[5] So the last idea left standing was the idea they went with: buy the CDS from FPs counterparties. The only issue was how much to pay. The CDOs underlying the swaps were then worth on average maybe 50 cents on the dollar and were dropping every day. It seemed only logical then for the Fed to offer to pay market value in return for closing out the swaps.

It didn't happen that way, though. On November 6 and 7, 2008, Fed executive vice president Terrence Checki and a team of colleagues reached out to FPs eight largest counterparties and asked them to take a "haircut," or discount from par value. They were politely told "no way."[6]

Under oath, the brokers said they stood their ground for a host of reasons: they were contractually obligated to par, they had spent tens of millions on hedging via CDSs and incurring losses to help out the Fed put them squarely against their shareholders interests.[7]

Goldman's officials, for example, testified that they had already spent $100 million to hedge the firm against an AIG default and argued they were owed an additional $1.2 billion by FP by their calculations. Publicly, they proclaimed they were hedged; privately, their senior executives had long fretted about the very sort of deal the Fed was now proposing in which they had to take a haircut from FP—in this case, the Fed—yet be legally obligated to pay out the full 100 cents on the dollar to their counterparty.

In reality, conversation with senior executives at Goldman and other brokers shows that they understood full well that the Fed had miscalculated the amount of risk that was embedded in AIG. Calling up and asking multiyear, complex derivative contracts to be broken in a few business days was an impossible request and would have subjected firms—such as Merrill Lynch—that were literally on death's door to losses that might have been fatal. The right thing to do from a market citizenship perspective would have been for the brokers to band together and agree to a unified price concession and present it to a beleaguered Fed.

From a business perspective, however, refusing to take a dime less than what they were owed was common sense.

So the Fed folded and paid par (a combination of the market price of the CDSs plus allowing them to keep whatever collateral they had received.) It rankled immediately: the investment and commercial banks that played (to varying degrees) active roles in fomenting the credit crisis were paid par to terminate swaps whose underlying securities were worth barely half that. Société Générale was paid $6.9 billion, Goldman Sachs was paid $5.5 billion, and Merrill Lynch—whose CDO depravity was at the core of the crisis—was paid $3.1 billion. . . . The list goes on.

Though the possibilities for debating this are endless and emotions often get heated—it is indeed nauseating to see the banks that were the economic handmaidens of the crisis get a pass on having to take their just desserts—a simple fact remains: AIG was dying and the Fed had no time left.

According to the people at the Fed who hatched the plan, their reasoning was akin to wartime decision making: there was the awful choice of paying par for swaps that were likely worth less, and an even worse choice of holding to principle and playing hardball with the banks and brokers as AIG suffered another collateral posting and took another $25 billion of taxpayer money with it, with no assurance that it was going to end.

In discussing their fervor to keep AIG alive, Fed officials conceded to me that once they focused on AIG, they were astounded at how often AIG touched the nonfinancial economy across the globe. It dominated the insurance of commercial marine and aviation shipments in areas of Asia, eastern Europe, and Africa, where rapidly securing a replacement policy at roughly the same price would be impossible. In retirement benefits and services, AIG was a massive player in stable value funds wraps, where it received premiums in return for guaranteeing the principal and interest payment of the bonds in these higher-yielding cash accounts. As of 2008, it had ensured $38 billion of these accounts for IBM, Wal-Mart, DuPont, and others. Assuming AIG's collapse, this would have been one of the first stops in the panic, as desperate retirees sought to liquidate holdings in individual retirement accounts (IRAs) and retirement plans at what would have been lower and lower prices.

So either choice was terrible, but there was a hierarchy of distastefulness. Paying FP's CDS counterparties par—involving a transfer of $27.1 billion of taxpayer cash—was less terrible than watching more than $105 billion of taxpayer money go down with AIG and whatever other large players and small fry that got sucked into its death vortex.

■ ■ ■

In the spring of 2008, New York Fed president Tim Geithner toured the magazine and newspaper offices of Manhattan, giving off-the-record talks about the Fed's role as a matchmaker in the Bear Stearns crisis. At stop after stop, one of the first questions posed to him was "How had things had gotten so out of control?" and "Why had the Fed seemingly done nothing in the multiyear run-up to the credit crisis?"

His answer in every case was brevity itself, "It's not our job to burst bubbles."

Narrowly, he is correct. The sudden—and, in hindsight, often unwarranted—expansion and contraction of various asset prices is of little concern to the Fed. The Fed's primary job is to effect the monetary policy of the United States and if the equities of U.S. computer companies or Russian commodity extractors are preposterously accelerating in price, that ultimately has little real bearing on American interest rates or the funding needs of the government.

Broadly speaking, however, what happened with the use and misuse of credit, especially real estate–backed credit, was no bubble. To use the parlance of software designers, the explosive use of mortgage bonds was no bug, but rather a feature, representing a concerted effort in organizational planning from the trading floor to the board room.

Geithner can fall back on the "Don't look at me" routine, known to parents of teenagers the world over, since the U.S. financial regulatory regime is a dysfunctional archipelago of competing and underfunded agencies. The Fed, especially the New York Fed, had no legal ability to force the Office of the Comptroller or the Currency or the Office of Thrift Supervision to step out of its silo and say something to the effect of, "We have a problem with Washington Mutual" or "There are things happening off balance sheet at Citi." It gets worse. In the case of WaMu, the same groups that had to wrestle with AIG also had to wrestle with a massive savings and loan that was growing its investment bank and building out a huge retail branch network. With Citi, there is a turn for the surreal: The Fed would audit the holding company, where accounting was relatively straightforward and liabilities understandable, and the OCC, smaller and less powerful, would have to audit the bank itself. The SEC would have control over the broker-dealer operations but much of what effectively killed Citi was its off balance sheet structured investment vehicles (SIVs), those perpetual arbitrage funds that seemed—from a risk-management basis—to belong to no department and no division. Because everyone regulated Bank of America and Citigroup, in essence no one did.

Much of this has a pre-September 11 sensibility to it. Reports of trainee pilots from foreign nations that were interested in learning how airplanes took off but not how they landed were caught in the ether of firewalls between the FBI and the CIA. Patriots all, no one at the FBI or CIA was indifferent to the horror of the attacks, but the system in place—the result of decades of bitter internecine power struggles—made the ability to pick off the eventual hijackers at their flight schools nearly impossible.

No one in the financial regulatory scheme, especially at the SEC whose responsibility the brokers were, seems to have discerned that a 10 percent drop in mortgage bond values would threaten the equity capital base of Merrill, Lehman, and a half-dozen other anchors of the global financial system. But even if they had, there was little interagency cooperation on issues like leverage that were as much philosophical as they were regulatory.

Many Fed executives had seen firsthand what the combination of leverage, mortgage bonds, and panicked capital withdrawal had wrought during the Long Term Capital Management debacle. There was indeed a template for what happened in 2008, and if everybody involved was acutely aware of it there was nothing, given the structure of things, they could do about it.

We can speculate though. If a more observant and gimlet-eyed Fed or SEC had forced a critical examination—the more public, the better—of repo collateral and especially bank balance sheet leverage, it would have likely brought some rationality on the fixed-income divisions at Merrill, UBS, Citi, and even Goldman. Bear Stearns's leverage-addicted hedge funds would have still gotten themselves into hot water—reckless is as reckless does—but in a different, smaller fashion since it wouldn't have been able to get loans of 99 cents on the dollar for nonsense like CDO-squared bonds from Citi and others.

The American love for a good guy and a bad guy is complicated by this alphabet soup of regulators and bureaucracies. The highly respected critic and author Christopher Whalen, whose consultancy, *Institutional Risk Analytics*, has long done the dirty work of examining the technical details of bank and Federal Reserve filings to develop independent views on financial sector health, took a stab and called out a woman named Sarah Dahlgren, who was in charge of the relationship management function of the Fed's Large Financial Institution group, where the largest banks—the J. P. Morgans, Citis, and so on—were examined. Whalen's argument is that Dahlgren led the unit that ignored the growing and systemic risks posed by AIG, Citi and its ilk. Nor is Whalen alone.[9]

It isn't clear how Dahlgren or the Fed can shoulder the blame for AIG since they would have had very little contact with the company. If FP fell though *all* the cracks, from a regulatory perspective, then AIG fell through most of them too. State insurance regulators and the OTS—the two sets of authority annually examining the company—likely did not put Greenberg off his feed.

It isn't to say that the Fed was wise to have ignored AIG; it wasn't. It remains unclear after a year of reporting why the senior-most decision makers of the Fed studiously ignored AIG's massive expansion of derivative exposure in the 2000's. On deep background some very experienced and sophisticated people at the Fed cop to having followed AIG's growth in the shadowlands of Wall Street's finance with interest. Perhaps in the future they will speak up.

Make no mistake: The AIG bailout has so many problems as to be difficult to quantify them all. No one at the Fed seems to have a reason for why Goldman Sachs and Morgan Stanley were allowed to become bank holding companies but AIG was not. Shareholders were wiped out and then had the cornerstone's of their remaining franchise—the foreign insurance operations—sold without a matter getting put to a vote, a clear violation of Delaware corporate law statutes. Government officials, many of whom condemned AIG for initially honoring the FP retention payments, as well as allowing a sales incentive award trip at a posh California hotel to go through, seems to make much less noise about the more than $40 billion profit the Treasury has with its AIG stake.

Tellingly, despite posting operating profits, Moody's Investors Services cut AIG's debt rating in mid-January citing concerns over the removal of governmental support. It is not idle speculation. The foreign insurance operations were both highly profitable and threw off healthy amounts of cash flow.

■ ■ ■

For all that though, the Fed's performance in rescuing AIG and keeping it viable was quite impressive.

Little remarked upon, for instance, was the way the Fed worked closely with a legal team from Davis Polk Wardell to find a way to actually inject $85 billion into AIG without running afoul of various other creditors. Because AIG had hundreds of billions of dollars in existing loans and debt, simply giving AIG an $85 billion check would have violated bond and lending covenants. Working in conjunction with Morgan Stanley, the lawyers eventually fashioned a way into AIG's capital structure that wouldn't land them in court.

Another problem was that AIG, in the words of one person involved in the deal, "had [already] pledged everything not nailed down" as collateral at some point, so to protect taxpayer capital, they received stock certificates in the regulated subsidiaries as collateral. (This gave rise to the one of the more comic scenes of the credit crisis as Federal Reserve policemen pushed mail carts down the street to AIG's headquarters to pick up massive amounts of dusty shareholder certificates and wheeled them back to the Fed.)

The Fed handled all of this with the dexterity and focus of an organization 100 times smaller in size.

Sarah Dahlgren, according to a half-dozen remaining AIG executives, appears to have had a certain genius for assisting a collapsed enterprise. In the crucial days after the collapse when AIGs leadership was in tatters and its employees truly stunned, she was a calming and rational presence that got a company that by all rights was dead back to doing business. Staying out of the way of the operations, she oversaw the meeting of AIG's obligations and ensured that none of the $85 billion was misappropriated. There were surely 1,000 people at AIG who knew more about management, insurance, and finance than she did, and Dahlgren—representing nearly 80 percent of AIG's capital—let them go about their business.

In the words of one AIG executive who worked with her at length, "[Dahlgren] allowed the rescue to be as minimal a factor in our lives as possible. She never once gave speeches or lectures and let business proceed. When she had to speak up, she usually said something that was smart longer term."

At bottom, it worked. The two Maiden Lane portfolios are up a total of more than $12 billion, net of loan paydowns, with Maiden Lane II up $2.7 billion alone.

Few Fed officials, including their public relations staff, try to assert that they handled their regulatory duties very well in the events leading up to September 2008; they remain a combination of bitter and astounded at the wellspring of bipartisan outrage directed at them over the AIG bailout.

Both sentiments are correct.

The Fed slept as a shadow banking system of investment banks, monoline insurers, structured investment vehicles, incredibly leveraged investment banks, hedge funds, and AIG all dropped billions of dollars' worth of nonrecourse hooks into the depository institutions they did regulate.[10]

Yet the Fed's bailout, however bitter a pill to swallow, was incredibly well structured, administered deftly and allowed perhaps the key player on the global capital markets—it does not appear that there was a single large financial enterprise on earth that did not have nine-figure exposure to AIG—to meet its obligations. Whatever the reader's recollections of the shape and pace of events in the fall of 2008, they would do well to consider that had the Fed not taken the actions it did, the global capital markets would have seized.

Regardless, in an Internet age, outrage is quick to spread, and given the sheer complexity of the issues at hand, AIG's bailout made an inviting target. Politicians and Internet demagogues made quick work of the issue, and given the Fed's secrecy and Geithner's political ambitions, the legitimate national furor over the nature and cost of the credit crisis quickly found an even more inviting target: the Fed itself.

Some of this has to do with what the Fed is and who works there. Long obsessed with keeping its deliberations secret from tipsters and traders alike; its New York and Washington, D.C., hubs; and natural remove from the everyday lives of Americans—some parts of which are obviously necessary—lends a menacing air to its doings, if seen in a certain light. Moreover, the people who work there—albeit for some of the higher civil service salaries—are more evocative of the elves from Tolkien's *Lord of the Rings* trilogy: wistful, deliberative, and academic, than modern financial operators. If ever an institution was primed for a walloping, it is the Fed.

There has been much talk about being more accountable and publicly engaged. Perhaps. The American people appear to understand that having their economic decision makers hash out policy on the talk show circuit is probably not in anyone's best interests. It is more likely, however, that they would gladly grant them their secret councils if they kept a closer eye on the less dramatic and mundane details of the marketplace and the firms that trade in it.

■■■

AIG is widely seen as having recovered and is now sporting, as of this writing, a stock price north of $54.

Considering the shape of AIG's future means taking into account the government's role as a majority share owner, and that is no light task, as it can be more convoluted than CDO analysis. In a nutshell, though, here it is: The government still owns a 70 percent stake in the company that, when some equity stakes in its Asian insurance operations are converted into actual tradable stock, gives the government a total ownership stake of almost 92 percent.

Ordinarily, this represents a nightmare scenario—who would invest in a company that has a 92 percent owner looking to get out? To allay concerns, the Department of Treasury has said it is going to pare down its equity stake over many years. As noted above, the Treasury has made massive unrealized profits on its investment on AIG. The future is less rosy. In the bid to pay down its loans, a sale of its key operating units, especially the Asian insurance operations, was staged. Successful enough on its face—more than $37 billion was raised from selling those units, with Nan Shan Life, its Taiwanese life insurance operations, slated to being in over $2 billion—the removal of this high margin earnings power will surely constrain future profits.

The costs of the bailout, in other words, to shareholders were not just the massive dilution of their investment but the dismembering of what made AIG the power it once was.

The Fed, as noted previously, has little beef with AIG and is up quite heroically in its investments as the mortgage market has come ripping back. Certainly, Marshall Huebner and his team of Davis Polk Wardell colleagues did a very good job in structuring the Maiden Lane deals to protect the taxpayer, but their client, the Federal Reserve Bank of New York, caught a lucky break with the Obama administration's willingness to bail out or subsidize most any sector and enterprise that had been a substantive U.S. employer. Indeed, the pumping of untold billions of taxpayer dollars into the real estate sector, as well as giving Fannie Mae and Freddie Mac a ceaseless subsidy—it is approaching $150 billion as of this writing—has wonderfully invigorated the secondary mortgage bond markets that devastated AIG in 2007–2008.

The currently robust capital markets owe much to the willingness of the government to spend in an amount and a fashion that is wholly apart from most any previous American administration to keep it so. It is very uncertain if an unemployment rate over 9 percent—it is in double digits in several areas, including California, where it is 12 percent—warrants a Dow Jones Industrial Average over 11,600.

A share offering slated to begin the process of divesting the government's stake was a subject of intense jockeying on Wall Street. To the surprise of no one, Goldman Sachs was among the four firms selected to lead the deal.

AIG's leadership appears to have solidified under Robert Benmosche, a former Credit Suisse board member and CEO of MetLife who assumed the reigns after what many concede was the ineffective tenure of Ed Liddy. In frequent contact with Greenberg, at least initially, he is now battling cancer and has not released any details of his long-term prognosis.

A surprisingly large percentage of AIG's corporate leadership during its disastrous forays into securities lending and writing credit default swaps remain in place. Of note is the continued employment of Kevin McGinn, the chief credit officer who signed off on Win Neuger's global securities lending program further expansion into asset-backed securities. Bob Lewis, the chief risk officer for the entire passion play, retired earlier in 2010.

Bob Willumstad, who had obtained a waiver from Jamie Dimon to go run AIG—J. P. Morgan was the largest investor in a private-equity fund he had set up as chairman, not knowing AIG would become all consuming—is back to running his PE firm, which he named Brysam, after the names of his grandkids. He declined a $22 million severance package from AIG. About AIG, he says he did everything he could with what he had available to him.

Martin Sullivan "retired" from AIG a very rich man and spent several years dealing with the litigation and congressional inquiry fallout from AIG's collapse. AIG alumni recall Sullivan, the man, fondly but view his complete detachment from AIGFP and the global securities lending program with varying levels of astonishment. In September 2010, he joined former rival The Willis Group as a deputy chairman in charge of selling insurance and risk-management advisory services for its multinational customers, directly competing against AIG in one of its long-running niches.

Former CFO Steven Bensinger joined the Hanover Insurance Group as CFO in January 2010; on December 15, 2010, it was announced that he was resigning "to return to the New York area." Bensinger's lawyers impressed the lawyers of his former colleagues, when, during the seemingly endless SEC and Department of Justice (DoJ) inquiries and investigations, he was able to obtain a release from any prosecution—a so-called will-not-prosecute letter.

In March 2010, Win Neuger successfully shepherded the sale of PineBridge Investments, AIG's hedge fund and alternative investment unit, to Hong Kong–based billionaire Richard Li's Pacific Century Group for $277 million. The CEO of a company with $83 billion under management, he is now shielded from the public eye. It is quite likely, however, that should performance of PineBridge's various funds be positive, per industry practice, Neuger stands ready once again to reap rewards into the many millions of dollars.

The Fed's $19.5 billion purchase of mortgage bonds (via Maiden Lane II) from the global securities lending portfolio is a fair starting point for calculating the 2008 era losses from Neuger's securities lending strategy. It is an inelegant calculation because any tally has to reckon with the $5 billion of cash AIG had to inject into it in June 2008 and what would have likely happened with the portfolio's investors and counterparties had AIG not been bailed out. However, the roaring mortgage market has put the portfolio in the black.

Neuger's deputy, fixed-income chief Richard Scott, who grew increasingly uncomfortable with the securities lending strategy, yet oversaw its implementation, is now the chief investment officer at Loews Corporation's CNA Financial Corp. subsidiary.

Michael Rieger, who had made it a point of honor to let his superiors know about his objections to the securities lending portfolio, is now a portfolio manager at Seix Advisors. In the summer of 2010 he spent his summer vacation helping run an eye clinic his church had built in Honduras.

FP is in full wind-down mode and has reduced its total derivative exposure to $505 billion from $941 billion at the beginning of 2010. It is not soliciting new business.

Though there has been no shortage of ugly episodes since the credit crisis developed, among the ugliest was the ways in which members of FP and their families were singled out for threats and scorn over the retention payments AIG agreed to pay FP. At least six of these families reported receiving death or other personal threats. Adding to the circus environment was the manner in which the Connecticut Working Families Party, a far-left political group, organized a "bus tour" of FP executives' houses.

There remains a profound rift between those who agreed to hand back their bonuses and those who did not. Many of those who did not agree to return the pay find themselves embroiled in protracted legal conflict with AIG over the matter.

Jon Liebergall remains at FP helping wind matters down, as does Andrew Forster in London. Both gave back their retention payments.

Gene Park left FP in 2007 to run a derivative products company selling protection on mortgage credit called Quadrant Structured Credit Products. It was a joint venture between Lehman Brothers and Magnetar, a hedge fund that has been accused of having sought to profit from the real estate crisis by structuring CDOs with problematic subprime mortgage loans and then buying CDSs on them.[11]

Jake DeSantis spends his time helping secure small loans for business start-ups in poor areas of Connecticut and maintains some parts of a nature preserve near his house in Redding, Connecticut. He rocketed to fame in 2009 when he penned a *New York Times* op-ed essay that was highly critical of how AIG handled the treatment of FP and its executives. He used his approximately $700,000 retention payment to fund the loan initiative.[12]

Alan Frost, the man who came up with the idea to aggressively solicit CDS business, does not appear to have launched any new ventures. He remains a figure of some affection and sympathy among his former FP colleagues despite the debacle, many of whom express relief that Frost appears to be financially secure given the notoriety of events.

Gary Gorton remains a tenured professor at Yale University's School of Management and produces widely read academic analyses of banking and financial affairs. In 2009, in a visit to C. V. Starr, he told Greenberg, Howie Smith, and others that much of the risk-management problems at FP were because Cassano forbade AIG corporate risk managers from having much input or oversight of the CDS portfolio. Cassano's lawyers argue that there is voluminous proof that this accusation is false.

Joe Cassano, who is indeed wealthy despite losing at least $100 million in FP's collapse, is apparently happy to be retired and spending time with his fully recovered wife. FP alumni who have run into him in the Westport area, where he keeps a house, say he refuses to discuss FP-related issues even in private. Both the SEC and the DoJ refused to initiate any claims against him.

Tom Savage lives in Brazil, where he describes himself as "warm and happy." He remains baffled that FP, something he said was "so rationally conceived and rationally executed," went so wrong.

Howard Sosin keeps a very private life, pursuing select endeavors like a nut allergy foundation and several small business ventures (described in previous chapters). He did, however, write a very detailed and thought-provoking article in May 2009 in which he posited some solutions for dealing with the market's wreckage.[13] He and Rackson, once the closest of friends, remain estranged.

Gary Davis and Robert Rubin, colleagues since the mid-1980s, are still friends and partners in a golf course development in the Hamptons. After leaving AIG in 2000, they opened DKR Capital, where Davis is still active in running it. Rubin has largely withdrawn from financial life and is pursuing a PhD in the history and theory of architecture at Columbia and is chairman of the Pompidou Center, an American group that supports the famous French museum.

■■■

Numerically, the fortunes of Goldman Sachs remain ever thus. In 2009, it earned over $13.3 billion in net income, and while 2010 has for a number of reasons not been so pleasant, it still has managed to clear $6 billion through nine months.

Goldman survived the crisis in large part because of its utterly ruthless risk-management regime and, to an extent, because the government made it a national priority to keep it—and other banks—alive. The Treasury invested $10 billion in the firm in October 2008 under its Troubled Asset Relief Program and because it took full advantage of all the lending facilities the Fed set up, borrowing $589 billion using corporate and mortgage bonds as collateral.[14]

In 2010, Goldman paid $550 million to settle charges that it misled investors in a series of CDO transactions known as *Abacus* about the quality of collateral in the deals as well as the role of real estate skeptic John Paulson and his hedge fund in selecting collateral for the deals.

Though this suit could well take up its own book, there are several observations that bear making. The first is the most obvious: The deals were indeed ugly and used some of the very worst pools of mortgage loans out there. That every rival firm did deals that were worse is no excuse. The buyer of the deal, the German bank IKB, was a victim for which it was difficult to muster much sympathy. Its portfolio management arm was well known in the CDO community as a yield addict in the truest sense of the word, with an established reputation for happily adding extra return by buying the most worrisome CDO tranches. The entire transaction resembles nothing so much as the bartender (Goldman) selling a man with *delirium tremens* (IKB) shot after shot of whiskey—for breakfast.

Goldman's executives emphasize in private that the suit was a public relations nightmare. They are correct, of course, but only executives who have left the firm seem willing or able to make the obvious connection: The Abacus transactions are the sort of deal that Goldman was famous for *not* doing. Drexel had done deals like this in high yield in the 1980s, Merrill and Citi underwrote and sold sketchy CDOs as a key component of their business plan, but Goldman had long marketed itself as standing apart from these deals. No longer.

The ugly and little remarked upon flip side of the Blankfein/Cohn maxim of "Do every trade!" was "Do every deal!" The bull market's earnings stream and the pressures of being a public company conspired to fog Goldman's common sense.

Dan Sparks remains retired at the age of 43. He was made the fall guy for the Abacus debacle, despite the involvement of a dozen other Goldman executives, and has told people that with respect to Abacus and the charges: "The truth no longer matters." The images of him being battered by angry Senators in April 2010, their questions and accusations mounting as he furiously tried to flip pages to get to various emails they cited, is burned in many minds at Goldman. They are profoundly bitter at having Sparks (and Goldman) singled out for business practices that were the core of their rival's business plans, though several will admit that they were thankful it was Sparks, and not them.

Ram Sundaram was made partner in 2008 when his unit earned nearly $1 billion. He had an even better year in 2009 when his group bought $6 billion in corporate bonds at record low prices and rode the trade (and the bond prices) all the way back.

Andrew Davilman is happily spending time in Larchmont with his wife and children, pondering his next move. Like many Goldman executives, both current and former, he remains both angry and astounded at how the firm at which he spent 14 years did not mount a more aggressive defense when its motives were questioned in dealing with AIG. The firm ignored his suggestion to hire a trio of eminent historians to assess the matter and publish their findings.

■ ■ ■

Despite his frustrating bet on AIG, Jim Chanos's Kynikos funds made more than 30 percent return on its $4 billion in assets in 2008, giving him a pay package of nearly $200 million. He is quite vocal about his view that China is headed for major economic trouble and has shorted many of its leading companies.

■ ■ ■

Gradient Analytics' Donn Vickrey is still analyzing companies with an eye towards highlighting what he and his staff see as looming accounting or financial problems. Despite an impressive track record in doing so, the economic and personal toll of the two lawsuits has forced Vickrey and his staff to adopt a minor but telling shift of tone in their reports: they avoid the use of the word "fraud" or anything like it.

■ ■ ■

After 15 years in and around Wall Street, Andrew Barber moved back to the Finger Lakes region of western New York State with his wife and children and opened Waverly Advisors, a money management firm.

■ ■ ■

Hank Greenberg and C. V. Starr continue to prosper, investing in real estate and private-equity deals far and wide, writing profitable insurance in niche areas. It could be fairly said that the company is up to something everywhere, a reflection of the globe-trotting, restless sensibilities of its 85-year-old CEO. As always, he is fully engaged in Asian-American relations and has been to the White House repeatedly to discuss the Korean peninsula situation with national security staff.

Greenberg's anger over AIG remains palpable. He disagrees with selling the Asian insurance operations to pay back the government and he disagreed with their strategy in dealing with Goldman. In the former, he thinks it absurd to sell an enterprise with a competitive advantage in the biggest market in the world as demand for their product intensifies; in the latter, he can't understand why anyone would take the word of an investment bank at anything, let alone in an opaque over-the-counter market.

There is a point that Greenberg *doesn't* make in a direct fashion but has implied in several conversations: AIG gave up its greatest source of leverage when it started conceding to Goldman's collateral demands. Taking Goldman to court would have forced them to make, in his view, massive concessions. It is a variation on the old banker's adage, "If you want to be owned by the bank, borrow $1 million; if you want to own the bank, borrow $50 million." The thinking behind this is simple and ruthless: desperate for cash due to its own collateral posting obligations, Goldman would have taken much less cash and the notion that AIG's CDS portfolio was an intractable problem would never have emerged.

These are, naturally, only several of the issues he can discuss at length when the subject of AIG comes up. In recent months, he has again considered writing, or having written, his memoirs.

Despite settling SEC charges, without admitting or denying guilt, for $15 million over the Gen Re matter, he remains (along with CFO Howie Smith) in a legal battle with the New York attorney general's office, the third administration since he left AIG. He and Smith have received a total of $210 million in settlements from AIG and insurance companies for expenses and legal fees from their battles.

Ed Matthews is now president of C. V. Starr and is wrapping up his fourth decade of working alongside Greenberg. He seems to be resigned to the fact that no one ever truly leaves Greenberg's inner circle.

■ ■ ■

Seen in the most charitable light possible, Eliot Spitzer's legacy as the attorney general of New York is at best a mixed one. His initial efforts to reform broker research assuredly focused attention on some appalling conflicts. From there in, starting with a defeat in the mutual fund timing case, his record of courtroom losses and reverses in his most defining and high-profile cases is stunning. The claims against Ken Langone were dropped and the NYSE's Dick Grasso was allowed to keep his compensation package. Every last bid-rigging conviction and plea has been overturned, most due to prosecutorial misconduct for withholding "multiple forms of exculpatory evidence," according to Judge James A. Yates. Spitzer and Smith refused to fold on the Gen Re matter.

After a landslide gubernatorial victory, Spitzer resigned on March 12, 2008 after it was revealed that his credit card payments to a brothel had been caught by a bank's suspicious activity report monitoring program and forwarded to the Southern District of New York.

He now cohosts a nightly television show called *Parker-Spitzer* with *Washington Post* columnist Kathleen Parker on CNN. As of this writing, it is widely held to be a flop.

In the fall of 2010, during a lunch with Sandy Weill at the Four Seasons hotel in New York City, Spitzer came upon their table and tried to shake hands with the pair. Greenberg refused to shake his hand, saying only, "I don't think so."

Spitzer then invited Greenberg to come on his about-to-launch show as a guest. Greenberg dismissed him and said again, "I don't think so."

■ ■ ■

A final note: In doing dozens of interviews with current and former Wall Street executives at Goldman, Bear Stearns, HSBC, Lehman, J. P. Morgan, and numerous hedge funds, one theme consistently emerged: the elimination of Glass-Steagall and the warping effects it has had on the financial system.

It cannot be escaped: AIG's near collapse was intensified because it was operating in a market dominated by commercial banks and their awe-inspiring funding capabilities. When that capacity is married to shoddy management throughout the market, 2008 is the result. Though the point of this book is not polemical, from the vantage of 2011, the evidence that the repeal of Glass-Steagall would stimulate competition in the marketplace and benefit consumers large and small is mighty thin on the ground.

The remedies provided for this—the quest to curtail proprietary trading at commercial banks, for instance—are designed to be less than even half-measures. That banks want a piece of the pie is no great threat; that they do so wielding their own massive, internal investment banks—Bank of America Securities Corporate and Investment bank was larger than Bear Stearns—twists and skews the market. If no one else will say or write this, then it needs to be heard here: the marketplace for both securities and human capital used to involve dozens of separate investment banks and trading firms; the U.S. capital markets are now dominated by seven or eight global commercial banks, only a few of which have roots in the United States.

Among the men and women who have to channel the market's animal spirits to provide liquidity to buyers and sellers, there is widespread resignation to the circumstances of 2008 being played out again: huge banks, stuffed to the max with securities there are no longer markets for, simply spew billions of dollars' worth of inventory on a market that cannot handle it. Because they have access to both public funding (the Federal Reserve) and the capital markets, it is the rare situation in which they are critically stressed. However, before Glass-Steagall's repeal, investment banks and trading firms, for whom capital was more difficult to replace, tended to avoid overly concentrating risk in one area. When one did and paid the price, its death was readily absorbed by the market.

More than a dozen years after its repeal, there are no more major U.S. investment banks, and the commercial banking sector is riddled with bad loans and tattered finances. It is unclear how a return to a defined separation between commercial and investment banking—adjusted for the realities of modern commerce (like allowing banks to have money-management or venture capital arms)—could possibly be anything but a massive benefit to the American citizen.

■ ■ ■

In the two years post AIG collapse, Congress passed a series of regulatory reforms called Dodd-Frank Wall Street Reform and Consumer Protection Act that President Obama signed into law on July 21, 2010.

Among other things, it created a Financial Stability Oversight Council that is designed to analyze capital markets for systemic risks. It shut down the OTS and gave greater regulatory power to the Fed. At every junction, there is to be greater cooperation and information sharing among regulators at the Treasury, SEC, the Fed, and OCC.

Asked if it would have detected a concentration of CDSs at an otherwise unregulated institution like FP, a Fed analyst said, "Honestly? No. We would have been alerted to the mortgage market problems earlier and maybe from there we could have moved faster on the securities that [price off of mortgages.]"

On paper, every trade is a winner, counterparties pay you off, and all of the rules work.

Until they don't.

Notes

Chapter 1

1. There is probably no more consistently available story to the investigative reporter than the myriad ways in which municipal borrowers grievously wound themselves using Wall Street's services. Specifically, interest rate swaps are a graveyard of good intentions. When politics, Wall Street campaign donations, and "outside advisers" are salted into the mix, much hilarity does not ensue. Just ask the residents of Birmingham, Alabama, whose city—the state's largest—is on the verge of bankruptcy (as of this writing) because of a series of spectacularly ill-advised derivative bets made on the advice of politically connected cronies of the now former mayor (who is serving a 15-year federal sentence for receiving bribes).

2. There is nothing new about this service save for the fact that AIGFP could do it anonymously, very quickly, and, perhaps most importantly, without the presupposition of investment banking or research conflicts of interest that all large brokerages bring to the table. As an AIGFP trader said, "The corporation knew we would use our own capital and not ask them for other [investment banking] business."

3. An option, or the right to purchase or sell 100 shares of a company's stock at a set price for a finite amount of time, is valued according to the underlying stock's price and volatility (or expected swings in price over a given time frame) and by the amount of time left until expiration.

4. In risk analysis, something with a "fat tail" has an abnormally thick end in a risk distribution, indicative of a sharply higher likelihood of a catastrophic event.

5. The losses from Goldstein's trading were even more striking once it emerged that UBS's computer systems were not integrated globally, making it nearly impossible for risk managers in Switzerland, or a trading colleague in New York, to know what the bank had positioned in real time, according to author Dirk Schutz, whose book, *The Fall of the UBS: The Reasons Behind the Decline of the Union Bank of Switzerland*, explores this in great detail. Of course, 11 months later, Swiss Bank's worries over risks from Goldstein's unit became small potatoes when it emerged that UBS lost over $675 million in connection with the collapse of the Long Term Capital Management hedge fund. As will be discussed later, UBS's repeated and consistent failure to manage risk and generally ill-informed management has few equals in Wall Street history.

6. Called the PE ratio, or more frequently, "the multiple," this calculation represents the multiple of next-year's net income an investor is willing to pay to own a share of stock. If a company is expected to earn $5 per share next year and is currently trading at $50, it has a PE of 10.

7. The exception to this was the shares of General Electric (GE) and Berkshire Hathaway, where investors had long ago made a sort of separate peace with the diverse nature of those enterprises. In GE's case, it was the regular increases in net income over multiple decades that stayed their fears. In Berkshire's case, it was Warren Buffett's incredible track record of growing the value of corporate investments. In 2008, however, investors panicked and fled GE's shares in droves.

8. One of the surprising things about Greenberg is that, despite his richly deserved reputation for being a demanding manager, he truly disdained the process of using layoffs as a tool for boosting earnings. He feels that if you are asking people to work 60 hours a week for less base salary than competitors (this will be elaborated more fully further on) in a pressure-filled environment, it is a truly disastrous policy to use the threat of layoffs as a cost saving every time earnings needed to be improved. He argues that people have to believe in your company and that they need a degree of safety to do that. Sadly, this is an increasingly anachronistic position in American business.

9. Greenberg saw little divergence between AIG's interests and those of the United States. More relevantly, his encyclopedic knowledge of the political and economic realities of China (and all of Southeast Asia), Russia, and Japan made him a truly valuable addition to the Rolodexes of senior CIA and State Department officials. Accordingly, Greenberg's deep influence on foreign policy has made him a favorite of Internet conspiracy sites.

10. Ribicoff and Greenberg had a long-standing relationship, but this introduction came with an implicit understanding. If AIG went ahead and hired Sosin et al., in lieu of the finder's fee paid to an executive recruiter, AIG would use Kaye Scholer to set up the necessary legal framework.

11. Wall Street public relations and marketing operations work hard to develop language that disguises the risk of what their firms do. After the junk bond–fueled recession of 1989–1990, they worked successfully to rebrand risky junk bonds into the more innocuous sounding "high-yield" securities. In the early 2000s, when crummy corporate loan underwriting and trading—including the loans made for the most preposterous leveraged buyouts imaginable—made the high-yield mix even riskier, the nomenclature again shifted downward to the truly benign "leverage finance."

12. He has also denied having made this statement (albeit with varying degrees of intensity). This is a shame.

13. Robert O'Harrow Jr. and Brady Dennis, "The Beautiful Machine," *Washington Post*, December 29, 2008.

14. Sosin and Rackson were prescient. In February 1990 Drexel collapsed when, overnight, creditors grew wary of its credit rating in the wake of a $650 million fine for a series of trading violations. Still, in 1987, when it was earning well north of $1 billion annually, it seemed like a lot of cash was being left on the table.

Chapter 2

1. There is no gainsaying the investment brilliance and discipline of Warren Buffett, but he has profited much from being the presumed safe harbor for "good" corporations in some sort of a pinch. Because Berkshire had ample cash and a triple-A rating, he is the first call for investment bankers and chief executives looking for a "friendly" investor and who are not too concerned about what they need to give up to get the deal done.

2. The reason for this is simple: investment banks had proven to be demonstrably lousy companies to bet on in the long term. A corporate executive who assumed in 1989 that Drexel would be around in a few years to meet all its obligations under a swap agreement was an executive that most likely found his career trajectory rerouted.

3. Another factor came into play to grant AIGFP the financial equivalent of "Most Favored Nation" status for corporations wanting to do long-dated swaps: Glass-Steagall. While the large commercial banks were players on Wall Street in the 1990s, the Depression-era Glass-Steagall division between commercial and investment banks firmly constrained what they could do in terms of trading with customers. The upshot was that AIGFP's only competitors were thinly capitalized investment banks.

4. Merton would tread this path in an epic fashion when he helped found (and lend incalculable credibility to) John Meriwether's Long Term Capital Management hedge fund. Its 1998 collapse—after nearly four years of massive profits—and Federal Reserve–led rescue was a foreshadowing of the U.S. governments 2008–2009 support of dozens of poorly managed and capitalized businesses. We may safely conclude that no lessons were learned from the 1994 credit crisis.

5. Litzenberger was Sosin's PhD adviser at Wharton and had a specialty in risk-management theory. A plain-spoken man, he came to FP from consulting jobs at Nomura and Lehman Brothers. In the days prior to its sale to the public, he would go on to become Goldman's first partner in charge of risk management.

6. This is not entirely true. Goldman did let several people know he had written a novel of some sort during the past decade but to date hasn't sought a publisher.

7. It was probably one of AIGFP's growing ranks of "marketers," a position of some definitional flexibility within the unit. A marketer dealt with Wall Street's brokers and money managers to screen and bring in potential transactions of interest. Over time the position became specialized, with several eventually taking a hand at structuring transactions as well.

8. The story of Edper and its dozens and dozens of subsidiaries occupied the Canadian media for several years in the mid-1990s not only because of the saga of the financial woes befalling the Bronfman family, long one of Canada's richest, but because of the sheer complexity of the enterprise.

9. By the end of 1993, AIGFP's competitors were anxious to use their large bank or insurance company balance sheets to do longer-dated swaps and lots of other complex derivative trades, including Gen Re Financial Products, Credit Suisse Financial Products, Deutsche Bank, and Bankers Trust.

10. AIG never broke out FP's specific performance in these years. This number can be backed into, however, via adding up the Financial Services unit's pretax income for 1987–1992 and attributing about 90 percent of it to AIGFP. A rough methodology, but both Howie Smith and Sosin's longtime lawyer, Ron Rolfe at Cravath, Swain & Moore, agreed that it was a good approximation of what the unit earned.

11. Robert O'Harrow Jr. and Brady Dennis, "The Beautiful Machine," *Washington Post*, December 29, 2008.

Chapter 3

1. In the name of full disclosure, I should note that I spent a happy year working for Time-Warner's *Fortune* magazine until they decided to take a more than $20 billion charge in 2008 to eat the final crow from the AOL merger. In a bid to cut costs, the corporation fired hundreds of reporters, myself included.

2. www.robertliebman.com/text_NYLS_Greenberg.html. This references a 1981 interview Greenberg gave the New York Law School's *Alumni* magazine.

3. While a concentration camp, Dachau was not an extermination center for the liquidation of Jews like Auschwitz or Treblinka, but rather a prison camp for the multitudes of German and foreigners the Nazis deemed political and cultural "undesirables." As such, the prisoners who died there more likely died from privation, diseases, and overwork than mass execution. The exception to this was a large number of Soviet prisoners executed in 1941–1942 by an SS unit garrisoned there for, incredibly, target practice.

4. In May 2006, Greenberg parried with Iranian President Mahmoud Ahmadinejad at a private Council of Foreign Relations affair. To the Iranian leader's assertions that the Holocaust didn't occur, he replied in anger, "That's just a lie. I went through Dachau during the war." Ahmadinejad then replied to him that he looked too young to have served in WWII.

5. Two accounts have Greenberg using the word ass.

6. Some of these stories have been told to me by AIG long-timers, including Greenberg, some are available in official archives and on sundry Internet sites like Wikipedia, and all are in a book by Ron Shelp called *Fallen Giant: The Amazing Story of Hank Greenberg and the History of AIG* (John Wiley & Sons, 2006). Its work on the background of Starr, the early days of AIG, and Greenberg is quite illuminating.

7. From a sociological perspective, this was akin to bringing Jackie Robinson to the Major Leagues around 1919. Adding to this, Starr's company would become the first Western insurance underwriter of life insurance to the Chinese. In Shelp's *Fallen Giant*, he notes that Starr's rationale was simplicity itself: Chinese people were underserved, the market was massive, and with improved sanitary conditions, they could well double their life spans, meaning that his liabilities—payouts upon death—would be pushed out years while greater and greater amounts of premium flowed in for decades more.

8. Shelp, p. 25.

9. Starr was correct. The officer, George Moszkowski, proved to be a superior hire and became Starr's primary global troubleshooter, smoothing ruffled customer feathers, favorably negotiating seemingly impossible contracts, and opening offices in what would become key markets.

10. Starr was not a saint nor was he on a social mission. He didn't run a modern university humanities department with strict guidelines for racial representation; he ran a business that simply departed from the norms of the day because it was good business to. His companies, for example, didn't have any Blacks because in that era there weren't multilingual or expatriate Blacks to be found in Asia.

11. Shelp, p. 37.

12. Insurance is the rare business in which a new company can have remarkable growth merely through chopping the price of the premiums they charge to insure risk. A certain sort of customer loves this and happily sends them business. Unless and until the claims start rolling in, the company's owners are in clover.

13. There was good cause for this. According to Shelp and other AIG veterans, an accepted practice among small- and medium-sized Chinese business owners was to try and salvage a bad year economically by burning a building down or sinking a ship and claiming full value for the loss. After a few years, the rigorous claims process proved to be a significant deterrent.

14. Shelp, p. 97.

15. James Bandler with Roddy Boyd and Doris Burke, "Hank's Last Stand," *Fortune*, September 28, 2008.

16. Ibid.

17. In 1994, Hank Greenberg, as a practical matter, was virtually immune from shareholder unrest not only because of his excellent track record of building investor returns but because he personally owned 2.23 percent of the shares outstanding. Based on an $80 price, the stake was worth $567 million; he owned nearly half that again via stakes in various private companies that owned large blocks of stock, Starr, and SICO.

18. Charlie Munger is vice chairman of Berkshire Hathaway and Warren Buffett's long-time "partner." Generally more reserved than Buffett, he is every bit the value-investing devotee of the work of Benjamin Graham and David Dodd.

19. This is actually an incomplete list for 1994. To wit, David Askin's Granite fund collapsed and lost $630 million of investor capital, Procter & Gamble dropped $157 million on interest rate derivatives, and Ohio's Cuyahoga County lost $110 million and blew its credit rating apart speculating on a series of complex, leveraged derivatives tied to municipal securities.

20. Medium-term notes are bonds that a corporation issues with maturities of between 1 and 10 years that require only one Securities and Exchange Commission (SEC) registration statement, allowing them to be issued at will. As such, they are popular with finance companies or other companies that have highly predictable cash flow needs.

21. The deal had a large cash component, but the stock swap portion—ILFC had been public since 1983—was structured in such a way as to make it tax advantaged.

22. Technically, ILFC's debt was its own obligation and initially traded with its original, pre-AIG triple-B rating. On Wall Street's trading floors, it was assumed that AIG implicitly guaranteed its debt rating. Over time, with its

increasing success—a function of AIG's perceived strength—ILFC's debt was increased to double-A.

23. It goes without saying that there is no shortage whatsoever of analysts, portfolio managers, and other market sorts who *swear* they saw everything and told everyone what was coming as far back as the early 1990s. Maybe. It's just that none of them seem to be able to back it up.

24. *Macro* in this context implied a thematic approach to investment as opposed to a more narrowly defined investment style. Specifically, these funds would put on trades designed to capture some overarching or macro theme like the convergence of interest rates in Europe and Japan.

25. The reputation of trading floor culture as being alternately harsh and locker room sprang from the 1970s and 1980s because they were indeed loud, confrontational, and often sophomoric. This was before workplace harassment and expensive discrimination suit judgments forced firms to enforce rules and before communications equipment was modernized, and shouting across the floor became unnecessary. Though plenty of pressure and behavioral groupthink remains, the daily culture of a trading desk is much more professional.

Chapter 4

1. In "spray and pray" deals, ordinary coal is sprayed with a substance that includes some combination of diesel and starch and, according to one source, byproduct of paper manufacturing processes. As one could imagine, the billions of dollars of tax credits industry has gotten from this loophole has aroused the ire of budget watchdogs like Taxpayers for Common Sense. See www.progress.org/tcs103.htm.

2. It is a quirk of Greenberg's personality that he would happily scream at Davis and Rubin for the risk of having $5 million unhedged, but was fully understanding in the face of a possible $10 to $20 million loss.

3. Though nothing would have forced Russia off its disastrous path, that July the structured-product market and other derivative markets were walloped when Sandy Weill, the head of the newly cobbled together Citigroup, ordered the closure of Salomon Brothers' bond-arbitrage desk, and billions of dollars of positions were sold.

4. Lehman Brothers, it is now known, was stressed to the point of near collapse from bond-market-related losses in 1998. Goldman Sachs, in the midst of completing its paperwork to go public, was forced to delay selling its shares to the public after it booked a more than $1 billion loss from trading that summer.

5. Savage, as noted, was foursquare on the side of the bond-market skeptics. While CMOs could be relatively plain vanilla, even in the early 1980s it was

apparent to him that an "arms race" of sorts was under way between investment banks to redirect principal and interest payments into uses that were impossible to model and hedge, and thus, he thought, served no real investment purpose.

6. An excellent account of the J. P. Morgan side of this episode is found in Gillian Tett's very worthwhile read *Fool's Gold* (Simon & Schuster, 2009).

7. Both FP and AIG had close relationships with J. P. Morgan; in AIG's case, one that went back decades. In this instance, however, the deal was attractive to FP because as an unregulated financial unit of an insurance company, it would not have any meaningful capital reserve requirements. So if the deals didn't go south, the $194 million was the easiest "insurance premium" they ever earned.

8. These deals were seen as a tremendous boon for the banks and, presumably, their governments. They got capital relief, which prettied up their balance sheets, and were able to make more loans or investments and increase their income. Governments approved of anything that could keep banks willing and able to lend to local employers.

9. The full quote from O'Rourke, a former *National Lampoon* satirist and *Rolling Stone* writer, is: "Giving money and power to government is like giving whiskey and car keys to teenage boys" (P. J. O'Rourke, *Parliament of Whores*. Grove Press, 1991).

Chapter 5

1. The reply from the magazine's editor, Bill Emmott, was poisonous in kind: "I can see no reason to share your rude, defamatory and bullying letter with our readers."

2. The first reporter to mention this transaction, per Schiff, was Douglas McLeod of *Business Insurance* in 1995.

3. The Starr foundation had given money before to the museum, but never in this scale.

4. There are other, internal benefits to "growth stock" status. In a company like AIG, where many employees held the stock, it was a way to hold onto employees longer and attract new employees. There was, in other words, absolutely tremendous internal pressure on the CEO of an anointed growth stock company to keep the price up.

5. It is no surprise that most of the giant corporate accounting frauds of the past decades came from once-crucial growth stocks. The pressure to "make your numbers" is indeed that intense.

6. Much of this growth was the annuities they assumed control of in the SunAmerica and American General deals. Obviously, the cash and assets they

received from the annuitant gave AIG tremendous investment opportunity—read: potential for profit—and liquidity as well.

7. According to an SEC led deposition of Grasso that was released as part of New York Attorney General Eliot Spitzer's suit against the former New York Stock Exchange (NYSE) chief in New York State Supreme Court on June 14, 2006, Grasso and other NYSE officials began hearing from Greenberg "within months" of its listing on the NYSE in 1984.

8. Precisely what he hoped to accomplish is anyone's guess. Though Grasso was a legendary string puller behind the NYSE scenes, he had little to do with shaping the actual bids and offers of the marketplace. Greenberg says that he thought the specialist was hesitant and passive in using his capital to set reasonable trading floors for AIG shares. Perhaps. But the specialist's capital was designed to *stabilize* a company's share price in order to facilitate an orderly market, not compete against the money managers who decided throughout 2002 and 2003 to sell AIG's shares. In any case, Grasso and Greenberg would soon drop the animus and frustration each had with the other as Eliot Spitzer presented himself as a common enemy.

9. Greenberg says he never considered a leveraged buyout (LBO), but that was his only option to rid himself of the annoyances of life atop a publicly held company.

10. See www.sec.gov/litigation/complaints/comp18340.htm.

11. Their official reasoning for approval involved a series of accounting and legal arguments that, while full of curves and entirely against both the spirit of the law and accounting standards, is somewhat plausible. Their unofficial reasoning involved the centuries-old Japanese cultural mandate to preserve public credibility, better known as *saving face*.

12. Greenberg insists that he did not order the transactions to be carried out "as is," but to be adapted to U.S. rules.

13. It remains unclear if AIGFP did not show Ernst & Young certain aspects of the deal or if the accountants missed it. Ernst & Young would pay a $1.7 million fine in March 2007 for its role in the affair.

14. The ironies abound. After its institutional collapse in the credit crisis, and failure to detect the Madoff and Allan Stanford Ponzi schemes, the dot-com era SEC seems vibrant in comparison. The DoJ, however, probably hit its apex with the Enron trial and proved to be of little use in both the lead-up to the credit crisis and its aftermath.

15. Paula Dwyer and Diane Brady, "AIG: Why the Feds Are Playing Hardball," *BusinessWeek*, October 18, 2004.

16. Cassano and Greenberg had actually grown quite close. They talked most every Sunday for a few hours about FP, the markets, and other financial and

economic matters. Much more quietly than Savage, Cassano had also sought to make Greenberg a partner in FP's success. These phone calls stopped when Martin Sullivan became CEO.

Chapter 6

1. He would also sue Ken Langone, a veteran private-equity investor, for misleading the board.

2. The remarks were made at a press conference announcing the complaint against Marsh. The actual complaint can be found at www.ag.ny.gov/media_center/2004/oct/oct14a_04.html.

3. Indicting a corporation the size of Marsh & McLennan would almost certainly be a death sentence. Its Putnam Investments unit was a high-volume trader in the short-term borrowing and lending markets, and it would have devastated the ability to attract new investors for its funds.

4. The hiring of Qorvis was bound to be controversial as its role as the PR shop helping revitalize the image of Saudi Arabia in the wake of the 9/11 attacks for $200,000 per month had sparked an uproar.

5. Greenberg, whose animus toward the attorney general was hardly secret in the autumn of 2004, denies having ordered anti-Spitzer op-eds, nor do former AIG PR executives have any idea who gave Qorvis the approval to solicit op-ed contributors.

6. Scandals and fines of this magnitude usually result in leadership changes throughout a corporation. Perhaps Spitzer concluded after dealing with Wall Street firms in the global research settlement that too much of the leadership at Merrill Lynch and Citi was not held accountable.

7. Actually, he didn't. Most of the pleas and convictions in the bid-rigging cases were heavily modified, reduced, or vacated throughout 2010 for the attorney general's office's withholding of evidence.

8. Finite reinsurance is a type of reinsurance that transfers only a limited, or "finite," amount of risk to the reinsurer. The benefit of this to the insurance company is the lower cost for laying off risk. Problems mounted in this era when accounting methods were used to reduce the remaining risk, thus improving the financial picture of the company.

9. This is perfectly legal. AIG, in standard practice, would accept a lower premium payment for the losses because, using the time value of money, they could (presumably) invest in low-risk securities and make up the difference.

10. He certainly also had one-to-one meetings as well as private discussions. But AIG veterans point to the manic atmosphere of Greenberg's office as being their lasting impression of his management style.

11. Wolosky had been a White House official and director of transnational threats for Presidents Clinton and Bush. Wechsler was a key official in President Clinton's efforts to begin a national terror-finance analysis effort. He is now deputy assistant secretary of defense for counter-narcotics and global threats.

12. Council of Foreign Relations: *Terrorist Financing*, Maurice R. Greenberg, Chair; William F. Wechsler and Lee. S. Wolosky, Co-Directors, October 2002, 55 pages.

13. Stock buy-backs made after 3:50 PM were forbidden because of the 4 PM close of trading. If a company's large market order was executed at 1 PM, purchasing all available stock for sale within a given price range and pushing the stock price higher, interested sellers would have time to offer their shares. With a few minutes to spare before trading closes, they might not. Without this check, corporations could use their working capital to ensure a higher close most every day.

14. This quote was used in an excellent *Wall Street Journal* article, April 1, 2005, written by Monica Langley: "Palace Coup, After a 37-Year Reign at AIG, Chief's Last Tumultuous Days."

15. The official releases described Greenberg as "stepping down" and Smith as "taking a leave of absence."

16. Matthews had formally retired in 2002, but to Greenberg that meant nothing, as Matthews kept his title and merely swapped his salary for a consulting fee.

17. The lasting effect of Paul Weiss's mistake was bad blood between the two firms that transcended typical courtroom bravado and competitiveness. Boies Schiller's lawyers were paid well in the multiyear quest to litigate on behalf of Greenberg and both Starr entities, but their bitter and relentless courtroom and procedural efforts against Paul Weiss and its client were very clearly personal.

18. These analysts and investors place a lesser emphasis on the *accuracy* with which questions are answered. As will be made clear, at AIG and other companies ensnared in the credit crisis, investors were continually heartened by answers that were firmly and forcefully delivered, yet utterly wrong and incomplete.

19. In certifying compliance with the Sarbanes-Oxley regulations, a corporate officer risked federal prosecution if he was found to be aware of shortcomings in corporate controls. There were even penalties for failing to make good faith efforts to find weaknesses.

Chapter 7

1. That's how it's supposed to work on paper. In reality, the potential losses of short-sellers are unlimited: a share sold at X can appreciate 100-fold.

2. Bethany McLean, "Is Enron Overpriced?" *Fortune*, March 5, 2001 (http://money.cnn.com/2006/01/13/news/companies/enronoriginal_fortune/index.htm).

3. Dean Rotbart, "Market Hardball: Aggressive Methods of Some Short-Sellers Stir Critics to Cry Foul," *Wall Street Journal*, September 5, 1985.

4. Chanos had nothing but contempt for the ratings agencies, and in fact would profitably short Moody's in 2007.

5. Chanos is quite open in noting that this was only a working hypothesis and that they had no concrete grasp of how large AIG's efforts were in this area, or that it was to guarantee collateralized debt obligations (CDOs) specifically, until everyone else did.

6. *This Week with George Stephanopoulos*, April 10, 2005.

7. The irony is that the perception of FPs balance sheet "strength" was largely derived from AIG, which in turn had much of its flexibility legally segregated in insurance subsidiaries that it had no access to.

8. Green Tree Finance was one of the great pre–credit crisis missed warning signs. Rife with fraud and self-dealing, the mobile-home lender was one of the asset-backed securities market's largest issuers. In just under two years, its awful lending standards and accounting shenanigans forced the once mighty Conseco to its knees.

9. Adams, now a lawyer in private practice, has written extensively on this and other related issues at www.nakedcapitalism.com/. The site's founder, former banker Yves Smith, wrote a book in 2010 that deals with these and related issues (*ECONned*, Palgrave Macmillan).

10. "The highest yield possible" meant that lenders were incentivized to go out and find the most marginal borrowers, that is, those who had no choice but to borrow money at a high interest rate.

11. If there was a mismatch skewed toward liabilities, the lending program manager would have to replace the "missing" assets—representing investment losses—out of their own cash.

12. Greenberg's idea to start a securities-lending business had not been without its critics internally, who declared the idea beneath a triple-A-rated company. They derided everything from the business line's reputation as having the most ethically challenged people on Wall Street to the business' risk-reward equation. No one, as far as I was able to tell, however, made these arguments directly to Greenberg, especially in 1999.

13. Smith insists that he brought up to Greenberg at this time the idea of scaling back the program but Greenberg told him to "forget it." Greenberg also continued to publicly support and praise Neuger for his work in streamlining Asset Management, which, to be fair, it appears he did to good success.

14. In the course of reporting, I interviewed two former AIG GIC executives who described telling an AIG official, when they were interviewing for the job, that in addition to their professional attributes and experience, they had dealt with Rieger before and felt they could get along with him. They were offered jobs on the spot.

Chapter 8

1. The marketing call was to keep everyone abreast of developments and was broad in scope; Trade Review was to analyze the specific risks of a transaction before engaging in it.

2. There is a rich literature critical of VaR. One of the more accessible essays is by author and risk-management guru Nassim Taleb, of *Black Swan* fame, dating back to 1997. It can be found online at www.fooledbyrandomness.com/jorion.html.

3. This was detailed in the Financial Crisis Inquiry Commission's interim report on AIG from June 30, 2010, found in Section III (the pages are unnumbered.) Online, it may be found at www.fcic.gov/hearings/pdfs/2010-0630-AIG-Risk-Management.pdf. My own reporting confirms this: absolutely no one at AIG corporate headquarters appeared to have had any knowledge of CSAs.

4. Ibid. Frost led FP to assume an additional $36.4 billion in 2005. At the end of 2007, it would be a total of $72.7 billion, although the majority of the additional swap obligations between the end of 2005 and 2007 were on the much safer European capital relief CDO deals.

5. In Greenberg's era, they wrote just under $18 billion in various CDO swaps. They appear to have been among the best-performing CDO swaps that had ABS collateral. This was function of the loans in the underlying collateral pools having been structured well and made before the mania of 2005–2006.

6. Matthews and Greenberg were said to be astounded at the size and profitability of FP's swap with Italy. The reporting on the preparations for the swap comes from a series of interviews with FP alumni of that period. For more context on the swap itself, see Robert O'Harrow Jr. and Brady Dennis, "The Beautiful Machine," *Washington Post*, December 29, 2008.

7. His colleagues, 23 years later, do not think Sosin was really joking.

8. Surely, the prospect of having their equity stakes valued at between $50 million and $60 million made them more inclined to go public.

9. Everything in the bond market is measured in terms of the amount of extra yield, or spread, one bond has to another. In turn, the risk of all bonds is assessed relative to the spread to Treasuries, the risk-free rate of return.

10. AIG FP was one of the key swaps providers in this transaction. Goldman was able to lay off some of its risk via FP, and FP made what has proved to be riskless money in guaranteeing the airport construction debt.

11. The same J. P. Morgan team that developed the BISTRO CDO deals that FP issued swaps to "insure" in 1998 was instrumental in getting this market off the ground in 1994 when they got the European Bank for Reconstruction and Development to guarantee the credit risk of a $4.8-billion credit line to Exxon.

12. This opinion, which was universally held at Goldman across numerous desks and departments, appears to have been arrived at in 2004 when someone from its credit department looked at a few annual reports, ran some models, and concluded that trouble was brewing. Incredibly, this view never publicly emerged. In contrast, the high-profile hedge fund investor Bill Ackman, of Pershing Square Capital Management, discussed his bearish conclusions on the monolines' dubious prospects publicly around the same time, to much controversy. Indeed, Ackman was widely accused of trying to drive the company into bankruptcy.

13. There was a two-basis-point fee for acting as a middleman.

14. Wise but ironic. Goldman, along with other brokers, worked mightily to gain regulatory exemptions for CDSs, which classified them—absurdly—as neither futures nor securities so they were exempt from SEC and Commodity Futures Trading Commission oversight. Naturally, Congress fell for it. That's how $62 trillion in swaps, just under five times U.S. gross domestic product (GDP), came to get written.

15. A copy of the paper is available for download at www.defaultrisk.com/pp_corr_05.htm.

16. The first and last word on this grim development is Felix Salmon's incisive recap of David Li and his theory: "Recipe for Disaster: The Formula that Killed Wall Street," *Wired*, February 23, 2009.

17. Much of the push to use mortgage-backed paper as CDO collateral was due to its abundance, but also because in 2001–2002 there had been a mini credit crisis and the concentration of downgraded or defaulted high-yield loans within CDOs had spooked underwriters and asset managers alike. The decision to use securities with better default characteristics gave everyone, at the time, a greater sense of safety.

18. Another $1 trillion would be brought to market by the end of 2007, the majority of which contained collateral of a much lower quality.

Chapter 9

1. Michael Lewis, *The Big Short: Inside the Doomsday Machine*, W.W. Norton & Co., 2010. Destined to be the iconic take on the credit crisis' most enduring characters: the handful of cynics, skeptics, and obsessives who bet against it.

2. The story of Park is more deeply told in what is destined to be the last word on the credit crisis: Bethany McLean and Joe Nocera, *All the Devils Are Here: The Hidden History of the Financial Crisis*, Portfolio/Penguin, 2010.

3. After this was written, but prior to publication, Bob Lewis retired from AIG.

4. As noted previously, a monoline insurance company is one that guarantees the credit of a debt issuer for a fee.

5. In New York State, the attorney general has the authority to regulate charities.

6. The Utah senators were willing to combat short-selling because they had a key campaign contributor who had made it his life's work to stop something called "naked short sales," where a short-seller does not seek to secure a borrow before selling stock short. Done in a high enough volume, this could serve to temporarily depress a company's share price; it has long been illegal. The contributor, Salt Lake City–based Overstock CEO Patrick Byrne, had developed a worldview in which naked short sales threatened western civilization. To wit: "dishonest" short-sellers, like Jim Chanos, fed "corrupt" reporters, like myself, stories about innocent companies that would be blindly transcribed and promptly devastate a company's share price. At the center of everything was the man who gave people like Jim Chanos orders: "the Sith Lord," former Drexel Burnham high-yield bond kingpin Michael Milken. I'm not making this up.

7. Chanos, via a lobbying group he set up, *The Coalition of Private Investment Companies*, spends an inordinate amount of time fighting off political attempts to curtail, eliminate, or politically demonize short-sellers and short-selling. His group, according to OpenSecrets.org, spent $840,000 in lobbying in 2010, far behind Goldman's $3.5 million.

8. The concern being that as long as the accounts are in proper order many accounting firms—even big ones—let a whole lot slide.

9. AIG FSB came to plenty of grief apart from the larger drama swirling around it. In March 2010 AIG settled charges with the DoJ that it had systematically charged Afro-American borrowers up to 20 basis-points more in interest expense than Caucasian borrowers of similar credit. Without admitting or denying anything, they paid a $178-million settlement.

10. The terms *savings-and-loans* and *thrifts* are interchangeable. Most so-called mutual savings banks are privately held and owned, although in recent years several have gotten quite large. The best (and worst) example of this is Washington Mutual Savings Bank, which collapsed into bankruptcy in 2008.

11. Though it did not become apparent until much later, one of the footnotes of the credit crisis was something called *regulatory arbitrage*, where large companies would "shop" around the regulatory community to get the most "agreeable" regulator. For many large companies that owned a thrift, such as GE, the agreeable regulator became the OTS.

12. Chief executive Lloyd Blankfein would make $53.4 million that year. Incredibly, it appears he was not even the highest paid in his firm; several traders were reputed to make between $60 and $70 million.

13. One of the more unique aspects of Goldman Sachs culture is that after a period of years, the head of one group or product area is often reassigned to run a different area. Sobel, an 18-year veteran of the mortgage desk, moved over to run a proprietary real estate investment portfolio.

14. Merrill had an equity investment in Ownit and had people on its board, so it was supposed across the mortgage community that Merrill closely monitored Ownit's investment and health.

15. The belief that Merrill would manage its investment in Ownit professionally and conservatively was among the more naive suppositions held in this era of foolish thought. Charlie Gasparino's *The Sellout: How Three Decades of Wall Street Greed and Government Mismanagement Destroyed the Global Financial System* (Harper Business, 2009) does an excellent job detailing how Merrill's policies of expanding loan production destroyed an otherwise decent mortgage company.

16. New home sales were a daisy chain made of cash that amounted to about 6 percent of GDP in 2006. Just as importantly, it provided ample work and revenues for both blue- and white-collar job holders. The high wages lost would not readily be replaced.

17. This is even more impressive when you consider that a risk controller earning maybe $400,000 annually was doing this to a trader who could be earning $4 million or more.

18. This sentiment is that of other Goldman traders, not Sparks.

19. In conversations with a half-dozen senior Goldman traders and bond managers, they all had a remarkably similar assessment of Cohn: they were deeply grateful for a boss who had been an exceptionally gifted trader and who had an encyclopedic understanding of markets; they were equally put off by his brusque and impatient manner.

20. Though the legal status of "partner" ended with its 1998 sale of shares to the public, Goldman maintained the tradition in the guise of "partner managing directors." In most years, the 300 or so partners share in a bonus pool of between 20 percent and 25 percent of the total compensation pool.

21. The informal Sullivan was universally referred to as "Martin" at headquarters. Greenberg, though called Hank by fellow executives, was known equally as "Mr. Greenberg" in public and "MRG" behind his back. For his part, 42 years after his death, Greenberg calls C. V. Starr "Mr. Starr."

22. A CDO-squared is a CDO whose collateral is tranches of other CDOs. If a standard CDO was too much for many analysts to effectively analyze circa 2007, a "CDO/2," as it was referred to in shorthand, was utterly opaque.

23. The BSAM managers were in the "troubled hedge-fund managers conundrum": if they accepted the distressed bids, they were shown they would have locked in severe losses that would have forced the balance of the fund's investors to panic and withdraw their capital, forcing the highly levered fund to sell more bonds, at lower prices until the capital was exhausted. However, if they did nothing, the market would have likely declined further or even seized.

24. The DoJ indicted Cioffi and Tannin on June 19, 2008, for purportedly misleading investors about the status of their fund's health; the SEC filed a claim soon after. On November 11, 2009, they were acquitted.

Chapter 10

1. It is not clear what this would have entailed legally for FP, although given it was a large and important customer for Goldman and other firms they likely could have gotten out of their obligations with some settlement.

2. An entire series of books might begin to do justice to the failure of the ratings agencies to adequately address risks in the credit crisis.

3. It appears that the majority of the other swaps they had with more than a dozen brokers had CSA trigger provisions of 8 percent or greater.

4. According to Goldman's risk chief Broderick, Goldman had made margin calls to FP starting in November 2006 but for amounts that ranged between $500,000 and $2 million. Each of these calls was paid in full, with no questions asked.

5. Collateral substitution occurs when a bond in a CDO collateral pool matured and the CDO manager replaced it with another bond. Cut and dry, save for the fact that post-2005 the collateral being substituted into most CDOs was most likely dubious subprime-backed paper. *Bloomberg News* did an excellent investigation into the matter in March 2010: Bob Ivry and Jody Shenn, "How Lou Lucido Helped AIG Lose $35 Billion with CDOs Made by Goldman Sachs," *Bloomberg News*, March 31, 2010. See www.bloomberg.com/news/2010-03-31/how-lou-lucido-helped-aig-lose-35-billion-with-cdos-made-by-goldman-sachs.htm.

6. Jeff Gerth, "Was AIG Watchdog Not Up to the Job?" *ProPublica*, November 10, 2008. See www.propublica.org/article/was-aig-watchdog-not-up-to-the-job.

7. Though the CDO market was deteriorating in real time in late July 2007 and a sudden drop in the price of CDOs was to be expected, a drop of that much over one day is, per Ram's argument, indicative of not paying close attention to prices. It also supports his broader argument that the sudden and large margin calls that were sure to result from such a price shift were avoidable if a more careful approach were taken.

8. Ram would later say that he reserved his biggest frustrations for other dealers who, in Merrill's case in particular, wouldn't even provide marks that were indicative of where trading could take place, noting that any numbers the firm provided were "for information purposes only."

9. Karen Bretell and Ed Leefeldt, "AIG Stock Falls on Fear over Possible Write-down," *Reuters*, October 25, 2007.

10. Alt-A loans are a category of mortgage between prime and subprime. In reality, from 2004 and on the credit quality of these loans deteriorated just as rapidly as other classes.

11. Generally shorthand for media relations staff.

12. Kirkland's facility with math astounded even FP's brightest. After leaving FP when Tom Savage was made president in the 1990s, Kirkland, a native Oregonian, spent some time at Cambridge University working with noted mathematician and theoretical physicist Stephen Hawking.

Chapter 11

1. Though it cost them their reputations, departing at this point was a lucrative move for both CEOs. Merrill's Stanley O'Neal, whose idea it was to throw the weight of the firm's balance sheet into the subprime/CDO business, received a departure package valued at $161.5 million. Citi's Prince, whose management style (and knowledge of CDOs) was more akin to Martin Sullivan's, took home a more modest $147 million "retirement" package.

2. A former Bear Stearns banker and merger arbitrage specialist, Paulson made an epic bet against the real estate bubble and overlevered banks in 2007 and 2008, for which he earned at least $2.3 billion in 2008.

3. It's doubtful there would be any dispute. Goldman underwrote the Abacus deals and provided the prices the CDS were valued from.

4. Since the collapse of Arthur Andersen in 2002 after its criminal indictment for bungling the Enron audits, members of the Big Four accounting firms had become much less passive in accepting management explanations for issues that bordered on the "materiality" threshold.

5. Incredibly, Sullivan would later testify that he has no recollection at all of this meeting. That it actually happened is not in doubt, as about six other people were on the call.

6. This was based on the recollection of Willumstad, which is congruent with what PwC produced for the Financial Crisis Inquiry Commission investigation. See www.fcic.gov/hearings/pdfs/2010-0630-AIG-Risk-Management.pdf.

7. As the spreads increased in value, it indicated a greater concern over debt-repayment ability. So if a company's swaps went from being quoted at 250, or

$250,000 to insure $10 million in debt for between one and five years, to 500 ($500,000), the company's default risk was popularly perceived to have doubled.

8. The corporate likelihood for default had definitely *not* increased absent new, material information about cash flow or, perhaps, assets and liabilities.

9. That's because with low rates and ample liquidity, investors and traders aren't really price sensitive. Everything everyone put on in the MBS-ABS world, with some exceptions, of course, appreciated or provided easy excess spread from 2003 to 2006 because of the low funding costs.

10. The $1.1 billion figure probably was understated.

11. The DoJ and SEC, in their investigations of Cassano, placed great emphasis on the fact that he discussed a write-down of $1.5 billion but not, as he had provided to AIG management, a possible valuation adjustment of $3.6 billion. True, but that spreadsheet had it as a worst case scenario and one that he had documented as highly unlikely. Of course, FP would completely blow through that number in short order, suggesting that Cassano was just as unprepared for the velocity of collapse as the average investor.

12. He got to keep $34 million in unvested stock.

13. The companies were Biovail, a Canadian pharmaceutical company, and Utah-based Overstock.com, an Internet closeout retailer (whose CEO, Patrick Byrne, was a vocal proponent of the naked short-selling conspiracy discussed earlier). As noted previously, I wound up doing much investigative reporting on these companies. On several occasions, in reporting on both companies, I used Vickrey as a source.

14. Biovail settled its suit with Vickrey and another hedge fund, apologized, and paid several million dollars. Gradient, having nearly run out of insurance coverage, paid the balance of its coverage—several hundred thousand dollars—and Overstock dropped the suit against it.

15. Since American General and its massive life insurance operations is based in Houston, the Texas Department of Insurance is considered the lead regulator of AIG's life insurance companies.

16. Miles Weiss, "AIG to Absorb $5 Billion Loss on Securities Lending," *Bloomberg News*, June 27, 2008. See www.bloomberg.com/apps/news?pid=newsarchive&sid=aoGjre8ctFFk.

17. National Union, the company that was responsible for the Brightpoint disaster, was a specialist in director and officer insurance, covering executives and board members of corporations from lawsuits. It was considered a goldmine internally at AIG.

18. John Whitehead and John Weinberg ran Goldman Sachs from 1976 to 1984 (Weinberg stayed on until 1990). They were obsessive about avoiding conflicts

of interest with clients and highly adverse to publicity. Though this has no bearing on the story, Greenberg likely identified with their war records: Whitehead drove a landing craft on D-Day and Weinberg, whose father Sydney essentially put the modern Goldman together as its general partner, fought with the Marines in the South Pacific and again in Korea.

19. The role UGC played in the mortgage food chain was like this: A borrower who wanted to put down $50,000 for a $500,000 property would owe a $450,000 balance, an amount the lender might not feel comfortable with. But with UGC, the borrower buys insurance for 25 percent of the balance outstanding, or $112,500, giving the bank an effective 35 percent equity level should the borrower default.

20. On December 1, 2010, the Fed released details of just how dangerous the situation was for AIG's insurance companies. Without the emergency intervention of about $20.5 billion in cash, thousands of global securities lending program trades would not have settled, meaning that the banks and brokers that had borrowed from the program were unable to get their cash collateral back.

21. For the conspiratorially minded, this last paragraph is a doozy. Both Dudley and Boesky worked at Goldman Sachs prior to joining the Fed—Dudley as its chief economist and Boesky as an analyst—and, yes, her father is Ivan Boesky, the famous insider trader.

22. Maybe 15 years prior, Liddy had asked Greenberg to consider a merger between the companies. Greenberg flew out, toured the place, met with Liddy, and told him, "I think you should keep your company."

Epilogue

1. In calculating the massive profits of Wall Street from 2003 to 2007, the importance of mortgage-backed trading and sales activity cannot be underestimated. Not only were mortgage desks regularly 15 percent or more of their annual bottom lines, but they provided huge crossover business potential for other desks like government bonds, derivatives, and agency securities. As such, the pricing power of the mortgage departments went through the roof. According to veteran recruiters, the heads of these units often earned $10 million or more, with various desk chiefs earning between $6 million and $8 million and the "rank and file" earning regularly into the $5 million–plus range; frequently, these sums were earned on multiyear guarantees. At a mortgage-reliant firm like Bear Stearns, desk chiefs in a good year earned $15 million or more.

2. In November 2008, the Department of the Treasury purchased a $40 billion preferred share issuance from AIG that was in large part used to pay down

the Federal Reserve Bank of New York's loan balance to $60 billion from $85 billion. At the same time, the initial terms of the Fed's deal were adjusted because repayment would have been nearly impossible for AIG to repay without risking further collapse—at an 11.3 percent interest rate, the $85 billion line of credit amounted to $9 billion in annual interest expense.

3. Maiden Lane LLC was the $30 billion credit line set up to house Bear Stearns' portfolio of subprime mortgage loans and related derivatives in March 2008. The Fed hired BlackRock to manage the portfolio.

4. Based on interviews, the New York Fed was now fully aware of the fact that collateral calls were not just a function of an investment bank like Goldman issuing one-way demands to FP, but were a series of postings among FP, Goldman, and a counterparty like J. P. Morgan or Deutche Bank.

5. See the report of Neil Barofsky, the Special Inspector General of the Troubled Asset Relief Program, on the New York Fed's handling of the CDS termination: www.sigtarp.gov/reports/audit/2009/Factors_Affecting_Efforts_to_Limit_Payments_to_AIG_Counterparties.pdf (specifically, pp. 13 and 14). Fed insiders think the balance of the report is fair but deeply object to Barofsky's conclusions.

6. UBS was the one exception to this, agreeing to accept 98 cents on the dollar if the other seven brokers followed suit.

7. See the SIGTARP report, p. 16.

8. This was the job of other regulators, the ratings agencies, the investment banks, and investors. They didn't do their jobs, either. It's not clear that anyone really did their job in this crisis.

9. See: http://us1.institutionalriskanalytics.com/www/index.asp (registration and a fee is required). To get a sense of the article, and a corroborating view from another Wall Street iconoclast, see www.nakedcapitalism.com/2010/08/technically-incompetent-ny-fed-examiner-of-biggest-banks-pre-crisis-promoted-for-blowing-up-the-economy.html.

10. Geithner has given an insightful and eloquent speech on this very matter, demonstrating a clear awareness of the threats posed from the shadow banking system. Unfortunately, it was in June 2008, three months after the collapse of Bear Stearns and mere weeks before the great plunge south. As such, the speech has the feel of a bright and earnest politician warning of the threat posed by the Japanese to American interests—in the summer of 1942 (www.newyorkfed.org/newsevents/speeches/2008/tfg080609.html).

11. See www.propublica.org/article/the-magnetar-trade-how-one-hedge-fund-helped-keep-the-housing-bubble-going.

12. www.nytimes.com/2009/03/25/opinion/25desantis.html.

13. http://bigthink.com/ideas/14583.

14. Goldman paid off the Treasury's investment in 2009 with a 23 percent interest rate. For information on this program, see www.federalreserve.gov/newse vents/reform_pdcf.htm. Also, Warren Buffett's Berkshire Hathaway struck a favorably priced bargain in September 2008 and invested $5 billion in the firm.

Acknowledgments

As noted below in more detail, there are many people I'd like to thank, but most of them would be subject to civil litigation and certain job loss if they were to be identified as having helped me, so I have thanked them privately.

I would like to offer profound thanks to my agent Sandra Dijkstra and her colleague Elise Capron of the Dijkstra Literary Agency. They were patient, enthusiastic, and forceful advocates for me, and I am grateful they were on my side. Many agents claim to love books; I have never seen anyone as passionate about the art of books as Sandy and her staff. Whatever shape written words take in the future, Sandy and her team will have a hand in getting the better work out there.

There would be no Sandy Dijkstra if there were no running into David Einhorn—yes, *that* David Einhorn, the hedge fund manager, poker player, and author—miles away from New York a few years back. I told him I had a book in my head and he emailed Sandy the next day. A stout fellow, but then I knew that already, as I'd shared a trench with him on occasion on a few investigative projects I had been involved with.

Every author thanks his editors and it all seems so obligatory, you know? Then I wrote a book and I understand fully why F. Scott

Fitzgerald was so passionate about Maxwell Perkins. It's asinine to even attempt to explain how much an Emilie Herman or Pamela van Giessen from John Wiley & Sons turned a series of connected fact sets on paper into a book. Like Sandy, they love books; that they do so even in the face of the sausage-making process that editing entails is beyond me.

On a personal level, I would like to list a few people who had kind words and extended courtesies for me along the way.

The staff at Rinaldi's Country Deli in Cos Cob are among the nicest people on the planet. They also have a fantastic deli that doubled as a permanent work break for me since I lived 50 yards from the place. Everyone should have a Rinaldi's in their life.

Chris Crotty and Chris Rossman are two close friends from Fordham who are just excellent people and were very supportive during moments when I doubted if I could pull this off.

In Greenwich, I went to a Bible study Tuesday mornings for years with Scott Greenlee, Steve Gilbert, Mark Scarlata, Tom Wells, Dave Tilly, Rick Watson, Dan Walker, Peter Jayes, and Bill Rainford. There may well be better examples of caring, decent Christian men out there, but I have never encountered any.

Also in Greenwich, I met Will and Susan Suarez, Jerome Kenny, and Suzanna Borthwick, as well as quite a few other friends from Tuesday nights. Good people who happily spent hours and hours getting me and others back on the proper road. They should rest assured that I am still on it and doing the same. The first 164 pages, indeed.

Professionally, Tom Lamont and Steve Murray took a shot with me years ago at *Institutional Investor News*. Polar opposites, they both drilled home the lessons of journalism on a weekly basis. At II, people like Dan Freed, Mark DeCambre, Jen Ryan, Hal Lux, and Jenny Anderson were friends and colleagues who went on to bigger things as well. I learned much from all of them over the years, but their decency and laughter is what stays with me.

At the *New York Sun*, Robert Messenger hired me and I think it worked out. Seth Lipsky, a garrulous and eccentric genius, and Ira Stoll, a stern taskmaster who sadly kept his encouraging, helpful side a well-kept secret from too many (though not from me), taught me much. A brief recollection: I had written a devastating exposé of a big hedge fund's general partner and how he had not told his clients about how

Citigroup had fired him in the 1990s because he had misvalued his trading portfolio when it declined. The piece relied heavily on background sources, and Ira killed it straightaway. He told me that he loved it but that allowing people to snipe at other people without identifying themselves is grossly unfair and the only thing worse than a reporter's being wrong or lazy is a reporter's being unfair. A fine lesson, even if that was a great frigging story he squashed. Ken Magill—a truly underrated editor—and Pia Catton were friends and colleagues who made the time there memorable.

The *New York Post* is a difficult place to write about since everything that has been said about it is mostly true but never totally catches the spirit of the place. Jenny Anderson, whom I replaced, put it best when she said the *Post* was the coolest job in the world until that one day when you just get tired of it. Dan Colarusso took a shot with me and stayed in the trenches with me fighting off the many, many angry executives and lawyers I attracted. A reporter cannot ask for a better editor because there really isn't a better guy to work with. Jay Sherman stepped in for Dan and never missed a beat. Holly Sanders, Rich Wilner, Keith Kelly, Suzanne Kapner, Zach Kouwe, Tim Arango, John Crudele, Peter Lauria, Paul Tharp, Chris Byron, and Janet Whitman were great colleagues and better people. Mike Cameron was probably happy to see me go, but only because he had to defend me constantly. Maybe in another life we could hang out and talk about whatever Australian lawyers talk about outside of story vetting. I would be remiss if I forgot to say that Brenda Walsh, Joe Barracato, and Mike Gray came up with the headlines and were a constant source of laughs.

Fortune magazine was the opposite of the *Post:* refined, witty, and urbane—a genial culture that in ordinary times would have been a fine place to hang your hat for a few decades. Xana Antunes recruited me out of the *Post* and said that life would be very different and she was right. Jim Ledbetter was a great assistant editor for me and became a friend—and then my editor again, at *Slate's The Big Money*. When I left to join *Fortune*, Dan Colarusso said, "Colin Barr is the best story editor I've ever seen." Dan, as usual, was right. Colin is a great editor, encyclopedic and keen in his understanding of financial journalism, and, naturally, *Fortune* has taken his talent and made him its in-house blogger or something. Scott Moritz and Devin Leonard were colleagues and friends, along with Nick Varchaver and John Brodie, who had some wonderful lines and introduced me to Bill Cohan. Working with Bethany McLean was cool, and just getting to watch Carol Loomis do her thing was great. Few gilded reputations are truly deserved in big media, if any, but she is the exception. Allan Sloan is the best translator of the raw data and fact sets of investigative reporting into something the common man understands that has perhaps ever been. He is also a great guy—patient, friendly, and encouraging.

My parents, Mike and Diane Boyd, deserve much more than a passing mention, but then they have long deserved more from me. My mother let me stay up late reading and sparked a curiosity with words that has yet to abate. My dad is a man who is often my role model and has long been one of the very few men on Wall Street that is a moral role model for other people. My sister, Meredith, put up with me for years and deserves all of the very best.

Many relatives of mine have shown me kindness that went above normal family obligation: My aunts Adrienne Foran and Judy and Marie Doris have been love itself. My cousins Mike and Walter McNulty have traveled many miles with me, Walter especially in that I lived with him for two years in college, and all I'll say is that I could not have asked for better companions in tight spots and strange places. My aunts and uncles Terri and John McCauley, Ann and Wally McNulty, and Mary Boyd, who along, with my late godfather, Tom Boyd, have always kept up support and interest in my reporting career. Deep thanks to them all.

My children, Samantha, Graham, Johanna, and Ben Boyd, made sacrifices as I worked long hours in New York City and then often at home as well. I love you all and pray that I have been able to provide you with the hope, love, and kindness you have given me. I am blessed to be your father. May your days be better than the ones I describe in these pages, and may you find the courage to stand for your beliefs and the right in this world, knowing that God will be your judge and ally.

Lou and Kathy Caprioglio have been excellent in-laws, and Laura's grandparents, Emilio and Alda Caprioglio, have been equally generous and warm in their affection.

I have dedicated this book to my wife, Laura. She has paid a price as I have spent hours chasing the financial filth in this world, and she said little, loving me all along. She could have done better than me but has remained my most loyal supporter, convincing herself she was lucky and being a great parent throughout. I aim to change that and show her who was really the lucky one.

Ultimately, all men reckon with God, either on the way up or on the way down. I'm glad I caught him in Greenwich: He and his family saved me and my family and continue to do so.

■ ■ ■

In a broad sense, a nonfiction book represents a contract between the author and the reader in which the author asserts that he or she has made every possible effort to include or obtain all information related to the work.

I'll assert that I have, with one (big) qualification.

A company the size and scope of AIG is literally too big and expansive to condense into one work, let alone a book focusing on a narrow aspect of it like the credit crisis. In the text, I argue that AIG's founding and early days alone probably warrant a substantial effort from some economic historian; its entire history would probably take several volumes. The stories about how AIG managed to consistently obtain favorable legislative or regulatory edicts across generations and in multiple countries is worth a good read in and of itself. (*Hint:* having a Washington fixer nicknamed "Mr. CIA" report directly to Hank Greenberg was probably helpful.)

So my work focuses exclusively on AIG's decision to enter the capital markets and its attempt to continually generate outsized returns in a marketplace where its competitive advantages—balance sheet and brainpower—gradually diminished. My reasoning for this was simple: This is how AIG was nearly killed.

To that end, a word on sourcing is appropriate.

AIG's collapse has been a boon to lawyers across the white-collar defense bar. The preponderance of civil litigation and (for several years) potentially criminal investigations has left most people who were in a decision-making capacity at AIG between 2005 and 2008 deeply traumatized. It was quite common for me to interview a source who had recently been interviewed or subpoenaed by some combination of the following: the Securities and Exchange Commission and the

Department of Justice, the Connecticut attorney general's office, the New York attorney general's office, the Financial Crisis Inquiry Commission, the Congressional Oversight Panel, and so many plaintiff law firms it is not really possible to go into them.

The upshot is that in this context, when a reporter calls someone up and seeks to interview them, they are not too thrilled to give a wide-ranging interview on the record. Much of the work I did thus involved not using people's names. To combat the effects of shifting memory and exaggeration, I did not use information that could not be verified by another colleague or supported by documents. I fear that the thrilling narrative arc that characterizes so much of today's nonfiction was minimized in some places, but perhaps the reader can take some solace from the fact that though some drama fell by the wayside, many events that are laid out in this book actually occurred somewhat as described.

In addition to dozens of interviews with current and former AIG executives and board members, I also relied heavily on official filings, especially the footnotes buried in annual reports, a host of lawsuits and related filings, lawyers (both plaintiff and defense), and the press—both in the insurance trade press and mainstream media.

I actively sought AIG's cooperation with this book. In seeking it, I provided their media relations team a detailed written framework of the thrust of my work, who I sought to interview, and what I was interested in and waited many weeks for an answer. Though Lauren Day, the spokeswoman assigned to deal with me, could not have been nicer, more courteous, or seemingly interested in what I was asking, AIG's final position also could not have been more clear: my book and I could go pound sand.

Everyone who was named in this book was contacted one way or another; if they declined to comment, their lawyer(s) were contacted and informed of my interest. In a less litigious age, Martin Sullivan and his lawyer would not cancel a long-scheduled interview and make up some blather about being "pro-Greenberg." Win Neuger, comfortable in his Sutton Place apartment, would have more courage than to say, "I don't think so." But we live in the world of our own making.

This brings up a final point concerns the reporting of this book. At least two dozen former senior executives told me that they would have been happy to talk in some fashion but they had signed exit agreements that included extraordinarily thorough nondisclosure agreements. In essence, they were (generally) paid sums of between $400,000 and $750,000 for up to three years silence. An executive getting a little something extra on the way out of the door is standard enough and is probably a sound practice—it keeps memories favorable—but AIG literally ran out of cash.

It set me to thinking: If I interviewed dozens of men and women who violated the agreement to get the story out—and encountered a few dozen more who declined to—and knowing fully there must be hundreds more who I never even considered, the numbers start to mount. It's conceivable that post-bailout at least $400 million, if not more, was spent in exit payments. Where did that money come from? At least indirectly, you and me. Because AIG was spared its fate, and since cash is fungible, the company was presumably able to take some of the $85 billion the United States was forced to inject and use it to fund these payments. Put another way, if AIG collapsed, as it was 12 hours or less from doing, then many people would have hit the street with no legal barriers in the way of their saying their peace.

This is perhaps a minor point within the constellation of absurdity that brought AIG to mid-September 2008, but it is fitting somehow: In preventing the greatest man-made financial disaster of the modern era, the U.S. government is going to allow many of AIG's secrets to remain hidden, trapped in hard drives and filing cabinets, to gradually be shredded and erased. In turn, for a year's salary or so, the people who know and did what happened will say nothing and move on.

In the last few years of its life, AIG's investors and employees deserved better; in its near-death experience, the American people, AIG's rescuers, deserve a better accounting than an occasional government panel's white paper.

Into this breech comes *Fatal Risk*.

Roddy Boyd
Wilmington, N.C.
January 2011

Index